Social Policy and the Commonwealth

Also by Catherine Jones Finer

IMMIGRATION AND SOCIAL POLICY IN BRITAIN

PATTERNS OF SOCIAL POLICY

PROMOTING PROSPERITY: The Hong Kong Way of Social Policy

Also by Paul Smyth

AUSTRALIAN SOCIAL POLICY: The Keynesian Chapter

Co-Editor with Bettina Cass: CONTESTING THE AUSTRALIAN WAY: State Market and Civil Society

TALKING POLICY

Social Policy and the Commonwealth

Prospects for Social Inclusion

Edited by

Catherine Jones Finer and Paul Smyth

palgrave
 macmillan

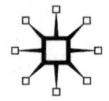

Editorial Matter & Selection © Catherine Jones Finer & Paul Smyth 2004
Chapter 2 © Catherine Jones Finer 2004
Chapter 12 © Paul Smyth 2004
Remaining chapters © Palgrave Macmillan 2004

All rights reserved. No reproduction, copy or transmission of this publication may be made without written permission.

No paragraph of this publication may be reproduced, copied or transmitted save with written permission or in accordance with the provisions of the Copyright, Designs and Patents Act 1988, or under the terms of any licence permitting limited copying issued by the Copyright Licensing Agency, 90 Tottenham Court Road, London W1T 4LP.

Any person who does any unauthorised act in relation to this publication may be liable to criminal prosecution and civil claims for damages.

The authors have asserted their rights to be identified as the authors of this work in accordance with the Copyright, Designs and Patents Act 1988.

First published 2004 by
PALGRAVE MACMILLAN
Houndmills, Basingstoke, Hampshire RG21 6XS and
175 Fifth Avenue, New York, N. Y. 10010
Companies and representatives throughout the world

PALGRAVE MACMILLAN is the global academic imprint of the Palgrave Macmillan division of St. Martin's Press, LLC and of Palgrave Macmillan Ltd. Macmillan® is a registered trademark in the United States, United Kingdom and other countries. Palgrave is a registered trademark in the European Union and other countries.

ISBN 1–4039–2166–0 hardback

This book is printed on paper suitable for recycling and made from fully managed and sustained forest sources.

A catalogue record for this book is available from the British Library.

Library of Congress Cataloging-in-Publication Data
Social policy and the commonwealth : prospects for social inclusion
  / edited by Catherine Jones Finer and Paul Smyth.
     p. cm.
Includes bibliographical references and index.
ISBN1–4039–2166–0 (cloth)
  1. Commonwealth countries–Social policy. 2. Social service–Commonwealth countries. 3. Marginality, Social–Commonwealth countries. I. Jones Finer, Catherine. II. Smyth, Paul

HN380.8.A8S63 2004
361.6′1′0917241–dc22   2004042731

10   9   8   7   6   5   4   3   2   1
13   12   11   10   09   08   07   06   05   04

Printed and bound in Great Britain by
Antony Rowe Ltd, Chippenham and Eastbourne

Contents

List of Tables	vii
List of Boxes	viii
List of Figures	ix
Preface	x
Acknowledgements	xii
List of Acronyms	xiii
Notes on Contributors	xv

1. Introduction 1
   Catherine Jones Finer and Paul Smyth

Part One   Introductory Overview

2. British Social Policy Tradition in Relation to Empire and Commonwealth 11
   Catherine Jones Finer

3. Social Inclusion Globalisation and the Commonwealth 29
   Patricia Harris

Part Two   National Case Studies

4. The Paradox of Exclusion/Inclusion in Jamaica 51
   Joy Moncrieffe

5. Three Decades of Community Development in Botswana: Is There Social Inclusion? 68
   Morena J. Rankopo

6. Social Welfare and Social Development in South Africa: Reshaping the Colonial and Apartheid Legacy for a Global Era 81
   Leila Patel and James Midgley

7. Socially Inclusive Social Security in Rural Tamil Nadu, India 94
   Barbara Harriss-White

8. Social Policy and the Sri Lankan Welfare State: The
   British Colonial Legacy 109
   Laksiri Jayasuriya

9. Balancing State Welfarism and Individual Responsibility:
   Singapore's CPF Model 125
   Tan Ern Ser

10. After *The Malay Dilemma*: Colonial Heritage and Ethnic
    Exclusion in Malaysia 138
    Souchou Yao

11. The Tyranny of Home Ownership: Housing Policy and
    Social Exclusion in Colonial and Post-Colonial
    Hong Kong 151
    James Lee

12. The British Social Policy Legacy and the
    'Australian Way' 167
    Paul Smyth

13. Redesigning the Welfare State in New Zealand 181
    Susan St John

14. Canada, Social Inclusion and the Commonwealth 197
    Malcolm J. Stewart

Part Three   The Commonwealth as a Transnational Institution

15. The Commonwealth and Social Inclusion 215
    W. David McIntyre

16. Prospects for a Commonwealth Future 236
    Catherine Jones Finer and Paul Smyth

Name Index 243

Subject Index 244

List of Tables

7.1	Estimated Coverage of Old Age Pensions	100
7.2	Demographic Position of the 65+	101
7.3	Household Composition and Extreme Poverty	103
7.4	Old Age and Poverty	104
7.5	Analysis of Cases of Old Age Pension	105
7.6	Analysis of Old Age Pension Cases According to Eligibility and Need	105
7.7	Political Affiliation of Beneficiaries	106
11.1	Three Models of Housing Policy in East Asia	154
11.2	Inclusion and Exclusion in Hong Kong's Housing Ladder	162
13.1	New Zealand Tax Schedule for Personal Income Tax	190
13.2	Weekly Maximum Rates of Family Support and Child Tax Credit	190

List of Boxes

2.1	Leading Characteristics of the British Empire	14
2.2	Three Guiding Principles of Recommendations	18
2.3	1905 Aliens Act and 1962 Commonwealth Immigrants Act	22
2.4	Immigration Controls and Race Relations Legislation	23
13.1	Welfare changes (NZ) 1990–1993	187

List of Figures

3.1	Four Conceptual Spaces for Thinking about the Impact of the Market on Society	31
3.2	Key Theorists in the National Era	33
3.3	The Strands of the Present: Uses of Social Inclusion/Exclusion Discourse	39
11.1	Tenure Trend and Composition	158
11.2	House Price Inflation and Economic Growth	159
13.1	Mean Household Equivalent Disposable Income Changes (NZ) 1982–1998	192

Preface

The idea of this book arose from an international academic conference, doggedly held and attended, in Brisbane, in the shadow of '9/11', on the theme of 'Promoting Social Inclusion in the Commonwealth'. It was convened by (the then) Dr Paul Smyth, Senior Lecturer at the University of Queensland, and was timed to coincide with the Commonwealth Heads of Government Meeting (CHOGM), which was also scheduled to take place in Brisbane in the first week of October. In the event, the CHOGM was postponed then relocated to a 'more secure' location further up the Queensland coast; but our own conference went ahead as planned.

In part, it could have been a product of this timing and circumstances that those present at the conference came away enthused with the idea of taking the theme of 'Commonwealth and Social Inclusion' a stage further. The striking absence of a distinct Commonwealth dimension to the international literature on comparative social policy, had been remarked on throughout the conference; whose list of contributors had itself borne out the difficulties of securing a 'representative spread' of papers from the huge variety – economic, political and cultural – of countries notionally united under the banner of the Commonwealth.

Once the idea of a book had been agreed on, we were committed to a twofold race: first, to recruit additional contributors to improve the balance of the collection and, second of course, to interest a reputable publisher in the value of this novel enterprise. This last involved confronting the present-day academics' classic conundrum head-on: Viz.

- without relevant university courses there can be no mass market for their books;
- without the requisite books, there can be little prospect of such courses ever being developed.

We are more than grateful to Palgrave Macmillan for responding to our challenge; just as we are no less grateful to the recruited band of expert additional contributors – mostly from way beyond conventional international/comparative social policy circles – for responding so positively to our invitations to participate. We thank *all* of the contributors for the work they have put into both the preparation and revision of their papers over time; and, above all, for their willingness and determination to stay with this project.

May it prove worth all our efforts, by signalling not merely a fresh line in social policy research and publications, but in social policy outcomes for the future.

Catherine Jones Finer and Paul Smyth
December 2003

Acknowledgements

The Publishers would like to thank the following for permission to reprint their material:

Senior Minister Lee Kuan Yew (Singapore) for permission to quote his words from the BBC Radio 4 programme *Lowering the Flag*, broadcast on September 9, 2002; and the BBC for permitting the same.

The *Daily Mirror* newspaper for permitting the reproduction of an extract from its issue of May 9, 1945.

The *Daily Telegraph* newspaper for permitting the reproduction of an extract from its issue of May 8, 1945.

[Both as quoted in Barnett, C.(1986) *The Audit of War*, Basingstoke: Macmillan; p.3]

The original version of the chapter by Barbara Harriss-White first appeared in her edited collection *Rural India Facing the 21st Century* and is reprinted by permission of Anthem Press, an imprint of the Wimbledon Publishing Company.

List of Acronyms

ABC	[members of the Commonwealth] Australia, Britain, Canada
ACP	Africa Caribbean Pacific [trade/aid] Group
ALP	Australian Labour Party
APEC	Asia Pacific Economic Cooperation
BDP	Botswana Democratic Party
BIDPA	Botswana Institute of Development Policy and Analysis
BOCONGO	Botswana Coalition for Non-Governmental Organizations
CAIP	Commonwealth Association of Indigenous Peoples
CCCS	CHOGM Committee on Cooperation Through Sport
CD	Community Development
CER	Closer Economic Relations [Australia and New Zealand]
CFTC	Commonwealth Fund for Technical Cooperation
CHOGM	Commonwealth Heads of Government Meeting
CHRI	Commonwealth Human Rights Initiative
COL	Commonwealth of Learning
COMMACT	Commonwealth Association for Local Action and Development
COMMAT	Commonwealth Medical Association Trust
CPF	Central Provident Fund [Singapore]
CPII	Commonwealth Private Investment Initiative
CYP	Commonwealth Youth Programme
EEC	European Economic Community [as was]
EPF	Employees Provident Fund
EU	European Union
GEAR	Growth and Redistribution Strategy [South Africa]
HLRG	High Level Review Group
IDAPE	Interim Disability Assistance Programme for the Elderly
IDB	International Development Bank
JDP	Jamaican Democratic Party
JLP	Jamaica Labour Party
LDO	Local Development Organization
MOSP	Ministry of Social Policy [New Zealand]
NAFTA	North American Free Trade Association
NEP	New Economic Plan [Malaysia]
NGO	Non-Governmental Organization

NIEs	Newly Industrialized Economies
OECD	Organization for Economic Cooperation and Development
PAP	People's Action Party [Singapore]
PAS	Party Islam Malaysia [Malaysia]
PASB	Pan American Sanitary Bureau
PNP	People's National Party [Jamaica]
PRA	Participatory Rural Appraisal [Botswana]
RED	Redistributive Discourse
SIE	Subsistence Income Estimate [Tamil Nadu]
UMNO	United Malay National Organization
UNICEF	United Nations Childrens' Fund
USAID	United States Aid Organization
VIPPSOS	Voluntary, Independent, Professional, Philanthropic and Sporting Organizations
WHO	World Health Organization

Notes on Contributors

Patricia Harris is Professor of Sociology and Social Policy at Murdoch University and Director of the Centre for Social and Community Research. With her colleagues Jan Currie and Bev Thiele she has recently published *Gendered Universities in Globalized Economies: Power, Careers and Sacrifices* (2002). Her current research centres on the linkages between fictional and political theory texts dealing with totalitarianism in the mid-twentieth century.

Barbara Harriss-White is Professor of Development Studies and Deputy Director of Queen Elizabeth House, Oxford University's centre for the study of development. Her two complementary research interests, which she has pursued through primary field research, are i) markets and the character of India's informal capitalist economy and ii) aspects of wellbeing. Publications include *India Working* 2003 CUP; *Illfare in India* (1999, Sage, with S. Subramanian) and *Outcast from Social Welfare* (2002, Books for Change, with Susan Erb)

Laksiri Jayasuriya is an Emeritus Professor and honorary Senior Research Fellow, attached to the Discipline of Social Work and Social Administration, School of Social and Cultural Studies, University of Western Australia, Perth, Australia. His research interests are comparative social policy, ethnic affairs and multiculturalism, and Sri Lankan social development.

Catherine Jones Finer is Honorary Professor at the Institute of Applied Social Studies, University of Birmingham. She has published widely on issues of social policy development and on comparative social policy. Principal relevant publications include *Immigration and Social Policy in Britain* (1977); *Patterns of Social Policy* (1985); *Promoting Prosperity: The Hong Kong Way of Social Policy* (1990). She continues as editor of *Social Policy & Administration* for regional and special issues.

James Lee is associate professor at the City University of Hong Kong. He specializes in teaching and research on comparative housing policy. He did his undergraduate studies in Hong Kong and his PhD at the School for Policy Studies, University of Bristol. He is both a founder of the Hong Kong Housing Research Network and the Asian Pacific Network of Housing Research. His recent publications include *Housing and Social Change: East West Perspectives* (2003) and *Housing, Home Ownership and Social Change in Hong Kong* (1999).

Emeritus Professor W. David McIntyre of the Macmillan Brown Centre of Pacific Studies at the University of Christchurch is author of a dozen books on Commonwealth and New Zealand history. These range from *The Imperial Frontier in the Tropics* (1967) and *Colonies into Commonwealth* (1966) to *British Decolonization 1946–97* (1998) and *A Guide to the Contemporary Commonwealth* (2001). He has contributed Pacific and Commonwealth chapters to the *Oxford History of the British Empire* (1999), and the Pacific War and Anzus entries in the *Oxford Companion to New Zealand Military History* (2001).

James Midgley is Harry and Riva Specht Professor of Public Social Services and Dean of the School of Social Welfare at the University of California, Berkeley. He has published widely on issues of social development and international social welfare. His most recent books include *The Handbook of Social Policy* (2000), *Controversial Issues in Social Policy* (2003) and *Social Policy for Development* (2004).

Joy Moncrieffe completed her PhD on Jamaican health policy administration in 1999 at the University of Cambridge. Her background is in Development Studies and in Social and Political Sciences. More recently she has been a Research officer at the London School of Economics and Political Science and is currently with the Poverty and Public Policy Group at the Overseas Development Institute. Joy's current interests are in governance, accountability, health, social exclusion/inclusion, and in evaluating poverty policy and participatory assessments.

Leila Patel is Professor of Social Development Studies and Chairperson of the Department of Social Work at the Rand Afrikaans University in Johannesburg, South Africa. She has been active in the formulation of welfare policy in a post apartheid society and in promoting research in social development in an African context.

Morena J. Rankopo is a Social Work Lecturer at the University of Botswana. Over the past 12 years he has been actively involved in research on community intervention and HIV/AIDS. He has publications in the areas of community participation, indigenous health practices, and poverty alleviation in Botswana. He is currently involved in a national study on stigma associated with HIV/AIDS.

Tan Ern Ser is an associate professor at the Department of Sociology, National University of Singapore. He received his PhD in Sociology from Cornell University. He is principal investigator of the World Values Survey-Singapore Chapter. He has written on industrial relations, welfare policy, ethnic relations, social stratification, and political values. He is co-editor of *Understanding Singapore Society* (1997) and *Tourism Management and Policy: Perspectives from Singapore* (2001).

Paul Smyth is Professor of Social Policy at the Centre for Public Policy at the University of Melbourne and Director of Research at the Brotherhood of St Laurence, also in Melbourne. He wrote *Australian Social Policy: the Keynesian Chapter* (1994) and, with Bettina Cass, coedited *Contesting the Australian Way: State, Market and Civil Society* (1998). His most recent book is *Talking Policy* (2004). Current research interests include social inclusion as an alternative framework for thinking about disadvantage and the reconfiguration of social policy in terms of social investment.

Malcolm J Stewart is in the Department of Social Work at the University of Toronto. His academic interests include Canadian and comparative social policy, pension policy, social inclusion, the life course and retirement. As a former Executive Director of the Ontario Association of Social Workers, Dr Stewart has a continuing interest in professional standards and regulation, and the development of professional identity in social work.

Susan St John is a senior lecturer in economics and a social policy advisor and consultant. She has published widely in the area of child poverty and family incomes, issues of the ageing population, long term care and pensions. She has co-authored several textbooks on the New Zealand's macroeconomic policy. Former deputy chair of a year-long review of New Zealand's retirement policies in 1997, Dr St John is currently researching the role of pensions and annuities in the New Zealand retirement income mix.

Souchou Yao teaches 'anthropology of Southeast Asia' in the University of Sydney, Australia. His research interests are the culture of capital, modernity and representations, particularly, of the Chinese diaspora. His latest publications include *House of Glass: Culture, Modernity and the State in Southeast Asia* (2001), and *Confucian Capitalism: Discourse, Practice and the Myth of Chinese Enterprise* (2002).

1
Introduction

Catherine Jones Finer and Paul Smyth

This collection developed from a conference on *Promoting Social Inclusion in the Commonwealth,* designed to coincide with the CHOGM (Commonwealth Heads of Government Meeting) scheduled for the first week of October 2001 in Brisbane. That meeting was postponed for obvious security reasons but the conference went ahead as planned. The deterioration in global security which followed has given added edge to the concern of our authors with the current difficulties facing nation states in meeting the twin objectives of economic efficiency and social cohesion. To an original scholarly interest in the British social policy legacy was added a concern to assess the Commonwealth as a future vehicle for promoting social inclusion.

Commonwealth

The Commonwealth of Nations (British Commonwealth until 1948) was not a single creation so much as the product of an incremental process of evolution. Just as the former British Empire had been accumulated and run – at a devolved distance – in a variety of ways for a variety of purposes (Ch. 2 below), so its successor institution was to be no less an assortment of parts, accumulated over the decades from 1931 – and especially from 1948 – as successive British colonial possessions gained (or were presented with) their independence (Ch. 15 below). Perhaps the wonder should be that – uniquely in the history of latter-day empires – this institution of the Commonwealth materialised at all. True, not every former colony chose to join or remain within it (notably not Burma and not the Irish Republic after 1948) – and not all were, even initially, minded to continue with the British Crown as their titular head of state. Nevertheless the British Crown has remained titular head of the Commonwealth *per se* and arguably, in the person of Queen Elizabeth II, remains its most dedicated champion.

But what is the Commonwealth *for*, and what (aside from the Commonwealth Games) can it *do*? The impatience implicit in such questions is understandable. The fact that the Commonwealth exists because the British Empire *no longer* exists is scarcely an explanation. More convincingly – though still question-begging – the Commonwealth exists because sufficient of the Empire's champions, institutions and former possessions proved unwilling – for each their own reasons – to break off the accumulated ties of Empire altogether. By implication, the Commonwealth was expected:

- to ease the transition from Empire, from a British Establishment – and perhaps an Old Commonwealth/Dominion – point of view, by getting the British and their dispersed descendants somehow 'off the hook' of post-imperial guilt;
- to ease the transition from Empire, from the point of view of former colonies –members of the New Commonwealth – by somehow compensating them and their peoples for the burden of their ever having been colonies in the first place.

Such 'reasons' may be understandable enough, but they hardly point in themselves, to a forward-looking, pro-active role for the Commonwealth upon which all its members can be persuaded to agree. Hence, the Commonwealth's longstanding directional troubles – not to mention intergovernmental financing troubles – both ever more apparent as the 'Old' member states came to be more and more heavily outnumbered by their by their 'New Commonwealth' colleagues (Ch. 15 below). Expressions of friendship (as epitomised by royal tours of duty) and egalitarian respect (reflected in equal voting status) and even the host of good works organised under the aegis of the Commonwealth Secretariat (www.thecommonwealth. org) have proved no substitute for the sort of catch-up, 'inclusive' investment programmes geared to the needs of the majority of poor states (and/or their governments), but which the Commonwealth *per se* (thanks to its rich minority) has proved incapable of delivering. An 'inclusive' agenda, capable of convincing the Commonwealth's rich as well as poor states that it was in their interests to co-operate, could finally be the making of this institution, before whatever time it has runs out.

Social inclusion

To suggest that the Commonwealth needs a positive agenda is one thing; to propose that this be set in terms of social inclusion, quite another. As is evident from the bulk of chapters in this collection, the common Commonwealth experience has been more one of social exclusion than inclusion, whether on a social group or whole societal basis. Yet these concepts now constitute the *lingua franca* for the analysis of poverty and disadvantage. The discourse emerged in Europe in the latter 1980s and was soon to become the official rhetoric of policy makers in the European Union (EU). With the election of the Blair Government in 1997, social exclusion took centre stage in Britain and from there it has been amplified through English speaking, especially Commonwealth, countries. Furthermore this is a framework which has been taken up by international organisations concerned with anti-poverty policies. In this regard it has been seen as a way of re-conceptualising social disadvantage in ways that better connect understandings of deprivation in rich and poor countries. This seems particularly apt at a time when, through globalisation, the traditional north/south research & teaching demarcation lines between social policy studies (for rich countries) and development studies (for poor countries) have lost so much of their validity. The Commonwealth's economically diverse membership, could conceivably be the network best placed to benefit from such a directional thrust.

Whether the framework of social inclusion/exclusion can fulfil such a role for the Commonwealth remains open to question. The expression 'social exclusion' originated in Europe (specifically in France) wherein, unlike 'Anglo-Saxon' notions of poverty, it was supposed not just to be about lack of money but about lack of participation in – and hence contribution to – the workings of society. Yet, as the EU has discovered to its cost, notions of social exclusion can be no less culturally specific than notions of relative poverty. In other words, each member state is liable to have its own views about how best the 'good society' is to be brought about, via measures geared, on the one hand, to social control and protection and, on the other to promoting maximum participation and self-realisation (cf. Ch. 3 below).

Thus, in attempting to apply standards of social exclusion/inclusion to the potential business of the Commonwealth, there are two key questions to be addressed:

- is the pursuit of social inclusion to concern itself simply with local notions of social inclusion within each nation state; or is it to refer to

common standards of social inclusion, somehow graded to accord with levels of economic development?
- is it to refer, ideally, to the inclusion of whole nations (and their governments) within this Commonwealth 'family of nations'; or should it refer simply to the most excluded segments of any member state's population, if need be in despite of its government?

The layout of this book

The twin themes under review – legacies of Empire and contemporary issues of social inclusion/exclusion – differ in their meaning and significance for each and every former British colony or Dominion. Yet the fact of the Commonwealth implies some sense of common interest and capacity-pooling potential between its members; large and small, rich and poor.

(i) Introductory overview

Catherine Jones Finer offers an historical review of 'The British Social Policy Tradition in Relation to Empire and Commonwealth', demonstrating the extent to which social policy development in Britain, from the nineteenth century onwards, was bound up with considerations of Empire and post-Empire. Unsurprisingly (in retrospect), the inauguration of the Welfare State in post-war Britain was to prove anything but 'inclusive' so far as citizens of the New Commonwealth were concerned.

Patricia Harris writes of 'Social Inclusion, Globalisation and the Commonwealth' primarily in conceptual terms, albeit with a strong sense of historical perspective. She shows how the *idea* of social inclusion – with its 'long past but short history' – predates the invention of this now fashionable expression. Her analysis hinges on a two-by-two matrix: social order versus social justice; solidarity versus participation. Social *polarisation* rather than social inclusion should, in her view, be the term of the moment; though the Commonwealth – as a key 'staging post between global forces and nation states' – could conceivably head an international drive to hit back in the interest of human rights.

(ii) National case studies

Twelve chapters offer empirical examples of Commonwealth members' experience. We have grouped these in broad ethno-geographic terms, the only part-exception being the final coupling of Canada with Australia and New Zealand as being all 'western' ex-Dominions.

Caribbean and Africa: the Third World

Here the emphasis is upon social exclusion as a whole society phenomenon. The Caribbean predates the acquisition of imperial possessions anywhere else and was based, of course, on the operation of the infamous trading triangle – cheap goods from Britain to Africa; slaves from Africa to work the Caribbean plantations; sugar from the Caribbean to Britain.

Joy Moncrieff's essay on Jamaica questions the applicability of notions of social inclusion/exclusion to the internal relations of societies where economic polarisation remains linked to shades of skin colour; and especially where these societies are so overwhelmingly poor that they are socially excluded in interstate terms.

Morena Rankopo narrates the experience of Botswana: a nation upon whose chiefdoms a system of Westminster-style parliamentary government had been super-imposed, but in whose actual governance the British were allegedly not interested. He details the costs and consequences of Botswana's diamonds-led, economic miracle and suggests this be taken more seriously by the Commonwealth – as an equivalent of the 'Tigers' of South East Asia.

Finally in this section, Leila Patel and James Midgely offer a penetrating review of 'social welfare and social development' in post-apartheid South Africa. The burdens of the colonial past remain evident in a 'nation' still struggling to come to terms with massive political and economic transformation. Social exclusion remains the majority experience, both within South Africa and between this country and other members of the Commonwealth; paradoxically more so than ever, now that South Africa no longer counts as a Dominion (white settler enclave) of the Commonwealth.

Indian sub-continent

Here the picture is more mixed. There are manifestly parts of Indian and Sri Lankan societies which feel very much socio-economically included, in both national and international terms; just as there are the village dirt poor, equally excluded on every internal and external count. We have two contrasting examples to offer.

Barbara Harriss-White, drawing upon first-hand, contemporary field work experience, details efforts to implement 'Socially Inclusive Social Security' in three villages of rural Tamil Nadu – and spells out the lessons arising from this exercise, not just for the governance of India, but for the richer member states of the Commonwealth also. The one measure that seemingly no one can effect, over the short-to-medium term, is to level up the provision of government supports right across federal India.

Set against this, Laksiri Jayasuriya offers an historical account of the evolution of the Sri Lankan welfare state – the exceptional case, as he sees it, of a welfare state's having evolved in a non-industrial, Third World country. Sri Lanka's era of 'post colonialism' really dates, he argues, not from the onset of independence (1948) but from the oil crisis of the 1970s and the outbreak of ethnic conflict which came soon after. He argues that a stabilised Sri Lanka could become a standard bearer for the Commonwealth, with the *Third Way* (see multiple references to come) emerging as a potential model linkage between capitalism and welfarism.

South-east Asia

Here the distinctions between the socially included and excluded become much more subtle and their relationships to colonial legacy and Commonwealth more mixed.

Tan Ern Ser's account of the Singaporean balance between State welfare and individual responsibility reveals a self-proclaimed fair, *equal opportunities* society, whose key social security system (cf. Malaysia, below and Ch. 11), remains the British imposed, intendedly self-financing and ever since immensely flexible Central Provident Fund. Here it is up to individuals to include themselves and their families; just as it is up to their government to ensure that Singapore is 'included' internationally, with or without any help from the Commonwealth.

By contrast, Souchou Yao's pointed Chinese account of 'Colonial Heritage, Ethnic Exclusion and its Consequences in Malaysia, emphasises that country's continued post-imperial emphasis on the need to 'protect' indigenous Malay interests at the expense of its Chinese and Indian business communities especially. Malaysia is manifestly not like Singapore. Nevertheless, in Yao's view, it is global rather than Commonwealth forces which are now putting pressure on Malaysia's ethnic preferentialism. Specifically, the 'emergent cosmopolitanism of Malay middle classes' could yet prove crucial to mobilisation *against* forms of colonial-inherited ethnic positive discrimination in Malaysia as well as other parts of the Commonwealth.

James Lee focuses on the *middle-class* problem of social exclusion in metropolitan Hong Kong, as a result of the housing crisis. The British colonial housing policy of building homes for home-ownership has backfired in the context of a general property price collapse, leaving not the poor so much as the aspiring middle classes especially exposed. But Hong Kong – and especially middle-class, aspiring Hong Kong – remains unique. It is, after all, having to come to terms with a change of ownership rather than a passage to independence.

'Old Commonwealth' Dominions

These, with Britain at the apex, used to be the white man's club of the Empire and beyond. Welfare states created in these countries post World War II owed much to the British welfare state model. Britain's decision to join the then European Economic Community (now European Union) in 1971 inevitably meant a major realignment of economic, social and political relations. Nevertheless the shared history now finds New Labour's Third Way under consideration as a new framework for social policy in these countries.

The crisis of the welfare state in Australia is analysed by Paul Smyth in terms of an overemphasis on redistribution in post war Commonwealth welfare states. Australia is receptive to the new policy currents associated with the *Third Way* but, he argues that, in the Australian context, social inclusion must be about productive values as much as redistribution. Susan St John offers a related but contrasting account of the impact of 'Thatcherism' and (again) subsequent *Third Way* policies on New Zealand. She emphasises the continuing importance of redistribution, showing that the aged have remained this country's most included group precisely because their pensions were kept intact. Similar themes inform Malcolm Stewart's review of the Canadian federal experience. He emphasises that country's triangular relationship with Britain and with the United States, concluding that the *Third Way* may offer Canada a 'humane alternative to neoliberal retrenchment, US dominated economic globalisation and dismantlement of social protection'.

The Commonwealth as a transnational institution

David McIntyre's 'Commonwealth and Social Inclusion' constitutes an authoritative, definitive review of the twin themes of this book. The Commonwealth *per se* – rather than merely as a collection of disparate parts – is the sustaining focus of his chapter. Both its limitations and its potential as a prime forum for smaller states – in association with a few rich large ones – are here set out for all to see.

Our editorial chapter on 'Prospects for a Commonwealth Future' then concludes this collection.

Part One
Introductory Overview

2
British Social Policy Tradition in Relation to Empire and Commonwealth

Catherine Jones Finer

Introduction

British social policy development has been intimately bound up with traditions of Empire and Commonwealth. But it has not usually been presented in such terms. Students of the British welfare state have typically been schooled in accounts of its evolution geared much more to developments at home than abroad – and least of all to developments taking place outside Europe and North America. By the same token, accounts of socio-economic and policy developments within the Empire have made little if any reference to contemporaneous developments in Britain. It is as if the two sides to this story have been invisible to one another.

One reason for the disconnectedness is to be found in the unco-ordinated, part-unintended, certainly un-forward-looking quality of British policy making *per se*: both with regard to domestic affairs, in the wake of industrial revolution, and to the 'management' of Empire, then Commonwealth. This same quality has fuelled both the ambiguities of the British welfare state and the failings, to date, of the Commonwealth as a credible international force for democracy and social justice.

This paper will first comment on developments leading to the establishment of the welfare state in Britain, interspersed with observations on the relationship between this process and considerations of empire. Next, it will comment on post-war and post-imperial social policy trajectories, before concluding with comments on prospects for the future.

Development of social policy in imperial Britain

First industrial nation c. 1760–1860

This sub-heading is not here to convey a jingoistic point. The fact that Britain was first – for a combination of reasons – to experience industrial revolution was rich in initially negative, but nonetheless long-lasting, social policy consequences.

This was a spontaneous, piecemeal, drawn-out form of 'revolution'; unplanned, and undirected; not even to be named as such until long after its beginnings (Matthias 1969: 3–4). The British government was by definition not in charge – *domestic* governance being then presumed a matter for influential amateurs in any case (such as self-governing chartered borough councils, or parish vestries under the oversight of unpaid justices of the peace) rather than career politicians or professional civil servants (these last still a novel idea in 19th century Britain). Industrial Britain's trading triumphs abroad were thus based on the initial triumphs at home of relatively unfettered individualistic invention and competition in an evolving, 'de-regulated' marketplace (Matthias 1969: 35).[1]

Not surprisingly – in retrospect – the social and political costs were to be considerable. The chattering classes of the turn of the 18th/19th century (e.g. patrons of coffee houses in London and of vicarages in the southern counties[2]) proved so ignorant of conditions in the industrial north as to provoke not merely searing social novels from outraged, informed individuals – such as Benjamin Disraeli (e.g. *Sybil or The Two Nations* 1845) and Elizabeth Gaskell (e.g. *North and South* 1855) – but determined 'Utilitarian'[3] attempts to improve on Britain's domestic governance from the bottom up.

On the latter count: 1834 saw the introduction of locally elected Boards of Guardians to administer a newly nationalised and supposedly standardised Poor Law (effectively the first and last such attempt in Europe[4]) (Kidd 1999; Brundage 2002). 1848 saw the introduction of elected Boards of Health (where locally agreed) to administer new public health regulations (Finer 1952). 1862 saw the introduction of new Highways Boards and 1870 the introduction of School Boards, each of these being separately elected, on a separate basis. It was not until the 1890s that *multi-purpose* elective local government was to come about (Smellie 1968).

A motley empire

Likewise, the British Empire was no pre-planned, coordinated project so much as an accumulation of possessions, separately acquired, in different ways, for particular purposes, over a period stretching from well before the industrial revolution. The rationale was consistent: to sustain, defend and extend British patterns of trade and trading influence. But there was no one route to success in such a cause, and solutions, over time, were (in)famously eclectic: from the imported slave-laboured plantations of the Caribbean, to the superimposition of the British Raj over the Indian subcontinent, to trading posts such as Hong Kong and Singapore, to British *majority* settlements (as these became) in the 'virgin' Dominions of Canada, Australia and New Zealand and finally to the British *minority* settlements (as these remained) of Sub-Saharan Africa. The cumulative result, by the early 20th century, was a collection of territories 'upon which the sun never set', but about whose forms of governance and standards of socio-economic well being, few generalisations could be ventured (Box 2.1).

Mounting economic and demographic concerns

By the latter 19th century, new dimensions of international competition were making themselves felt, economically, militarily and hence socially. While the British had been creating and debating *social problems*, it seems the Germans had been pro-active in *sozialpolitik* (Buchi 1974; Cahnman and Schmitt 1979; Jones 1979). Bismarck's newly united Germany (1871) was geared not merely to a better regulated process of industrialisation in the wake of the British example, but to a better-ordered industrial labour force (e.g. Rimlinger 1971). Compulsory social insurance for industrial workers might not have been enough to save Bismarck's own career in the end (Tampke 1981: 81)), but it was enough to raise awkward questions about contemporaneous domestic management in Britain.

Indeed Britain's capacity for heading even its own 'free range' version of empire was increasingly being called in question. By the turn of the 20th century, opinion leaders across the political spectrum were warning that the 'Condition of England' could be unfitting its common people for this very task (Greenleaf I. 1983: 166–167). Much of the concern expressed was not so much humanitarian as socio-imperial, in respect of the standards of fitness (moral as well as physical) deemed necessary for a people in charge of the world's leading empire.

The humiliations of the Boer War (1899–1902) – and the ensuing Report (1904) by the Committee on Physical Deterioration with regard to the condition of too many of the British volunteers for military service – were proofs indeed (e.g. Jones 1977: 30). Hence the

Box 2.1 Leading Characteristics of the British Empire

Type of empire
- Geographically scattered: 'the sun never sets on the patches of pink' (cf. the contiguous Roman empire) because the British Empire was based on trade, which, in turn, was based on shipping.
- Economically diverse: from subsistence to commercial agriculture; from cheap trade to competitive manufacturing.
- Politically variegated: devolved 'least trouble' forms of government being the order of the day.

Types of imperial possession
(i) 'New World' settlements of British people elsewhere (whether voluntary, encouraged or enforced) from 17th century: e.g. North-east USA, then Canada, Australia, New Zealand.
(ii) plantation colonies, dependent on imported slave and indentured labour e.g. Burma and East Africa dependent on indentured labour; West Indies and south-east USA dependent on slave and indentured labour.
(iii) East India Company trade undertakings, evolving into British Raj: run by the best and worst of the British ruling classes (+ their families); with the cooperation/cooption of the best and worst of Indian and Anglo-Indian elites.
(iv) trading stations e.g. Singapore, Hong Kong, which depended on their capacity to attract a mix of independent traders: hence the requirement for 'moderated British rule' + self-financing status.
(v) 19th century 'Europe's scramble for Africa'; resulting in a mix of British settlements (amongst other Euro-settlements) superimposed on indigenous tribal populations and compounded by the missionary factor; eventual 'national' boundaries which made little tribal, linguistic or religious sense; massive black/white racial inequalities re access to land, education, political voice, etc.

expressions of eugenic concern over what was to do be done with those deemed seriously unfit (e.g. Jones, K. 1972); and hence also the parliamentary support for such preventive measures as the provision of school meals for necessitous schoolchildren (1906) and school health inspections (1907). Meanwhile it was still regarded as appropriate to maximise the contribution of 'surplus' healthy young people from Britain to at least the white-majority-settled portions of the Empire, by for instance exporting 'Poor Law children' to Canada in the 1900s (just as 'Children's Home children' were being exported to Australia until as late as 1967) (Bean and Melville 1989; Women's Group 1951; Parker 1990). Considerations of Empire (followed by Old Commonwealth), manifestly came before considerations of children's rights.

Socio-imperial elites

Missionaries famously travelled 'on the coat-tails of empire' – and thence, on occasion, could cause embarrassment to British officials ostensibly loth to offend native religious sensibilities (e.g. Mitchell 1973: 303–310; Ustorf 1998). The fact that missionary endeavours were also responsible for such a breadth of health, welfare and education developments outside of the White-settled British Empire, says as much about the imperial government's lack of interest in such concerns, as about the capacities of the various missionary societies for providing schools, hospitals and welfare centres, *en route* (as was hoped), to the conversion of entire colonial peoples to a particular Christian affiliation. At home, the contrast between what such societies were inspired to attempt across the colonies, as opposed to within Britain, did not go unremarked. Salvation Army founder William Booth's *In Darkest England, And The Way Out* (1890) stood in eloquent protest to what he saw as the contemporary missionary obsession with 'Darkest Africa' at the expense of the poor at home.

Other sorts of elite were easier to categorise, hierarchically. The first grade (in every sense) comprised British military/civilian officials – and their wives and families. The second comprised leading local (British) settlers. The third could comprise leading Asian or Eurasian families (in the case of India), members of the Chinese Establishment (in the case of Hong Kong) or light-skinned Afro-Europeans (in the case of the Caribbean). The one potential slot, never significantly filled or recognised, was that of an Indigenous or Euro-Indigenous elite, within what were to become the White majority-settled Dominions of Canada, Australia and New Zealand.

Whereas missionaries were presumed to have gone out to 'do good' (or to try to win souls by doing good), British colonial officials, settlers and their hangers-on were more about trying to create something of a British lifestyle for themselves in an alien environment (e.g. Edwardes and Dilkes 1973: 280–294). The white-settled Dominions apart, this led to people of often quite modest social origins back in Britain 'putting on airs and graces' in the colonies and 'taking servants for granted', in a way which would scarcely have been tolerated (let alone been affordable) 'at home'. But they were not at home – any more than, in a different sense, were the local Anglophile-elites with whom they were supposed to be on terms. The end result was something of a British colonial lifestyle which was at once as much removed from native contamination *in situ* as it was from the realities of life in Britain.

Paradoxically, it was a world whose social and hierarchical certainties were to take longer to unravel than was the case for the home, mother country, before, during and after the Great War 1914–18.

20th century war and social policy

The idea that engaging in war could be socially constructive (i.e. socially *de*structive from an establishment point of view) was famously propounded, in retrospect, by Richard Titmuss (World War II's official British historian in respect of *Problems of Social Policy*, 1950) after the event. The closer the war, and the more encompassing the popular effort, he argued, the greater its potential for boosting domestic social policy development (Titmuss 1958 – and see below, p. 17). Hence, by comparison with the Boer War (let alone the distant Crimea), the relatively huge impact of the Great War 1914–18 on the lives of ordinary people in Britain and the even greater impact of World War II – mass conscription, the *Blitz*, food rationing, mass evacuation, emergency labour mobilisation, and all – saw Government becoming ever more responsible, in its turn, for safeguarding the wellbeing of the people.

By comparison, for the white-settled Dominions, World War II was an occasion for sacrifices abroad thereafter to be remembered, as proofs of the quality, loyalty and steadfastness of these 'British-born peoples', when called to serve on behalf of the mother country. Whereas, for men from such as the British West Indies, the fact of their having volunteered so extensively for World War II service (e.g. Ferguson 1998: 249–50; 253) was construed *only by them*, after the event, as constituting a 'ticket' into this white man's club. It was precisely such feelings of 'just desserts' – in combination with the unthinking open-endedness of the 1948 British Nationality Act (Box 2.4 on page 23), coupled with Britain's own massive post war labour shortages – which help explain the sustained immigration to Britain from the British Caribbean from as early as 1948, with the docking of the *Empire Windrush* (below and Panayi 1999: 38–39).

To be sure, the conclusion of World War II had been hailed in the British press as being not merely a British but a British imperial triumph.

> The whole Empire has played a valorous and ungrudging part... It is the Empire's 'finest hour' too.' (*Daily Telegraph* May 8, 1945, as quoted in Barnett 1986: 3)
>
> The grand Canadians who, when our peril was greatest, came to nourish and sustain our resistance ... the Australians and New

Zealanders who bore the brunt of the battle in Egypt and Greece ... the South Africans who tore from Mussolini's grasp the first fruits of his treachery ... the loyal Indians and sons of Colonies who won battle honours in Egypt and Italy. (*Daily Mirror* May 9, 1945, as quoted in Barnett 1986: 3)

This was high-sounding talk – for all that, none of the imperial subjects so recruited could be said to have been fighting directly in their own country's interest, let alone for their own 'national' survival – something of an anachronistic idea for the British Empire, even by the 1940s (e.g. Clark 1973).[5]

So when Richard Titmuss opined that

> The waging of modern war presupposes and imposes a great increase in social discipline; moreover, this discipline is only tolerable if – and only if social inequalities are not intolerable... . It follows that the acceptance of these social disciplines – of obligations as well as rights – made necessary by war, by preparations for war, and by the long-run consequences of war, must influence the aims and content of social policies not only during the war itself but in peace-time as well (Titmuss 1957: 85)

he was speaking of and for Britain, not the British Empire. For the youthful Lee Kuan Yew of Singapore, it had rather been the experience of Japanese occupation which provided 'the most lasting education I could ever have' (BBC 2002).

Against such a backcloth, the 'wartime-halo' of the British welfare state (Marshall 1975: 79) was understandable and much needed at home. Legislation already half-promised in wartime – if not actually introduced, as in the case of the 1944 Education Act – had the status of a just recompense for the nation's feat of solidarity, courage and endurance thereafter to be eulogised as its finest hour(s). For Clement Atlee's landslide-elected 1945 Labour government,[6] it was a great chance to legislate for a new sort of Britain. And the period 1945–1950 did see a deal of social legislation – to which the title 'welfare state' was subsequently applied.

Nevertheless the title *was* applied only after the event – and to the distinct un-enthusiasm of key social reformers, preoccupied as these were with practicalities rather than rhetoric.

> ... I must say that I am no more enamoured today of the indefinable abstraction 'The Welfare State' than I was some twenty years ago

when, with the advent of the National Health, National Insurance and other legislative promissories, the term acquired an international as well as a national popularity.... Generalized slogans rarely induce concentration of thought; more often they prevent us from asking significant questions about reality. Morally satisfied and intellectually dulled, we sink back into our presumptive cosy British world of welfare.   (Titmuss 1958: 124)

Furthermore it was evident that, for all the thrill of Labour's sweeping, election victory of 1945, there had been no grand plan in readiness. Those who subsequently seized on the Beveridge Report of 1942 as the equivalent of a blueprint for a welfare state, were in effect clutching at straws – or rather at the Report's opening, ringing, rhetorical, declarations of principle (Box 2.2). The main body of this report amounted, by contrast, to precisely the sort of meticulous tidying-up and gap-filling exercise Lord William Beveridge had been commissioned to produce.

To be sure Beveridge had strayed well beyond his brief in arguing so grandly (and with such a sound command of the media) for a single comprehensive system of national insurance, itself to be part of a composite attack on all of his *Five Giants on the Road of Social Progress*. But

Box 2.2   Three Guiding Principles of Recommendations

- The first principle is that any proposals for the future, while they should use to the full the experience gathered in the past, should not be restricted by consideration of sectional interests established in the obtaining of that experience. Now when the war is abolishing landmarks of every kind, is the opportunity for using experience in a clear field. A revolutionary moment in the world's history is a time for revolutions, not for patching.
- The second principle is that organisation of social insurance should be treated as one part only of a comprehensive policy of social progress. Social Insurance fully developed may provide income security; it is an attack upon Want. But Want is one only of five giants on the road of reconstruction and in some ways the easiest to attack. The others are Disease, Ignorance, Squalor and Idleness.
- The third principle is that social security must be achieved by co-operation between the State and the individual. The State should offer security for service and contribution. The State in organising social security should not stifle incentive, opportunity, responsibility; in establishing a national minimum it should leave room and encouragement for voluntary action by each individual to provide more than that minimum for himself and his family.   (Beveridge (1942) pp. 6–7)

in reality his conceptions of *Want, Disease, Ignorance, Squalor and Idleness,* were as static as was his underlying notions of social and familial relations. So it seems less of a wonder, in retrospect, that he should have spoken of his Plan (p. 17) as 'in some ways a revolution, but in more important ways ... a natural development from the past. It is a British Revolution' – than that others should ever have credited his report with more than wartime rhetorical significance (e.g. Jones C. 1993).

The Welfare State: inclusive potential, exclusive actuality

There were three party political pillars to the eventual welfare state construct:

- W. Beveridge's (Liberal) 1942 plan (above) for universal, flat-rate, national insurance (legislated for, with modifications, 1946–1948);
- R.A.B. Butler's (Conservative) 1944 plan for secondary education to be free for all, according to age, ability and aptitude (legislated for in 1944);
- Aneurin Bevan's (Labour) 1946 plan for a National Health Service, free to all at the point of use (legislated 1946, to come into effect 1948);

It was, to say the least, a disparate collection of foundations upon which to build the new Britain. It was consensual to the extent that few leading politicians in the major political parties were to feel it practicable, over at least the next 20 years, to speak openly against the very idea (though what precisely *was* the very idea?) of Britain's welfare state. Such a degree of party political stand-off was to prove more than sufficient for the spate of 'non-controversial' welfare state expansionism of the 1950s and 1960s.

By the same token, it was also a good time for the launch of a new welfare state university subject under the leadership of Richard Titmuss, its first named professor at the London School of Economics (LSE). Like its object, Social Administration was deemed to be beyond (mere) ideological debate, by virtue of its being presumed non-party-political. Yet the fact that the beginnings of both welfare state and welfare state-*subject* in Britain should have coincided with the end of empire and of the growing movement of large numbers of colonial and ex-colonial immigrants into Britain, was destined to bring the two sides of this story together at last.

20 *Social Policy and the Commonwealth*

So far as aspiring individuals within the Empire/Commonwealth were concerned, there were three categories of career prospect in evidence:

- the production/confirmation of post-imperial elites
  Just as the British Colonial Service had long been able to attract potential administrators from the likes of Oxford and Cambridge, just so, in its closing days, was it more than willing to encourage 'top flight' colonials (backed by their fee-paying families) access to ostensibly just the same forms of education in Britain. In the paraphrased words of Lee Kuan Yew (BBC 2002): 'We learnt Shakespeare. We learnt poems about flowers I never knew in my home country... . But whenever I had occasion to meet with my generation of Commonwealth leaders thereafter, I found we had this common ground of having experienced the same sort of "good British education"' (BBC 2002). More self-importantly, the History of the London School of Economics and Political Science, as narrated by its former Director Ralf Dahrendorf sees the LSE as having been a source of inspiration right across the pink-shaded portions of the then global map by the simple fact of its existence as a magnet for ambitious members and would-be members of an emergent Commonwealth elite (Dahrendorf 1995: 402ff)
- the distribution of academic and other support personnel around the Commonwealth (mainly from the Old to the New Commonwealth)
  As any middle-ranking British social science academic with a yen for travelling abroad without having to learn another language used to know, the postwar Empire/Commonwealth was a mine of opportunity. Universities around the former-imperial world are yet still staffed with some of them, many reputed to be over-paid and over-promoted, by comparison with what they could conceivably have achieved at home (or, for that matter, in the more truly competitive academic markets of North America and Australasia).
- mass economic migration into Britain, initially as of right, thanks to the terminology of the 1948 British Nationality Act (see below).
  The key practical distinction turned out, once again, to be between the Old Commonwealth (i.e. the white-settled Dominions[7]) and the New (of successively liberated British possessions in Africa, Asia and the Caribbean). Visitors from the Old Commonwealth were presumed to be 'basically British', self-supporting – and unlikely to stay long; whereas incomers from the New Commonwealth were presumed to be in search of a better life, all too likely to take up per-

manent residence, bring in their families and 'take advantage' of the welfare state. All of which was pointed evidence of just how little the 'ties of Empire' (other than those of the Anglophone conglomerate) counted in the domestic British consciousness.

The social residues of empire

The British empire had worked by moving people 'usefully' around: slave labour from Africa to the Caribbean; the transport of 'criminals' to Australia; the inducement of indentured labour from the Indian subcontinent to other parts of Asia, Africa and the Caribbean; the 'free trade' migration of individuals from one to other parts of the empire (aside from Britain); the export of charity children from Britain to the labour-hungry Dominions; the 'inspired' migration of British missionaries to some of the empire's least reachable parts; the induced emigration of low income settlers from Britain to the so-called 'virgin' territories of Canada, Australia and New Zealand; above all, the Colonial Office's distribution of generations of aspiring colonial civil servants right around the world.

The long-term, cumulative effects of all this remain hard to estimate. That its post-imperial phase should have involved the spontaneous movement of hard-pressed colonial and Commonwealth citizens into Great Britain after World War II, was something which might with hindsight have been anticipated but which manifestly was not. This time, however, the very institution of popular democracy was to ensure a more targeted response on the part of government. Unlike the *Aliens Act* of 1905 (designed to keep out anyone who might become a charge on the rates), the first Commonwealth Immigrants Act of 1962 sought to discriminate between categories of Commonwealth immigrant – albeit without specific reference to their racial origins. (Box 2.3) This it contrived to do by linking acceptability to employability (see Panayi 1999: 48), despite the fact that preceding racial tensions had stemmed not from employment so much as from inner-city housing conditions (Jones 1977); and that the public sector recruitment campaigns of the labour-hungry 1950s (e.g. on behalf of London Transport, British Rail and the NHS) had been directed precisely at the unskilled of the British Caribbean, (e.g. Panayi 1999: 40–41). In short, this was a continuation of an old imperial tradition: of moving surplus, cheap labour around[8] – except that this time the movement was spontaneously from the bottom up, in the face of opposition from the top down.

Box 2.3   1905 Aliens Act and 1962 Commonwealth Immigrants Act

1905 Aliens Act	1962 Commonwealth Immigrants Act
Declared purpose: To prevent 'undesirable and destitute aliens', or persons who were likely to become a charge upon the rates, from landing on these shores.	**Declared purpose:** To be able to control the numbers and employability characteristics of Commonwealth immigrants entering Britain.
Implicit purpose: To limit the entry of 'New Jews'.	**Implicit purpose:** To cap levels of 'New Commonwealth' immigration.
Key provisions: Unless they could prove themselves to be *bona fide* refugees from religious persecution, penniless aliens were not to be allowed to land. Those who were allowed to land, might be expelled by the Home Secretary within one year of their arrival, should they be found to be in receipt of poor relief.	**Key provisions:** Three categories of vouchers to be issued, based on notional employability: a. For those who had specific jobs to come to; b. For those with specific marketable skills; c. For unskilled workers without definite prospects of employment.

As intended, the 1962 Act advantaged members of the Old Commonwealth (though even more obvious was the need to exempt the Irish from the same employability criteria – Jones 1977). But it also – perhaps un-intendedly – advantaged immigrants from the Indian sub-continent *vis-a-vis* those from the Caribbean, the former's traditions of extended family networking being that much more entrenched (e.g. Jones 1977).

The 1962 Commonwealth Immigrants Act was a first response to the British popular intolerance which had culminated in the infamous Nottingham and Notting Hill riots of 1958. It was an intolerance responded to by relevant constituency MPs, irrespective of political party. Out-and-out racist expressions of rejection were not admissible within Parliament (though MP Sir Cyril Osborne's reputed determination 'to keep Blacks out, irrespective of race, colour or creed' came pretty close to the limit); but they were rampant in the national and local press.

Hence there was a *civil liberties* reaction to this xenophobia, which explains why there had to be a cross-party *race relations/integrationist* complement – albeit behindhand – to the sequence of measures taken to control Commonwealth immigration post-1962. (Box 2.4). The ostensible logic of this dual approach was that keeping the flow of incomers down to 'manageable proportions' was a prerequisite for improving race relations and hence promoting the integration (*social inclusion* not being a term then in use) of those (New) Commonwealth communities already present in Britain. Yet the race relations component never carried the clout or credibility of the immigration controls component, precisely because it was attempting to legislate for consensus, on what were issues of conspicuous dissensus.

The Old Commonwealth and its 1970s moment of truth

It was not merely Britain which was taken unawares by the speed and scale of the Commonwealth's transformation after World War II. For many in the Dominions – who had hitherto thought of themselves as *the* authentic British Commonwealth – the accession of 'brown-skinned' India must have been momentous enough – let alone the succession of small nations to the self-same, exponentially expanding, so-called Commonwealth club. The events of the 1970s – the decade not merely of oil crisis and of the questioning of the economic credentials of the western welfare state *per se*, but also of Britain's entry into the then European Economic Community (EEC) – were of landmark implication.

For the Dominions, Britain's entry into the EEC was a final signal that the preferential trading ties of Empire were at an end. Whereas for the miracle little tiger growth economies of Asia Pacific, it was the west's oil-provoked but seeming welfare-exacerbated *economic* crises of government which confirmed their notions of the welfare state as being a form of western disease to be avoided at all costs. This was also the period from which western social scientists began, in turn, to take

Box 2.4 Immigration Controls and Race Relations Legislation

Immigration Controls	Race Relations Legislation
1948: British Nationality Act	
1962: Commonwealth Immigrants Act	
	1965: Race Relations Act
1968: Commonwealth Immigrants Act	1968: Race Relations Act
1971: Immigration Act	
	1976: Race Relations Act

the performances of East Asian economies increasingly seriously (e.g. Doling and Jones Finer 2000). In a quite different sense, however, it was the period from which 'senior' members of the Commonwealth also began to take the downwardly spiralling performances of numbers of its smaller states no less seriously.

Margaret Thatcher won the 1979 general election in Britain, with a promise to free ordinary British workers from the tyranny of the trades unions *and* to 'roll back' the burden of the free-for-all, alleged dependency-inducing, tax-hungry welfare state. Her stance was to prove of striking, albeit accidental, import for the Commonwealth. On the one hand, Mrs Thatcher was no great fan of the 'hand-out' school of (New) Commonwealth Relations – but then she was no great fan of what she saw as the 'hand-out' school of European Community relations either. In the end, nevertheless, she both signed over Hong Kong to China in 1984 (Jones 1990) and signed over Britain (1986) to the European Single Market (Kavanagh 1990).

It was in the wake and ostensible despite of Thatcherism that *New Labour* was returned in electoral triumph in 1997. Ironically, however, this was comparable with Clement Attlee's loss of office in 1951. In that case it had been a reformed Conservative party which had convinced the electorate that they could manage the same (welfare state) show better than its instigators could. Whereas, in 1997, it was a reformed Labour Party which convinced sufficient of the electorate that it could – in effect – run and update Thatcherism better than could what remained of a tired and discredited Conservative Party (Jones Finer 1997).

The revised doctrine was revealingly titled 'Third Way': to neither the left nor right but something radically over and above. The imprecision of the expression proved sufficient not merely to generate a healthy quantity of books for student reading lists, but to stand comparison with the equally woolly years of so-called welfare state consensus in the 1950s. Only, this time, the consensus was about restructuring and monitoring the welfare state, rather than simply watching and helping it grow.

Even if Blair's *Third Way* might, for a time, have seemed consensual within Britain, it has so far proved a divisive force within the Commonwealth. At the heart of this honed-down version of Neo-Liberalism is a conviction that all can be well in a free market-led world – provided individuals, families and communities 'pull their weight' and make the most of their opportunities. The genuinely incapacitated will need to be supported, but there is no place for shirkers, either individually or collectively.

As such, the doctrines of the Third Way have resonated throughout the Old Commonwealth – *and* found ready audiences in the miracle economies of East Asia, whose example had helped fire the imagination of British and other western politicians in the first place (see Chs 8, 9, 12, 14 in this volume; and Jones Finer 1997 1999)[9]. But for the seeming perpetual losers of the Commonwealth – in South Asia, the Caribbean and above all sub-Saharan Africa – the behavioural criticisms relate seemingly to longer, deeper, societal characteristics.

Conclusion

Neither the British Empire nor the ensuing Commonwealth of Nations was designed with notions of social inclusion in mind. Nevertheless, this has been an Empire gradually wound-down in what, for the most part, has been a peaceable, intentionally amicable fashion. Uniquely, the Commonwealth of Nations, the scope of whose voluntary membership – irrespective of how many chose to continue with the British monarchy as actual head of state – is indicative of there being a sense of continuing common interests, if not so much as shared policy objectives. At the very least, the Commonwealth remains a decent sort of international club for its member states large and (especially) small to belong to – not least, perhaps, because the United States of America is not in it. Also, according to some of the same observers, because this is the best way for former colonies to be able to play, not merely upon Britain's 'imperial guilt', but upon the guilt of its white-settled Dominions in general.

What remains open to question, is how far such a piecemeal past can conceivably contribute to a cooperative, positive future. Notions of democracy (let alone *liberal* democracy) have proved the factor most difficult to export from Britain to places and peoples whose 'national boundaries' have been colonially imposed. To portray such as part of a conflict between 'North' and 'South', is as much an affront to geography as to the realities of post-imperialism.

Notes

1. i.e. Progressively deregulated from the trammels of mercantilism.
2. e.g. the Rev. Thomas Malthus who 'took charge of a small parish in Surrey' in the same year (1797) as he became a fellow of Jesus College, Cambridge.
3. 'Utility' in this context being a policy's practical capacity to promote pleasure and minimise pain. Jeremy Bentham, the founding philosopher of

utilitarianism, was determined to cut through and cut out the weight of non-functional illogical tradition in British law and administration.
4. With the partial exception of France (wherein statutory categorical rights to assistance – *assistances obligatoires* – whose amounts were nonetheless locally determined – were instituted from the early 1900s), near everywhere else was to come to rely solely on social insurance at the national level. Social assistance was to remain a local-run, discretionary, last resort.
5. Aside from the Raj in India, and the Dominions of the Old Commonwealth, there was seemingly no notion that other colonial possessions might develop sentiments of 'national' statehood for themselves.
6. Note, not Winston Churchill who, for all his revered abilities as wartime leader, was not noted or trusted as a 'man of the people' when it came to workers rights.
7. South Africa constitutes an ambivalent case here, being by far the largest white settlement in Sub-Saharan Africa, yet the whites remain a minority population in the territory.
8. Cf. the former use of slave and indentured labour.
9. The onset of the Asian Financial Crisis naturally dented the East Asian aura, since it seemed to indicate that the behaviour of entire financial and commercial sectors in East/South-east Asia had long been operating below notional western norms of probity and openness.

References

Barnett, C. (1986) *The Audit of War*, Basingstoke: Macmillan.
BBC (2002) *Lowering the Flag:* Episode 4, Radio 4, September 9.
Bean, P., Melville, J. (1989) Lost Children of the Empire, London: Unwin Hyman.
Beveridge, Sir William (1942) *Social Insurance and Allied Services: Report*, London: HMSO Cmd.6404.
Booth, William (1890) *In Darkest Africa, and the Way Out*, London: International Headquarters of the Salvation Army.
Brundage, A. (2002) *The English Poor Laws 1700–1930*, Basingstoke: Palgrave.
Buchi, W. (1974) 'La Politique Sociale comme Discipline Scientifique dans les Pays de Langue Allemande', in R. Girod and P. de Laubier (eds) *L'Etude de la Politique Sociale*, Berne: Commission Nationale Suisse pour l'UNESCO.
Cahnman, W.J. and Schmitt M. (1979) 'The Concept of Social Policy' (*Sozialpolitik*), *Journal of Social Policy*, 8.1: 47–59.
Clark, A. (1973) 'Global War', in S.W. Sears (ed.) *The Horizon History of the British Empire*, American Heritage Publishing Co., Inc. in association with BBC-TV/Time-Life Books. [Copyright Time Life International (Nederland). Printed in the United States of America.] pp. 455–464.
Dahrendorf, R. (1995) *LSE: A History of the London School of Economics and Political Science, 1805–1995*, Oxford: Oxford University Press.
Doling, J. and Jones Finer, C. (2000) 'Looking East, Looking West: Trends in Orientalism and Occidentalism Amongst Social Scientists', in C. Jones Finer (ed.) *Comparing the Social Policy Experience of Britain and Taiwan*, Aldershot: Ashgate.
Edwardes, M. and Dilks D. (1973) 'A Remote Elite', in S.W. Sears (ed.) *The Horizon History of the British Empire*, American Heritage Publishing Co. Inc.,

in association with BBC-TV/Time-Life Books. [Copyright Time Life International (Nederland). Printed in the United States of America.] pp. 280–294.
Ferguson, J. (1998) *A Traveller's History of the Caribbean*, Moreton in the Marsh, Gloucestershire: Windrush Press.
Finer, S.E. (1952) *The Life and Times of Sir Edwin Chadwick*, London: Routledge.
Greenleaf, W.H. (1983) *The British Political Tradition: Volume Two: The Ideological Heritage*, London: Methuen.
Jones C. (1977) *Immigration and Social Policy in Britain*, London: Tavistock.
Jones C. (1979) 'Teaching Social Policy: Some European Perspectives', *Journal of Social Policy*, 8.4: 509–526.
Jones C. (1990) *Promoting Prosperity: The Hong Kong Way of Social Policy*, Hong Kong: The Chinese University Press.
Jones C. (1993) 'Beveridge Abroad: from student to statesman', in N. Deakin and M. Willis (eds) *Social Services Research 1993 No 1: Beveridge Special Edition*, Birmingham: Department of Social Policy and Social Work, the University of Birmingham.
Jones, K. (1972) The *History of the Mental Health Services*, London: Routledge and Kegan Paul.
Jones Finer, C. (1997) 'The New Social Policy in Britain', *Social Policy and Administration*, 31.5: 154–170.
Jones Finer, C. (1999) 'Trends and Developments in Welfare States', in J. Clasen (ed.) *Comparative Social Policy*, Oxford: Blackwell, pp. 15–33.
Kavanagh D. (1990) *Thatcherism and British Politics: The End of Consensus?*, Oxford: Oxford University Press; 2nd edition.
Kidd, A. (1999) *State, Society and the Poor in Nineteenth-Century England*, Basingstoke: Macmillan.
Marshall, T.H. (1975) *Social Policy in the Twentieth Century*, London: Hutchinson Education.
Matthias, P. (1969) *The First Industrial Nation: A Economic History of Britain*, London: Methuen.
Mitchell, D. (1973) 'The Missionary Impulse', in S.W. Sears (ed.) *The Horizon History of the British Empire*, American Heritage Publishing Co., Inc., in association with BBC Time-Life Books.
Panayi, P. (1999) *The Impact of Immigration: A documentary history of the effects and experiences of immigrants in Britain since 1945*, Manchester: Manchester University Press.
Parker R.A. (1990) *Away From Home: A History of Child Care*, Ilford: Barnado's. (First published in 1968.)
Rimlinger, G.V. (1971) *Welfare Policy and Industrialization in Europe, America and Russia*, New York: Wiley.
Smellie, K.B. (1968) *A History of Local Government*, London: Kingsley Bryce; 4th edition.
Tampke, J. (1981) 'Bismarck's Social Legislation: a genuine breakthrough?', in W.J. Mommsen (ed.) *The Emergence of the Welfare State in Britain and Germany*, London: Croom Helm.
Titmuss, R.M. (1950) *Problems of Social Policy*, London: HMSO and Longmans, Green and Co.
Titmuss, R.M. (1958) 'War and Social Policy', in *Essays on the Welfare State*, London: George Allen and Unwin, pp. 75–87.

Titmuss, R.M. (1971) *The Gift Relationship*, London: Allen Unwin.
Ustorf, W. (1998) 'Global Topographies: the spiritual, the social and the geographical in the missionary movement from the west', *Social Policy and Administration*, 32.5: 591–604.
Women's Group on Public Welfare, Committee on Child Emigration (1951) *Child Emigration*, London: National Council of Social Service.

3
Social Inclusion Globalisation and the Commonwealth

Patricia Harris

Introductory

Social inclusion has been voted policy metaphor of the year. During the 1980s and 1990s it spread through continental Europe, achieving prominence in the deliberations of the European Commission and the European Union anti-poverty programes (Jones and Smyth 1999). It then became a central plank of Blair's New Labour and entered the field of policy analysis and development studies more generally (ibid.). Inclusion is, at first sight, a heart-warming notion, promising greater cohesion and more shared opportunities. But it begs a host of questions about who gets to belong, to what sort of collectivity, and on what terms. Equally, and most seriously, there are questions about who gets excluded and what happens to them. Given the pressures of globalisation, such issues are now as important at the level of the Commonwealth as at the national plane where they are traditionally posed.

In this chapter I locate social inclusion within an historic tradition whereby western theorists and administrators have pondered the relationship between market and society. In this respect, social inclusion is only the most recent of a long list of terms concerned with social relations in market economies. Behind it trail social capital, social participation, social solidarity, social cohesion and social bonds. Tracing this trajectory helps to reveal the peculiarities of the present. My undertaking is generally restricted to Anglophone countries, and, more particularly, to the 'British' tradition in welfare theory. As other contributors to this volume comment, it is highly debatable whether this tradition can be adapted to different nations, particularly in the face of wide economic, cultural and historical differences. I touch on this issue throughout the chapter, and consider the relevance of British theorising for the Commonwealth in the concluding section.

Structuring this analysis is a distinction between the 'national' and the 'global' era. The 'national' era refers to a period stretching from the late 18th century to the mid-1970s in which it was assumed that the national economy – and hence national welfare – were naturally co-extensive with the 'nation state' (even though this nation state was significantly shaped by membership of international bodies such as the Commonwealth and other major trading and political bodies). The 'global' era refers to the comparatively short time span of the last quarter century and is marked by the decreased autonomy of the nation state and its subordination to transnational capital.

A framework for analysis

The social cohesion motif arises in the face of a long standing concern that the competitive dynamics of the market will in fact drive people apart. This worry proceeds along two fronts. The first concerns the market's impact on the structural features of society, most particularly *social order* (stability, security and integration) and *social justice* (distribution of resources and benefits between individuals and groups). The second axis concerns the market's impact on social relationships. Here the main issues are *social solidarity* (people's sense of connection one with another) and *social participation* (people's involvement in the social and economic life of their community). These dimensions are not mutually exclusive or antagonistic – social justice, for example, may be positioned as an important aspect of social order, or social participation of solidarity. In any given theory or social metaphor, moreover, there are always elements of all four dimensions. Nevertheless, I suggest that theorists have a primary loyalty, a place where their thinking naturally comes to rest.

On this basis, the schema gives rise to four quadrants or 'conceptual spaces' within which the market-society problematic comes to be considered. It is illustrated in Figure 3.1. In this configuration the zones are numbered in an approximate relation to their chronological appearance. (My suggestion will be that the current thrust of government policy in Anglophone countries is located in Zone Four.)

Market and society: conceptual shifts in the national era

I now trace the changes occurring in the 'national' era. This involve consideration of changes in the way that order, justice, solidarity and

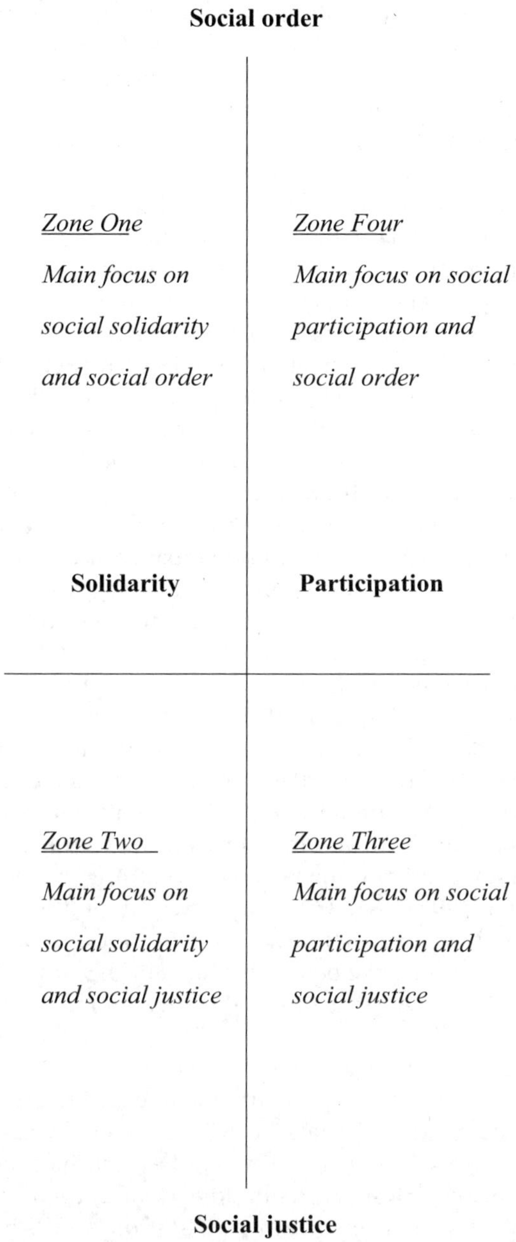

Social order

Zone One
Main focus on
social solidarity
and social order

Zone Four
Main focus on social
participation and
social order

Solidarity | **Participation**

Zone Two
Main focus on
social solidarity
and social justice

Zone Three
Main focus on social
participation and
social justice

Social justice

Figure 3.1 Four Conceptual Spaces for Thinking about the Impact of the Market on Society

participation are conceptualised as well as shifts in the conceptual spaces. The broad direction of my analysis is illustrated in Figure 3.2.

In the early industrial period, it was the market's consequences for order and solidarity that were at the centre of attention (Zone One). Social justice, as an identifiable sphere of government action, had not yet been invented. In any event, the market was then a signifier of justice, rather than antithetical to it. It marked the independent sphere of free economic exchanges, away from the network of monopolies, guilds and restrictions associated with feudalism. At that time, too, poverty was a problem of order rather than financial distributions. The main question was how to control the movements of the destitute and provide relief to those considered deserving. Further, it was assumed that the labouring poor – who made up the great bulk of the population – would participate in the daily grind by force of circumstance. But worries about social order and social solidarity there certainly were. Very early on, Adam Smith suggested that the division of labour could undermine social bonds unless 'government takes some pains to avoid it' (Smith [1776] 1979: 782). Further, sympathy or fellow feeling – 'one of the original passions of human nature' – was needed to moderate 'the injurious consequences of self-interested actions' (Smith [1759] 1976: 47). On the question of order, Smith took a wider view than most of his contemporaries, visualising it as a 'right ordering' between the three main classes. As part of this he assumed that the labouring poor faced landowners and industrialists as rational owners of labour. His recommendations for their support were relatively generous, including 'a liberal reward for labour; the establishment of a minimum wage rate consistent with common humanity and the improvement of the circumstances of the lower ranks according to the principle of equity' (Dean 1992: 231–232). The force of political deliberation, though, was in favour of the *laissez faire* notions of Malthus and Ricardo, thus jamming the possibility that Smith's 'principle of equity' would flower into a territory of social justice subject to the purposeful action of government.

As industrialisation progressed, so did worries about its divisive effects. In the outlying camps, Marx documented the degradations of capitalism and predicted that the whole system would fall on the sword of its own contradictions, while Herbert Spencer lobbied for the survival of the fittest. In the middle ground, theorists considered the divisive consequences of industrialisation and urbanisation. In this respect, Tonnies [1887] (1957) offered his classic account of *Gemeinschaft* and *Gesellshaft*, longing for the commitments of village

Social order

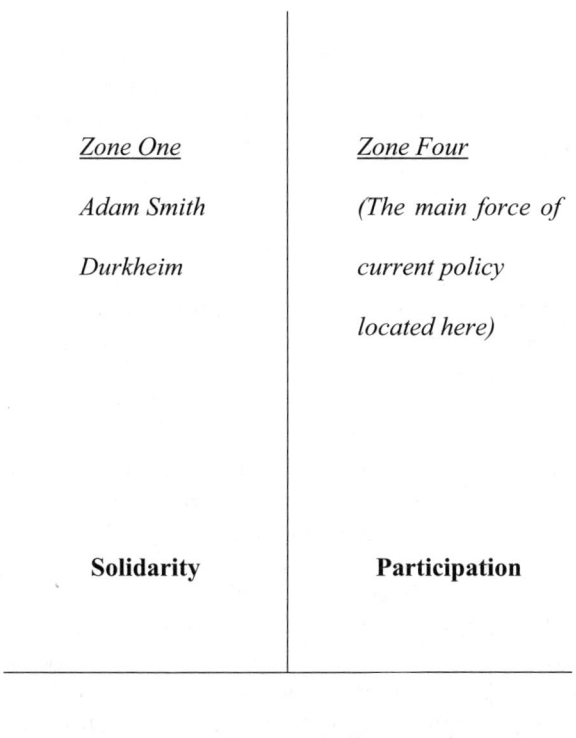

Zone One

Adam Smith

Durkheim

Zone Four

(The main force of current policy located here)

Solidarity | **Participation**

T.H. Marshall

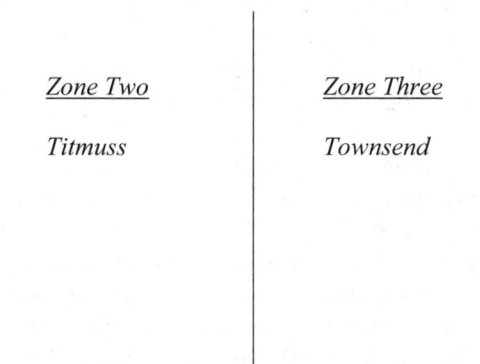

Zone Two

Titmuss

Zone Three

Townsend

Social justice

Figure 3.2 Key Theorists in the National Era

and family. In our context, though, it is Emile Durkheim who is most important given the way his ideas were subsequently adapted by Richard Titmuss (see below). Durkheim offers a classic representation of the relationship between social solidarity and social order (Zone One), while setting this relationship securely within a market-society problematic. His inquiries were prompted by a perception of massive industrial change, most particularly, the concentration of capital and the increased specificity of labour. On this he argued that:

> We need have no further illusions about the tendencies of modern industry; it advances steadily towards powerful machines, towards greater concentrations of forces and capital, and consequently to the extreme division of labour. Occupations are infinitely separated and specialised, not only inside the factories, but each product is itself a specialty dependent on others. (Durkheim [1893] 1933: 39)

Having made this diagnosis, Durkheim set aside Marx's critique of capital and Tonnies' pessimistic assessments of *Gesellshaft*. In their place he considered the market's capacity to produce a new form of 'organic' solidarity in which the individual 'becomes more closely dependent on society' while 'also becoming more autonomous' (Durkheim [1893] 1933: 37). Despite this optimism, Durkheim, like Smith, worried about the market's capacity to disrupt social order and undermine people's sense of connection with each other. In certain respects, these preoccupations with order and integration bear a surface resemblance to various forms of contemporary conservative discourse. Durkheim's analysis, however, was tied up with the structural features of industrial society and the obligations of those in power. It was a *sociological* interpretation of events and in this way quite different from today's quasi-psychological, behavioural renderings of social solidarity and social order.

Durkheim was writing in the late 19th and early 20th centuries – just when poverty, industrial unrest and concerns about public health were suggesting that governments needed to take a more interventionist role if the health and safety of the nation was to be secured. What he considered to be 'abnormalities' (anomie, personal isolation and industrial dislocation) were coming to be seen as regular features of capitalism. Rose suggests that a new formula of rule developed as a result, which 'lay somewhere between classical liberalism and nascent socialism' (Rose 1996: 48). However, governments took on their newly interventionist role in a patchy and halting fashion. The experience of the depression, together with J.M. Keynes' sense that unemployment was a normal feature of capitalism, were necessary to push the thing along. By the time of post-war reconstruction, theorists and administrators were prepared to argue that the market, if left to itself, would most likely produce considerable evils, most famously 'Want, Disease, Ignorance, Squalor and Idleness' (Beveridge 1942: 6). In such ways, social justice came of age as a proper sphere of government action.

In one influential stream of thought, exemplified by Richard Titmuss, these new commitments to social justice were combined with older allegiances to social solidarity (Zone Two in our analysis). Titmuss conceptualised justice in terms of the benefits accruing to people in different parts of the occupational hierarchy and took the division of labour as the primary influence on social solidarity. Trailing a debt to Durkheim, he proposed that an 'increasing division of labour in society and, simultaneously, a great increase in labour specificity' meant that 'more and more people at one or more stages in their life consciously experience the process of selection and rejection' (Titmuss 1963: 43). To counteract the tendency whereby 'the aims of equity ostensibly set for society as a whole, become sectional aims, invariably rewarding the most favoured in proportion to the distribution of power and occupational success' (Titmuss 1963: 55), Titmuss turned to social solidarity. In his hands, solidarity became a healing force, arising out of human compassion and able to counteract egotistical calculations. Herein lies the famous Titmusssian thesis that the 'gift relationship' – a reciprocal yet unconditional transfer – would transform the self-interested exchange of the market while universal services would offset sectionalism and express the collective conscience. 'All collectively provided services', Titmuss wrote, 'are deliberately designed to meet certain socially recognised needs; they are manifestations, first, of society's will to survive as an organic whole, and, second, of the expressed will of all the people to assist in the survival of some people' (Titmuss 1963: 39). Importantly, this vision was unashamedly *national*, being closely wedded to the building of a particularly 'British' welfare state. It was also quite gender-blind, in the sense that it assumed the unpaid household labour of women.

In Britain, the Titmusssian view of social policy was influential throughout the 1950s and 1960s, coming to represent 'an orthodox academic consensus, strongly collectivist in value orientation and characterised by a moral rather than theoretical identity' (Pinker 1981: 6). Over the same period, T.H. Marshall was providing a more theoretical, more sociological and, in a sense, more pragmatic view (which, nevertheless, remained Anglo-centric and gender blind). Of all the theorists considered here, Marshall is the most concerned to integrate questions of order, justice, solidarity and participation. He straddles the social solidarity and social participation zones of our analysis, with a strong weather eye to social order even if justice is his primary concern. This integrative, practical stance arose in part because Marshall visualised the state, Weberian style, as 'a delicate balance of opposing forces' rather than a Durkheimian organic whole (Pinker 1981: 16). It was also linked to Marshall's desire to work *with* the opposing forces of welfare-capitalism, rather than attempt to transform them. Believing that stability was essential to justice, and justice to stability, he aimed at striking some kind of workable balance between the democratic notion of equal worth and the capitalist ethos of individual competition.

As is well known, Marshall called on the social rights of citizenship to bridge the gap between the two. In this respect, citizenship rights were to provide 'the foundation of equality on which the structure of inequality could be built' (Marshall [1949] 1964: 91). Here citizenship is less about feelings of national belonging, more about people being treated in a similar fashion *simply because they are members of the same political entity*. It is in this respect that the Marshall thesis has the greatest potential for national transferability – and even for realisation at a Commonwealth level (an issue to which we shall return). What mattered most, he said, was that:

> There is a general enrichment of the concrete substance of civilised life, a general reduction of risk and uncertainty, an equalisation between the healthy and the sick, the employed and the unemployed, the old and the active, the bachelor and the father of a large family. Equalisation is not so much between classes as between individuals within a population which is now treated for this purpose *as though it were one class*. (Marshall [1949] 1964: 102) (my emphasis)

The hopes of the welfare theorists were challenged in the 1960s, as were the forces leading to the rediscovery of poverty. At this point the Left cried foul to the traditional welfarist position, pointing out that social rights were a weak instrument in view of the enormous inequalities of western capitalism. One of the main claims of the radical movement was that mainstream institutions operated in such a way that the poor were systematically excluded. As this contention moved to centre stage, notions of solidarity started to drop from view, and social justice became more exclusively articulated with participation (Zone Three). Here participation was understood as the capacity to engage in mainstream activities, while social justice revolved around the myriad of structural factors which affected this capacity. Peter Townsend's work, which formalised the connection between social justice, poverty and exclusion, was crucial. The crux of his argument was that poverty marked the point at which individuals and families were prevented from participating in the customary activities of their society due to a lack of resources. It was an 'objective condition' accruing to people whose resources 'are so seriously below those commanded by the average individual or family that they are, in effect, excluded from ordinary living patterns, customs and conditions' (Townsend 1979: 33). At this time, the logic of Townsend's thesis contributed to the post-war climate favouring distinctly 'national' solutions to 'national' problem. People were excluded because they couldn't share in a common, societal core, and it was up to the national government to do something about that. It was only later that Townsend turned to the related question of how prosperous nations – as members of a common world, regional or Commonwealth order – should respond to poverty in poorer nations (Townsend 1993a, 1993b). This is discussed in the concluding section of the chapter.

Townsend's *Poverty in the United Kingdom* was published in 1979, just when the 'national' period was giving way to globalisation. In the new era, the notion of participation was used for a number of different purposes, most in direct opposition to his intentions.

Social inclusion and the global era

Over the last quarter century globalisation has moved from being a vague possibility to an established 'thing' over which world leaders meet and protestors demonstrate. While there is no agreed definition of what globalisation actually means, certain key features predominate in most accounts. These include the internationalisation of the world economy, the increasing power of transnational corporations, a hollowing out of the nation state, and a dissolution of national cultures as well as national economies. In responding to globalising forces, governments in industrialised nations have helped to create the very conditions to which they are subject through deregulating the finance and banking sectors, dismantling tariff protection, privatising government services and deregulating industrial relations and taxation reform. It is against this background that social inclusion and exclusion have emerged as the dominant metaphors for considering the market-society problematic.

Contributors to the current discourse generally collapse into two opposing groups. On the one side there is a bottom-up, pro-social justice approach, in which claims are made by, or on behalf of, excluded groups. On the other, there is a top-down, pro-social order approach, which operates as a tool *of* government rather than a claim *on* government. Examples of the first include the claims made by the Child Poverty Action Group; of the second, underclass theory, conservative forms of communitarianism, and, I contend, the main thrust of government policy across Anglophone countries.

We now turn to explore this in more detail. The inclusion/exclusion discourse contains in miniature each of the conceptual spaces identified at the beginning of the paper. Figure 3.3 sets out the direction of the analysis.

I start with the bottom-up, pro-social justice view since it stands alone in making a claim *on* government. This space is now almost entirely the province of the radical welfare lobby, and is located in the social justice/social participation quadrant of our framework (Zone Three). It approximates what Levitas (1998) calls the 'redistributive discourse' (RED) in British social policy. Its proponents start out from the 'facts' of exclusion and concentrate on the political and economic forces seen to cause them. While similar to Townsend in orientation, they extend his analysis to a wider range of concerns. The Child Poverty Action Group, for example, developed a broad notion of social exclusion involving the span of social, cultural and economic life – seen, for example in its publication of Lister's classic *The Exclusive Society: Citizenship and the Poor* (1990) and its review of the legacy of almost two decades of conservative government by Walker and Walker (1997). This type of approach has been called on by the welfare lobby in numerous studies of marginalised groups – the homeless, street kids, ethnic minorities, nomadic workers – all suffering, one way or another, from the fallout of globalisation. Ironically, one of the effects of this approach is that attention tends to be diverted from poverty, institutionalisation or wage discrimination *per se* toward the general sequelae of exclusion. Such is one reason why the exclusion discourse accommodates such strange bedfellows: the political right is also deeply concerned about exclusion and its impact on society. The attention of the Right, however, is centred on the *behaviour* of the excluded, particularly if they are poor and black. In other words, we swing into the terrain of the top-down, pro social order, approach.

Social order

Zone One
Sub-cultural and underclass theory (Murray, Mead)

Communitarianism and social capital (Putnam; Etzioni)

Significant influence on government

Zone Four
The main thrust of government intervention, typified by New Labor, OECD, European Commission, and welfare reform in Australia

Solidarity | **Participation**

Zone Two
This zone has emptied out although government rhetoric appeals to it at times. It is also the location of certain social democratic analyses (e.g. Hutton, Cox, Latham).

Zone Three
Claims on the state by marginalised – groups (Child poverty action group)

Social justice

Figure 3.3 The Strands of the Present: Uses of Social Inclusion/Exclusion Discourse

Here the prime example is what Levitas calls the 'moral underclass discourse' (MUD). This occupies the social order/social solidarity quadrant of our analysis (Zone One), with solidarity interpreted as adherence to socially endorsed practices and social order as the stability of dominant values. At its heart is the insider/outsider problematic: the fear that the disorganised and unruly will disrupt the world of the hardworking majority. The crux of its proponents' argument is that the poor have become isolated from mainstream society due to misplaced welfare interventions and are concentrated in pathological and dangerous communities (Levitas 1998: 18). For Charles Murray (1984) the 'generous revolution' of the Kennedy era led to the poor deciding to opt for benefits rather than paid work (Murray 1984: 154). In contrast, Lawrence Mead (1986, 1992, 1997) maintains that the poor are 'not exploitative but inert, controversial because they do so little to help themselves, not because they hurt others in the pursuit of advantage' (Mead 2000: 113).

Coming alongside the underclass thesis, there are the communitarian claims about loss of community. The communitarians still interpret solidarity and order in relation to core values and practices, but their attention moves from exclusion to inclusion, and from inner-city locales to middle class suburbs. Above all, these writers want people reunited in a shared moral and social order. This is an attendant belief that something has gone terribly wrong with the social fabric (cf. Himmelfarb 1994; MacIntyre 1981, 1988; Walzer 1983). Robert Putnam (1993, 1995) argues that social capital is in decline because people have turned away from the community to their own inward-looking interests. In his famous example, people in the United States now bowl alone rather than in teams (Putnam 1995) His solution lies in civic associations that generate the 'networks, norms, and social trust that facilitate co-ordination and co-operation for human development' (Putnam 1995: 67). In his turn, Amitai Etzioni maintains that the 1960s produced 'rampant moral confusion and social anarchy' (Etzioni 1997: 65). Accordingly, he wants reforms centred on families, schools and local institutions, since it is there that 'individuals and groups in a good society encourage one another to adhere to behaviour that reflects shared values' (Etzioni 1997: 124).

Communitarian influences can be discerned in many official pronouncements (Zone One). The Australian Report on Welfare Reform insists on 'the bonds of trust and relationship and shared norms that communities build and renew' (McClure 2000a: 13; 2000b) and Senator Newman's suggests that:

> The income support system needs to be refocussed on participation, emphasising the principle of mutual obligation and recognising the

contribution that all people can make to society. A modern system ... should promote personal responsibility to support oneself and/or contribute to the community in other ways. Those of us who can contribute to the community should be encouraged and expected to do so. (Newman 1999: 10)

More generally, though, the focus comes to rest on matters of order and participation (Zone Four). Here inclusion is framed in an increasingly up-beat way, centred on participation in the economic life of the nation, with all the benefits which that implies. This emphasis has links with what Levitas (1998) calls the 'social integration discourse' (SID). In theory, it has a critical potential which is partially realised in the work of social democrats such as Cox, (1995), Hutton (1996, 1997) and Latham (1998). In contrast, governments reduce integration to participation in paid work, effecting a drastic narrowing of the broad understanding of solidarity typical of French republican thought (Silver 1994; Levitas 1998: 21-25). For them, it is workforce involvement that needs to be monitored, corrected and improved. This has a lodestone effect whereby official attention constantly veers to the behaviour of those out of work rather than class relations, organisational structure, or the distribution of resources.

Current policy and connections with globalisation

So far I have suggested that social inclusion has a long past and a short history. The long past is constituted by the market-society problematic and continued attention to order, justice, solidarity and participation; the short history by the manner in which these elements are assembled and understood. I have argued that government discourse now occupies a conceptual space characterised by the conjunction of social participation and social order, while noting that its tone and direction are also influenced by the fusion of communitarian and underclass sentiments. So how does all this link up with the globalising process? It is not enough to assume that economic logic *necessarily* brings about a particular reading of social inclusion and its component parts. Some attempt to articulate the particular pathways and consequences is needed. First, to solidarity.

In the national era, when the nation state was assumed to exercise sovereignty, solidarity was pitched at the level of society as a whole. For Durkheim, it existed beyond individual consciousness given that society was an external *fact*; for Titmuss and Marshall, there was a sense of nationhood in which solidarity and citizenship were created and upheld; for Townsend, there was a common core of national expectations against which relative deprivation could be benchmarked. In the contemporary period, the 'hollowing out' of the nation state (Jessop 1994) has been mirrored by local, interpersonal and particularistic accounts. Underclass theorists concentrate on inner-city locales; communitarians put their faith in civic associations and community affiliations; governments talk about self-sufficient communities and local initiatives – and so forth. Even the multitude of groups who bring their claims to bear on government have a localising and fragmenting effect. In brief, as globalisation renders the very idea of 'society' or 'national economy' obsolete, so social relations get re-conceptualised as a matter of interpersonal relations at the level of the small group.

In its turn, participation has come to be allied with social order rather than social justice, with behaviour rather than service provision, and with paid work rather than a broad range of social activities. The link to globalising forces is evident enough. In a context of heightened international competition, governments aim to increase labour force flexibility and reduce welfare dependence as a means of attracting corporate investment. Accordingly, participation as paid-work is part of a larger package including labour force reform, enterprise bargaining, individual contracts and supply-side economics. All have marginalising, individuating and exclusionary effects.

The changing trajectory of social order is more difficult to trace as it covers a particularly wide governmental terrain, stretching from social integration to law-and-order issues. While early and classical renderings were primarily concerned with right ordering between the major classes, current thought is firmly based on an insider-outsider problematic. The association between contemporary readings and globalisation appears more an offshoot of the neo-conservative presence than a deliberate attempt to forge new corporate alliances. However, benefits for corporate capital and the globalising process there certainly are. At a fundamental level, the insider-outsider issue, and its attendant law-and-order focus, turns attention away from class inequality to individual and local concerns. In this way, it acts as a force for containment, demonstrating that governments need to reincorporate disaffected entities in a system that, in itself, is quite OK. This, as Walters (2000: 197) suggests, 'normalises society by redefining and narrowing its boundaries to the contented majority. Society is not the problem. Society can look after itself'.

Finally, to social justice. To grasp what is happening we need to consider one of the central tasks of government: namely, safeguarding the on-going prosperity of the nation. In the national era, this depended on the effective management of internal affairs. Under globalisation, safeguarding prosperity takes on a new form, resting on a nation's capacity to remain afloat in an international competition (Hindess 1998). This has produced a fundamental re-casting of the relationship between prosperity and justice. In the welfare period, attending to social justice – understood as equitable access to public services and adequate income security – was a means of attending to prosperity – understood to be contingent on securing harmonious relationships between capital and labour. The two were mutually re-enforcing. Under current conditions, however, earlier notions of social justice are rendered antithetical to national prosperity with the charge that they protect inefficient groups against their more successful counterparts elsewhere. In these circumstance, social justice is either relegated to an optional extra or recast as a reward for competitive efficiency.

Where to from here?

These shifts in welfare theorising take place against a backdrop of mounting global inequality. Townsend and Donkor (1997: 19) estimate that four-fifths of global income and development resources are now owned by one-fifth of the world's population, with inequalities increasing sharply between 1960 and 1991. Inequality has also increased sharply within nations with malnutrition and starvation endemic in subsistence economies. Townsend and Donkor point out that there has been a devastating collapse of living standards in Eastern Europe and the republics of the former Soviet Union. In Georgia, for example, 'there are beggars of all ages on the streets, patients in psychiatric hospitals and old people in institutions who are on the brink of starvation' (Townsend and Donkor 1997: 30). The inequalities to which they refer are reproduced within the Commonwealth with its membership spanning some of the richest and poorest regions in the world. In such circumstances, how relevant are the Anglophone notions of social inclusion traced in this chapter – either now or previously? Could any assist the Commonwealth to redress such marked disparities between its member states?

In the case of current official renderings, the response must be negative given the preference for behavioural over structural solutions and the continued tendency to look inward rather than outward. The issue, then, is whether older social democratic notions – Titmuss, Marshall, Keynes and so forth – could be refurbished and made relevant for an international as well as national order. Here the answer is a qualified yes. The principles of universality, full employment and collectivism are surely essential to any decent welfare order, national or international. At the same time, these older principles – particularly in relation to assumptions about gender and the domestic division of labour – would need to be radically altered to meet current practices and expectations.

Critically too, the 'national' focus, so typical of these earlier readings, is no longer sufficient on its own, if it ever was. This does not mean that national welfare states are redundant. To the contrary, there is a need for an interactive process whereby nations formulate their own welfare programmes and relate these to an international welfare strategy. Townsend and Donkor call this the principle of *duality*. They contend that:

> The market cannot be regulated, or made to work efficiently, without introducing new rights, new public services, and new entitlements to give adequate meaning to social as well as individual development. This amounts to making a defence of the principles, and even many of the intentions, of 20th century welfare state practice while simultaneously preparing the ground for, and implementing, the early stages of an international welfare state. (Townsend and Donkor 1997: 36–37)

Such arguments are echoed in Hirst and Thompson's (1995) proposition that nation states should take on a new role in the global economic order – less as sovereign entities and more as members of an international polity. They contend that in an international and pluralistic society, the 'rule of law is more rather than less necessary' (1995: 436). In the field of social policy, such propositions might lend themselves to an international welfare state; something akin to a radically refurbished United Nations but with real international representation across both rich and poor nations. Similar possibilities exist at a regional level, with trading blocks using some of their gains to ensure welfare systems and human rights. Crucially, too, and as canvassed by other contributors to this volume, the Commonwealth could act as a staging post between global forces and nation states (cf. Ch. 16 below).

If the Commonwealth is to demonstrate genuine commitment to social inclusion amongst all its members, it will need to re-set older commitments to universality, full employment and collectivism to the circumstances prevailing in a globalised order. New readings of the four elements considered in this paper would thus be necessary. At an international level, the principle of social order (in its traditional guise as 'right ordering') would call for laws to keep transnational capital honest; social justice would require taxes on the world's wealthy to be used for redistribution across the globe; solidarity would demand the protection of human rights, while participation would depend on the democratic representation of all nations on international decision-making bodies. Parallel measures at a national level would involve regulations ensuring good corporate behaviour as well as the health and safety of workers; properly redistributive taxes; shared public services and democratic control over decision making at all institutional levels.

Earlier in the chapter I cited Marshall's hope that there would be:

> a general enrichment of the concrete substance of civilised life, a general reduction of risk and uncertainty, an equalisation between the healthy and the sick, the employed and the unemployed... . (Here) equalisation is not so much between classes as between individuals within a population which is now treated for this purpose as though it were one class. (Marshall [1949] 1964: 102)

This could now read as pertaining to:

> a general enrichment of national and international life, a general reduction of risk and uncertainty, an equalisation between health and sickness and between employment and unemployment, between and within nations. In this instance, equalisation is not so much between nations as between individuals within all nations which are now treated for this purpose as though they were one nation.

References

Beveridge, W. (1942) *Social Insurance and Allied Services*, London: HMSO.
Cox, E. (1995) *A Truly Civil Society*, Boyer Lectures, Sydney: ABC Books.
Dean, Mitchell (1992) 'A genealogy of the government of poverty', *Economy and Society*, 21, 3: 215–252.
Durkheim, E. [1893] (1933) *The Division of Labour in Society*, tr. George Simpson, New York: The Free Press.
Etzioni, A. (1997) *The New Golden Rule, Community and Morality in a Democratic Society*, New York: Basic Books.
Himmelfarb, G. (1994) *The Demoralisation of Society, from Victorian Virtues to Modern Values*, Vintage: New York.

Hindess, B. (1998) 'Neo-liberalism and the national economy' in Dean, Mitchell and Hindess, Barry (eds) *Governing Australia: Studies in Contemporary Rationalities of Government,* Cambridge University Press: Cambridge.

Hirst, P. and Thompson, P. (1995) 'Globalisation and the future of the nation state', *Economy and Society,* 24, 3: 409–442.

Hutton, W. (1996) *The State We're In,* London: Cape.

Hutton, W. (1997) *The State to Come,* London: Cape.

Jessop, B. (1994) 'Post-Fordism and the State', in A. Amin (ed.) *Post-Fordism: A Reader,* London: Blackwell.

Jones, A. and Smyth, P. (1999) 'Social exclusion: a new framework for social policy analysis?' paper presented to the 26th AASW National Conference, published in *Just Policy,* December, 17: 11–20.

Latham, M. (1998) *Civilising Global Capital, New Thinking for Australian Labor,* Australia: Allen and Unwin.

Levitas, R. (1998) *The Inclusive Society? Social Exclusion and New Labour,* London: Macmillan.

Lister, R. (1990) *The Exclusive Society: Citizenship and the Poor.* London: Child Poverty Action Group.

Lukes, S. (1973) *Emile Durkheim: His Life and Work: A Historical and Critical Study,* Harmondsworth: Penguin.

MacIntyre, A. (1981) *After Virtue,* London: Duckworth.

MacIntyre, A. (1988) *Whose Justice? Which Rationality?* London: Duckworth.

Marshall, T.H. [1949] (1964) 'Citizenship and Social Class' reprinted in Marshall, T.H., *Class, Citizenship and Social Development,* Chicago: University of Chicago Press, 1964.

McClure, P. (2000a) *Participation Support for More Equitable Society,* Interim Report of the Reference Group on Welfare Reform, Canberra: AGPS.

McClure, P. (2000b), *Participation Support for More Equitable Society,* Final Report of the Reference Group on Welfare Reform, Canberra: AGPS.

Mead, L. (1997) *The New Paternalism: Supervisory Approaches to Poverty,* New York: Brookings Institute.

Mead, L. (1986) *Beyond Entitlement: The Social Obligations of Citizenship,* New York: The Free Press.

Mead, L. (1992) *The New Politics of Poverty: the Non-Working Poor in America,* New York: Basic Books.

Mead, L. (2000) 'The new politics of the new poverty' in *The Welfare State Reader,* (eds) Pierson, C. and Castles, F. Cambridge: Polity Press, 107–119, reprinted from *The Public Interest,* 103.

Murray, C. (1984) *Loosing Ground: American Social Policy,* 1850–1980, New York: Basic Books.

Newman, J. (1999) 'The challenge of welfare dependency in the 21st century', Discussion Paper, Commonwealth Department of Family and Community Services, Canberra.

Pinker, R. (1981) 'Introduction' in T.H. Marshall, *The Right to Welfare and Other Essays,* Suffolk: Northumberland Press.

Putnam, R. (1993) *Making Democracy Work, Civic Traditions in Modern Italy,* Princeton: Princeton University Press.

Putnam, R. (1995) 'Bowling Alone', America's Declining Social Capital', *Journal of Democracy,* 6, 1: 65–78.

Rose, N. (1996) 'Governing "advanced" liberal democracies', in A. Barry, T. Osborne and N. Rose (eds) *Foucault and Political Reason*, London: UCL Press.

Silver, H. (1994) 'Social exclusion and social solidarity: three paradigms,' *International Labour Review*, 133, 6: 531–577.

Smith, A. [1759] (1976) *The Theory of Moral Sentiments*, London: Clarendon Press.

Smith, A. [1776] (1979) *An Inquiry into the Nature and Causes of the Wealth of Nations*, Oxford: Oxford University Press.

Titmuss, R.M. (1963) *Essays on the Welfare State*, London: Allen and Unwin.

Tonnies, F. [1887] (1957) *Community and Association*, New York: Harper Torchbook.

Townsend, P. (1979) *Poverty in the United Kingdom: A Survey of Household Resources and Standards of Living*. Harmondsworth: Penguin.

Townsend, P. (1993a) *The International Analysis of Poverty*, Hemel Hemstead: Harvester Wheatsheaf.

Townsend, P. (1993b) 'The International Welfare State', *Fabian Review*, 105, 2: 3–6.

Townsend, P. and Donkor, K. (1997) *Global Restructuring and Social Policy: the need to establish an international welfare state*, Bourmemouth: Policy Press.

Walker, A. and Walker, C. (eds) (1997) *Britain Divided: the Growth of Social Exclusion in the 1980s and 1990s*, London: Child Poverty Action Group.

Walters, W. (2000) *Unemployment and Government, Genealogies of the Social*, Cambridge University Press: Cambridge.

Walzer, M. (1983) *Spheres of Justice*, New York: Basic Books.

Part Two
National Case Studies

4
The Paradox of Exclusion/Inclusion in Jamaica

Joy Moncrieffe

August 5, 1938. The West India Royal (Moyne) Commission is appointed to investigate social and economic conditions in the British West Indies, and to make recommendations. This was not altruism; it was a matter of urgency. His Majesty's Government desired to understand the causes for the mounting discontent in the colonies, and to devise strategies for promoting social order.

According to the Commission's report, the 1930s disturbances were of distinct character: these were not sporadic and unfocused outbursts; they were unequivocal demands for 'a better and less restricted life' (Moyne 1938, Ch. 1, p. 8). The West Indian Negroes were removed from lands where – though they lived in primitive state – they had observed some valuable social norms. These norms were destroyed when they were transferred to the West Indies. 'Negroes', then, had a singular function, which was to provide cheap labour on the estates. Colonial governments had no interest in preserving traditional languages, customs or religion; they had even considered this unwise.

The Commission observed that social provisions were inadequate and had even deteriorated with the economic depression. However, missionaries were involved with providing education, and some West Indian governments had come to recognise that they had a responsibility to sustain the public health and general welfare of the population, as economic viability depended on it. Economic prospects were bleak: low wage rates, intermittent employment (particularly in the rural areas), growing populations, excessive reliance on traditional export crops, inadequate domestic food production; all these revealed the need for a new economic and, particularly, agricultural policy.

One part of the solution, as the Commission perceived it, lay in drastically increased expenditures for social development. Accordingly, members recommended that a West Indian Welfare Fund be established and administered through an appointed Comptroller, rather than the Colonial Office and Governments. This fund should prioritise teacher training, provide adequate school accommodation and equipment, and support a curriculum that included 'practical and agricultural subjects for boys and domestic training and child welfare education for girls'. Though the West Indies had made notable improvements in public health, it was now necessary to focus on preventive medicine. Housing conditions were deplorable and required urgent attention. Additionally, it was important to develop an agricultural policy, with the distinct aim of increasing subsistence production, providing agricultural education, ensuring efficient land tenure arrangements and better use of natural resources.

The report also encouraged profound social and cultural change, which was necessary for raising the status of women, addressing colour prejudice, and reversing 'the prevailing absence of a spirit of independence and self-help, the lack of a tradition of craftsmanship and pride in good work, and [the] tendency on all matters to appeal to government for assistance' (Ibid., p. 35). The Commission rejected proposals for complete self-government or for expanding the powers of the colonial governors. Members explained that the first would undermine attempts to control expenditures under the West Indian Welfare Fund, while the second would legitimise autocracy and, therefore, constitute 'a retrograde step'. Instead, 'more, and not less participation by the people in the work of government is a real necessity for lasting social advancement' (Ibid., p. 449).

We may well disagree with some of the Commission's value judgments and have questions about its policy proposals; however, this paper does not discuss these. Instead, we use the report to provide a background for our overview of processes of social exclusion and/or adverse or problematic inclusion (Kabeer 2000) – in one post-colonial country: Jamaica. The Moyne report provides a good starting point for it describes the legacies of multiple forms of injustice, including economic exploitation, social/cultural dislocation and discrimination. The report provides a damming account of conditions in the West Indies in the 1930s and suggests policy responses that could form the springboard for greater 'inclusion', particularly of the majority black populations. However, it also hints at the constraints: the institutional, political and social forces that would have significant influence on the direction, pace and scope of change. Indeed, close examination of processes of change in the West Indies reveal the weight that history, interest groups, political and other leaders, formal and informal institutions, and various policy decisions have had on the 'terms of incorporation'. In addition, change has long been influenced by external and, particularly since the 1980s, global requirements for greater *inclusion* in the market, often with attending *exclusion* from livelihoods, social services, welfare and security networks, especially among the poor (Wolfe 1995, pp. 81–101).

This chapter describes the British influence on political and social policy (particularly health) and highlights pertinent developments in the structural adjustment and post structural adjustment periods. It accentuates the 'paradox of exclusion/inclusion', with specific reference to the role of successive governments and departments. Additionally, the chapter demonstrates how global requirements for inclusion in the market have resulted in adverse incorporation of particular segments of the population. The concluding section outlines some of the potential challenges to Commonwealth and global solutions.

Jamaica – social and economic background

In 1938, when the Commission visited Jamaica, the island's racial composition was not unlike the patterns observed in a number of Caribbean post-slavery societies: over 78 per cent of the country's 1.2 million inhabitants were black, 17.5 per cent were coloured and 1 per cent were white. The minority white population owned and controlled the vast portion of the resources (Munroe 1972; Broom 1954, pp. 115–125). Between 1944 (when universal adult suffrage was granted) and 1962 (independence), there were important social changes: the capitalist class had expanded to include the immigrant Afro-Europeans, Lebanese and Chinese. A now multi-racial dominant upper middle class challenged white hegemony.

The economic boom of the 1950s and 1960s resulted in further changes to the class structure. During this period – with the aid of an open economy and significant foreign investments – manufacturing (and particularly bauxite) overtook agriculture as the major export earner. Correspondingly, a growing group of merchant-manufacturers gained ascendancy over the planters. The upper class now comprised some 21 families who, without entering politics, dominated the private sector and influenced government policy. Newly formed groups such as the Jamaica Chamber of Commerce, the Jamaica Manufacturer's Association, the Jamaica Hotel and Tourist Association and the Sugar Manufacturer's Association promoted their interests. The economic boom also favoured the business sectors and the middle class grew to approximately 22 per cent of the labour force.

In contrast, the majority of the population experienced little of these social and economic gains. By 1958, 'the lowest two deciles of households in the country had a 2.2 per cent share of total income, whereas the wealthiest 5 per cent ... had a 30.2 per cent share' (Wellisz and Findlay 1993, p. 172). This social and economic stagnation had much to do with the extent and manner in which the poorer segments were incorporated into the economy. The largest capital investors (Kaiser, Reynolds, Alcan and Alcoa) bought more than 600,000 acres of the farmlands in order to mine bauxite, which effectively displaced the agricultural labourers. However, there were no plans to re-integrate these workers into other forms of employment. In 1976, for instance, only 1 per cent of the Jamaican labour force were employed by the bauxite companies; that is, nearly 6,000 workers from a labour force of 883,600. Further, there was limited knowledge transfer, as much of the mined bauxite was processed abroad. Tourism, which became another major earner, developed little or no linkages with the agricultural sector and domestic agriculture, the main source of livelihood in the rural areas, stagnated.

The colonial legacy of social and cultural discrimination persisted beyond the introduction of universal adult suffrage in 1944, and this reinforced – and justified – the low economic standing of the majority black population.

> The privileged white and light-skinned elite was assumed to be inherently superior both racially and culturally and this assumption was reinforced by a white, racist, social ideology and the dependence of the society on a European imperial power, Great Britain. The dominant class ideology assumed that landowners, the wealthy, and the highly educated had a natural claim to national leadership, pre-eminent political influence, and social wisdom.   (Stone 1985, p. 15)

Palmer notes that one of the more harmful by-products of European domination was the effect of that rule 'on the minds of sections of the Jamaican populace ...'

> A white bias had come to prevail and with it a concomitant devaluation of the sense of self of the citizens of African descent who,

interestingly enough, comprised the vast majority of the people). (Palmer 1989, p. 114

However, the Rastafarian movement, which began in the 1930s, and the Black Power movement of the late 1960s instigated a welcome transformation of the black person's perception of self. Reggae music, in particular, became a powerful medium for expressing the frustration of the poor black majority; it was the prime avenue of protest against colonial and post-colonial oppression. Yet, most of the more tangible changes in the status of the majority took place under Michael Manley's earlier period of leadership. Manley, who first became prime minister of Jamaica in 1972, based his political platform on 'giving the poor a chance'. From 1972 to 1979, in particular, he introduced a distinctly socialist agenda (which his People's National Party described as democratic socialism) and complemented this with extensive social improvement programmes. Only then did it begin to become (gradually) acceptable for blacks to be included in the more visible and higher status occupations.

Jamaica – political background

The People's National Party (PNP), which was formed after the 1938 rebellion, originally dedicated itself to advancing middle class concerns. Its 1938 party paper stipulated: 'a more forceful leadership of the middle class is necessary if we are to prevent worse things than the Frome riots' (Munroe 1972, pp. 21–22). Further, effective middle class leadership required 'the type of self-government which was democratic and fundamentally British' (Ibid.). In 1942, Alexander Bustamante defected from the PNP and formed the Jamaica Labour Party (JLP). His prime mandate was to champion the cause of the black worker and to 'get the labourer a little more bread and a little more butter'. The less popular Jamaica Democratic Party (JDP) advocated a policy of free enterprise in its bid to represent upper class interests. Eventually, and especially in the 1970s, the PNP became associated with the working class and socialist policies, and the JLP – now dubbed the party of stability – became known for its capitalist rhetoric and alliance with Western interests. Between the 1970s and the 1980s, these ideological differences resulted in vastly diverging policy emphases. The distinctions were much less marked in the 1990s, for by then the PNP had abandoned its radical stance.

From the earliest elections, the PNP and the JLP established themselves as the dominant parties. To secure votes, both enlisted the support of the unions. However, union involvement in political outreach was to dissipate as the parties became increasingly successful at winning and sustaining their own support, particularly through party patronage and personalised politics (Edie 1991; Harrigan 1995; Stone 1985, p. 15; Waters 1985). Gray (1991, p. 9) points out that successive political leaders have adopted an authoritarian approach to political management. Similarly, Munroe contends: 'for much of the period of decolonisation and post-colonialism, party and state structures as well as economic enterprises reflected "master-servant", "boss-employee", "parent-child", "hero-crowd" relationships, reproducing the colour, class, racial and educational hierarchies of the wider social structure' (Munroe 2000, p. 9). Undoubtedly, many of these tendencies are legacies of the British era of domination, itself characterised by authoritarian leadership, the arbitrary exercise of power and various forms of suppression (Moncrieffe 2001b, pp. 26–50). Therefore, despite the political stability in Jamaica, there is justifiable concern about the terms on which certain groups, and especially the lower classes, are 'included'. Garrison communities and constituencies are extreme manifestations of this political subordination. In these communities, gang leaders maintain close relationships with the designated Member of Parliament, and have the important role of securing the territory. These political agents, who have access to high-powered weapons, then 'encourage' community members to support the designated political leader in return for scarce benefits and spoils (NCPT 1997). As politicians become increasingly incapable of providing the expected largesse, drug barons are now replacing them as the dominant authorities. These garrison communities, hitherto included on adverse terms, now operate as *de facto* 'mini-states', and have, on occasion, demonstrated their capacity to exclude state penetration.

Nevertheless, Munroe observes that with globalisation and improved forms of communication, citizens have now become much more aware of their rights and, accordingly, are making new demands for inclusion. Political leaders and government departments have not been sufficiently responsive or proactive and, in the absence of effective formal channels for democratic participation, emerging interest groups and community-based organisations have been advocating for select causes. There has also been an upsurge in protest movements – particularly among the poorer urban segments of the population – though through more costly avenues such as roadblocks and destruction of property. Unfortunately, there is a view that these 'active' forms of demonstration are the most productive and direct means of communicating with the political directorate (Munroe 2000).

Welfare politics/economics, structural adjustment and beyond: a review of health provision 1950–1968

Many agree that Jamaica has profited from the tradition of constitutional rule and from the welfare state policies and liberalism that formed part of the colonial heritage (Munroe 2000, p. 4). Admittedly, that influence has been somewhat mixed, as policy administration was usually highly centralised, hierarchical and primarily beneficial to the privileged. Nevertheless, there was a belief in the state's responsibility for social service provision and the political elite, many of whom were educated in British institutions (cf. Ch. 2 above, p. 11), implemented policies to that effect. This section uses a brief review of Jamaica's health policies between the 1950s and 1990s to illustrate, more broadly, the influences of the British welfare and more recent neoliberal traditions on social policy.

Up to 1972, the parties adopted similar approaches to health, despite their ideological leanings. The overarching philosophy, as Norman Manley expressed it, was that:

> ... There is no politics in sickness. There is only the desire to do, in this country, within our resources what we can do to help the sick people for we have a quasi-socialist scheme of medicine ... in the sense that the State has accepted responsibility for the provision of medical services for all who cannot afford it and there are medical services with fees which are virtually nominal for those who are able to pay.   (Jamaica Hansard 1963, p. 338)

The actual health strategies were also quite similar and consistent with the Moyne Commission recommendations. In 1956, the PNP, as had the previous administration, stressed the immediate need for improved nutrition, the importance of controlling contagious diseases and increasing access to health care. The sectoral presentation outlined a number of specific programmes that has already been attempted: 'a scheme for applied research into human nutrition', which was sponsored by the Colonial Development Welfare Scheme; the provision of milk for pre-school children and pregnant mothers, sponsored by the United Nations Children's Fund (UNICEF); insect control and efforts to eradicate malaria and yellow fever, sponsored by the PAN American

Sanitary Bureau (PASB) and the World Health Organization (WHO); hospital rehabilitation, which was seen as critical, given the 'woeful neglect of hospital buildings in the last ten years' (Jamaica Hansard 1956–57, p. 20). The PNP proposed to continue and expand on past initiatives; thus, there would be hospital expansion in the areas that most required it, the provision of dental officers, expanded mental health facilities, and the provision of additional health centres, considered the 'kernel of our development plans'. The reasoning, consistent with its socialist orientation was that these centres would substantially improve the public's access to care, so that 'instead of the difficulty of people going long distances to get medical facilities, medical facilities will be brought to the people' (Ibid., p. 20). Between 1962 and 1972, the JLP had a similar agenda. In his 1966–1967 presentation to Parliament, the Minister of Health emphasised his commitment to preventive health: Immunisation programmes were to be continued in earnest, the family planning programme was incorporated in the Ministry, and health education was endorsed as a critical component of the government's policies.

As the parliamentary debates revealed, the greatest dissent during the period concerned programme administration rather than policy/-programme content. For example, party representatives accused each other of partisanship and supplied supporting evidence. In the 1956–1957 sectoral debates, opposition member, Tacius Golding, accused the PNP of deliberately neglecting his constituency and of refusing to continue programmes that his (JLP) administration had started:

> 'Health centres are to be constructed in PNP constituencies, but they are to be constructed in JLP constituencies too because they are taxpayers and they form the inhabitants of this country'. (Ibid., p. 43)

In response, one PNP member justified his government's partisan practices and challenged the Opposition when he asserted:

> 'You didn't think of the people of St. Elizabeth [then a PNP stronghold] in your days'. (Ibid., p. 43)

Therefore, even from this early period, partisanship and patronage were to exclude select groups, with adverse and durable political and social consequences. (For a more comprehensive discussion see Moncrieffe 2001a, pp. 73–97).

In 1972, the new PNP administration asserted that a 'health policy' was necessary since 'there has so far been no conspicuous difference between medical policies of the JLP and the PNP' (McNeill 1972). Consistent with its democratic socialist principles, the party emphasised community participation, increasing the access to care, equity, and cost-effective care for all rather than the chosen few. Among the more bold initiatives were the discontinuation of hospital fees and the introduction of community health aides. The first was justified with the argument that individuals – and particularly the poor – should not have to pay for health care; this, as obtained in properly socialist countries, was the state's responsibility. The second was geared at boosting access to care in the rural communities. These health policies were reflective of a much broader social reform. Other initiatives included 'subsidies for essential food items, public works programmes, land lease to peasants, literacy programmes and training and educational reforms' (Kaufman 1988, pp. 45–71; Keith and Keith 1992; Davies and Witter 1989). There is little doubt that the Manley-led administration of the early 1970s contributed substantially to social gains for the lower classes and to addressing colour prejudice. Culturally, Manley stressed the value of 'blackness' and encouraged the poor majority to appreciate themselves. This was a new era that promised and, in large part, delivered economic and social/cultural inclusion in the interest of the lower classes.

However, with social reform there was a massive increase in current and capital expenditure. (Davies notes that total expenditure as a percentage of GDP increased from 23 per cent to 42 per cent between 1972/73 and 1976/77 (Davies 1986, pp. 73–109).) Further, Manley's anti-imperialist rhetoric and socialist programmes provoked and alienated many within his own class. The private sector objected to seemingly radical programmes, such as the nationalisation of the key industries and the imposition of a price control mechanism. Consequently, 'enterprises were closed, tax payments evaded and investments shelved. A climate of hysteria paralysed economic activity in the private sector, and the collaborative relationship it had maintained with the public sector in the two previous decades gave way to confrontation' (Wellisz and Findlay 1993, p. 179). Massive migration of administrators, managers, and professionals – among them numerous categories of health workers – followed. In addition, after the first oil shock in 1973/74, the PNP tried to obtain a greater share of rents from the bauxite companies by imposing a levy. Though this provided substantial revenues in the short term, the companies responded by cutting production or withdrawing from Jamaica. All these, combined with the deliberate opposition from the United States, culminated in the economic crisis of the late 1970s. This period, then, provided a classic example of the possible costs of social reform. Policies designed to provide for the majority can be perceived as a threat by the minority, who in most cases own the resources and have the expertise required to implement and sustain them. In the real world, effective social action often depends on political bargaining; it may require deals to appease various vested interests.

The Seaga administration, which assumed office in 1980, was as capitalist in rhetoric as the PNP had been socialist, yet expressed similar concerns for health. Minister Kenneth Baugh claimed that his administration saw health as an absolute priority and was committed to the philosophy that

> Health must be delivered in equity, both to the rich and poor, not only to urban citizens but to those in rural areas as well, and that easy access to all the facilities of the service is a basic and fundamental right of all the people. (Jamaica Hansard 1981, p. 36)

Baugh's emphasis, similar to that of the previous administrations – was on primary health care. The Minister's main disagreement with the PNP's approach was the lack of a comprehensive approach to primary, secondary and tertiary care. For example, while there had been some development in the building of clinics, there was also a 'progressive relentless deterioration of the hospital services' (Ibid.). Between 1980 and 1983, the JLP government received substantial multilateral and bilateral loans, which were conditioned, principally, on export growth. No devaluations or reductions in the number of public sector employees were required. However, by 1983, and in response to the worsening economic situation, the JLP government was forced to redefine its agenda. The dilemma – corroborated by World Bank and IDB studies – was that up until 1970, economic growth was sufficient to finance state expansion but the massive downturn that began in the 1970s meant new emphasis on efficiency and cost effectiveness. The key lending agencies proposed decentralisation, rationalisation and privatisation. In 1984, the loan preconditions included a large tax increase, devaluation and that approximately 20,000 government employees be laid off. The cost of medical supplies increased significantly, hospitals were actively downsized, the number of staff was reduced, and hospital fees were increased. Boyd (1998) notes that allocations to health decreased from J$70 per person in 1981 to J$47 per person in 1985 and, correspondingly, rates of malnutrition, undernutrition and gastroenteritis increased in both urban and rural areas. Successive Economic and Social Survey reports have linked the underfinancing of the health sector to the decreasing quality of care. The September 1994 Stone Poll also reported wide public dissatisfaction, particularly with the high cost of drugs, inordinate delays in getting treatment and the continuously overcrowded facilities.

By the early 1990s, the newly restored PNP administration had renounced its radical stance and acknowledged the merits of the market. Since then, this primarily externally directed market logic has entailed a progressive redefinition of state responsibility, from provider to regulator. In health, the World Bank, IDB and USAID have called for further rationalisation: 'scaling back the range of services that are, in any event, of dubious quality, and allowing the remainder to be sourced privately'. Government is to provide 'basic public health services and essential clinical care while the rest of the system becomes self-financed' (World Bank 1993, p. 11). Privatisation is to cure low quality and excessive expenditures. Decentralised management structures are to bring efficiency and financial and managerial autonomy to hospitals and health centres. Consistent with the recent emphasis on good governance and the celebration of new public management methods, these decentralised structures are to observe strict accountability principles, governed by a citizen's charter. Consumers should be encouraged to define their needs and to provide feedback on the quality of service; this is key to their inclusion.

There are key officials within the Ministry of Health who still adhere to the old philosophy and regard health provision as the state's responsibility. Though they acknowledge that welfare strategies may be untenable, they are wary of the privatisation and rationalisation agendas. (Perhaps this, in part, accounts for the laggard approach to change.) Analysts are concerned about the private sector's capacity to provide the quality of care envisioned and about its propensity to exclude those who cannot afford to pay. Rationalisation has assisted with cost savings and improved service quality in upgraded hospitals; however, particularly in the rural areas where facilities and services have been 'scaled back', surveys[1] reveal that community members are disillusioned with the very restricted access to care. In one farming community, for example, local health officials reported that the hospital was downscaled and re-classified as a poly-clinic and its hours of service reduced from 24 to seven. This effectively denied access to the majority of residents, who were normally occupied on farms throughout the day. Therefore, during the 'no-access hours', people had to travel 20 miles to reach the next health facility. However, there was no guarantee that these alternate hospitals would accept patients, as they normally operate at full capacity. The resident nurse explained that there had been a consistent shortage of drugs since the 1980s, that even minor illnesses had to be referred to other hospitals, and that the doctor on staff could only provide services on select days, as he was required to work in all the other clinics in the area.

Though globalisation has raised the profile of inclusion through mechanisms of accountability, consumer participation and voice, marginalised communities, such as this, scarcely benefit. Further, these mechanisms for inclusion are designed to facilitate the market. They are not concerned with building citizenship; neither do they prevent persistently ineffective political representation and, as a number of interviewees claim, inadequate responsiveness from the Ministry of Health. The widespread sentiment is that formal political channels are not operational and that the wealthy communities have easier access to government. One community leader expressed the commonly accepted position:

> There are no avenues to influence the Ministry of Health's policy. Ministries do not respond to anything but roadblocks. People like us do not get help from the people up there. We have to do it ourselves. The wealthier communities get more done.[2]

Another familiar critique – particularly among academics – is that the last two decades of adjustment and further integration into the international market may have produced some economic gains but have also resulted in significant social losses, particularly for the poor and already dispossessed.

Commentators in other parts of the region have expressed similar concerns. For example, Selwyn Ryan maintains:

> political failure and its attendant crisis of governance are closely related to the poor performance of most Caribbean economies and the persistence of poverty; increased criminal activity, especially as it relates to drug trafficking; the inability of Caribbean states to sustain the levels of welfare that were put in place in the post-independence era; and the redefined position of the state from its previous function as a development agency to that of a facilitator of market driven policies.   (Ryan 1996, p. 40)

Hall and Benn (2000, pp. xii–xiv) note that while – since the 1980s – some governments have been able to control inflation and to reduce public sector deficits, others have failed to achieve the expected levels of growth 'and the social impact of adjustment has borne heavily on the population in these societies'. Consequently, there is urgent need for strategies that secure growth with equity. Furthermore, 'the demand for increased social equity as a basis for social stability will require that greater attention be paid to the equitable distribution of the benefits of development and the adoption of specific measures to ensure increased allocations of resources to the poor and vulnerable in the society'.

The challenge to 'inclusion'

The social exclusion approach offers to investigate 'processes of deprivation' and to emphasise the institutional, economic, political and social factors and forces that produce differing and, often, persistent forms of injustice. Based on this 'deeper understanding', it would then be possible to design the antidote: the strategies for promoting social inclusion. However, conceptions of exclusion and inclusion vary; they are coloured by subjective political, economic and moral judgements. As Harris argues in this volume (Ch. 3 above), 'inclusion' can serve particular political ends – it can secure social order and smooth the way for economic transacting – which need not be consistent with social justice. Therefore, the underlying ideological and political persuasions matter for policy outcomes. Whether or not 'inclusion' prioritises 'just' social policies is of substantial consequence, particularly to the poor.

There is a persuasive argument that over the long term, social stability depends on social equity. Our case study supports this. Moreover, it demonstrates that state intervention is required, particularly in contexts of vast and persistent inequalities. This does not mean an unqualified endorsement of welfare politics and economics. The Jamaican experience demonstrates that there are significant economic and political costs to increased state provision, and that one of the more formidable challenges is to develop affordable and sustainable social policies and programmes. Sustainable social policies, in turn, require earnest attention to the institutions, politics, cultural and social norms that support adverse relationships. Furthermore, understanding class divisions and relations is essential for accounting for and addressing deprivation.

- These are familiar objectives; they top the mission statements of almost all 'well-meaning' social projects. Yet, while there has been some progress, old exclusions remain and new forms are developing. Arguably, few countries have genuinely prioritised human development. Many more have been satisfied with piecemeal and largely reactive strategies, even under the guise of social inclusion. How do we account for this? First, as Harris describes, there are real tensions between 'market and society' and 'capitalism and sociality'. Without a fundamental change in ethos, principles of social justice may be sacrificed in the interest of more conservative agendas.
- Second, the political and economic constraints to effective social action are frequently underestimated. National governments often have limited space for action and/or lack the political skill required to secure cooperation among contending groups. (The danger with pitting capitalism against sociality or market against society is that we may minimise the significance of sound macro-economic management for effective and long-term social policies.) However, governments can be irresponsible; there is no reason to assume that leaders would promote social justice if they were not constrained by globalisation. Further, there is disagreement on whether, despite the limitations, there is still scope to address long-standing inequalities. For example, Robotham (2001) contends that external obligations confine Jamaican governments to set courses of action; there are no alternatives to the market. Henke (2001), Antrobus and Peacoke (2001) maintain that government do have the space to 'address fundamental questions of social equality and collective realisation'.
- Third, effective national action depends on the wider terms of incorporation – regional and global. There are sobering questions about the feasibility of a regional or global strategy, particularly one that has noteworthy national and local reach. The more pressing challenges include securing cooperation across countries and interest groups, defining the depth and breadth of the agenda, identifying appropriate standards of inclusion and establishing effective means and mechanisms for securing them. These are formidable tasks since at these supranational levels the politics of inclusion/exclusion is equally, if not more, complex and daunting.

However, this is an exciting era, in which improved forms of communication allow rapid dissemination of ideas and practices. With increased information, more people are questioning the merits of various policy stances and the values that inform them. This is precisely the period in which the Commonwealth, as an organisation, could increase its call for 'terms of incorporation' that profit the excluded/adversely incorporated within member states. The Commonwealth should continue to pursue distinct social objectives, underlined by principles of justice and equity. It should recommend that member states prioritise these objectives and question policies and programmes (both internal and externally directed) that flout them. Indubitably, this would give the Commonwealth a political role and powers of observation and intervention that individual member states may resist. It requires that the Commonwealth practise objectivity, despite the economic and political clout of any member state involved. Such a mandate will likely lead the Commonwealth into debate and, perhaps, confrontation with some of the more dominant agencies and corporations. It is a tremendously bold initiative that has the best prospects where the leading institution is appropriately organised, and has the will and capability to influence change. Should the Commonwealth dare to consider such an agenda, and should it successfully organise its own operations to effectively lead this effort, then there are likely to be substantive gains for its member states, especially the poorest among them.

Notes

1. Surveys conducted for research on accountability and health provision in Jamaica, 1998. See Moncrieffe (1999c).
2. Personal interview, 1998.

References

Antrobus, P. and Peacoke, N. (2001) Yabba Still Empty: Comments on Holger Henke's Freedom Ossified: Political Culture and the Use of History in Jamaica and Don Robotham's Response to Henke, *Identities*, Vol. 8, No. 3, pp. 413–440.

Boyd, D. (1998) The Impact of Adjustment Policies on Vulnerable Groups, in [eds Cornia G.A., R. Jolly and F. Stewart] *Adjustment With a Human Face*, Vol. 2, Ten Country Studies, Oxford: Clarendon Press.

Broom, L. (1954) Social Differentiation of Jamaica, *American Sociological Review*, Vol. 19, No. 2, pp. 115–125.

Davies, O. (1986) An Analysis of the Management of the Jamaican Economy: 1972–1985, *Social and Economic Studies*, Vol. 35, pp. 73–109.

Davies, O. and Witter, M. (1989) The Development of the Jamaican Economy Since Independence, in [eds Nettleford, R.] *Jamaica in Independence: Essays on the Early Years*, London [Kingston]: Heinemann.

Edie, C.J. (1991) *Democracy by Default: Dependency and Clientelism in Jamaica*, Kingston: Ian Randle Publishers.

Gray, O. (1991) *Radicalism and Social Change in Jamaica 1960–1972*, Tennessee: The University of Tennessee Press.

Hall, K. and Benn, D. (2000) *Contending With Destiny: The Caribbean in the 21st Century*, Kingston: Ian Randle Publishers.

Harrigan, J. (1995) Jamaica; Mature Democracy But Questionable Accountability, in Healey, J. and W. Tordoff (eds) *Votes and Budgets: Comparative Studies in Accountable Governance in the South*, Basingstoke: Macmillan.

Jamaica Hansard Parliamentary Proceedings: The House of Representatives, Kingston: Government of Jamaica, Proceedings 1956–1957; April–August 1, 1963; September–December 1981.

Henke, H. (2001) Freedom Ossified: Political Culture and the Use of History in Jamaica, *Identities*, Vol. 8, No. 3, pp. 413–440.

Kabeer, N. (2000) Social Exclusion, Poverty and Discrimination: Towards an Analytical Framework, *IDS Bulletin*, Vol. 31, No. 4, pp. 83–97.

Kaufman, M. (1988) Democracy and Social Transformation in Jamaica, *Social and Economic Studies*, Vol. 37, pp. 45–71.

Keith N.W. and Keith, N.Z. (1992) *The Social Origins of Democratic Socialism in Jamaica*, Philadelphia: Temple University Press.

McNeill, K. (1972) Health Position Paper submitted to the Hon. Norman Manley and the PNP leadership. Unpublished.

Moncrieffe, J. (2001a) Problems of Parliamentary Accountability in Jamaica: Consequences for Health Administration, *Commonwealth and Comparative Politics*, Vol. 39, No. 2, pp. 73–97.

Moncrieffe, J. (2001b) Accountability: Idea, Ideals, Constraints, *Democratization*, Vol. 8, No. 3, pp. 26–50.

Moncrieffe, J. (1999c) Accountability: Principle, Practice and Implications for a Developing Democracy (with a case study of health provision in Jamaica). Cambridge: Cambridge University, Unpublished Thesis, 1999.

Munroe, T. (1972) *The Politics of Constitutional Decolonization*, Kingston: Institute for Social and Economic Research.

Munroe, T. (2000) Voice, Participation and Governance in a Changing Environment: The Case of Jamaica; The University of the West Indies: Discussion Draft.

National Committee on Political Tribalism (NCPT) (July 23, 1997) *Report*; [Kingston: Government of Jamaica]

Palmer, C. (1989) Identity, Race and Black Power in Independent Jamaica, in Knight F. and C. Palmer, *The Modern Caribbean*, Carolina: The University of North Carolina Press.

Robotham, D. (2001) Freedom Ossified or Economic Crisis: A comment on Holger Henke, *Identities*, Vol. 8, No. 3, pp. 451–466.

Ryan, S. (1996) Democratic Governance and the Social Condition in the Anglophone Caribbean, Caribbean Division, Regional Bureau for Latin America and the Caribbean, New York: United Nations Development Programme.

Stone, C. (1985) *Democracy and Clientelism in Jamaica*, New Jersey: Transaction Books.

Waters, A.M. (1985) *Class and Political Symbols: Rastafari and Reggae in Jamaican Politics*, New Brunswick: Transaction Books.

West India Royal Commission, 1938–39: Recommendations presented by the Secretary of State for the Colonies to Parliament by command of His Majesty, February 1940 [London: HMSO, 1940]

Wellisz, S. and Findlay, R. (1993) *The Political Economy of Poverty, Equity and Growth: Five Small Open Economies*, Oxford: Oxford University Press.

Wolfe, M. (1995) Globalization and Social Exclusion: Some Paradoxes, in G. Rodgers, C. Gore, J. Figueiredo (eds) *Social Exclusion: Rhetoric, Reality, Responses*, Geneva: ILO.

World Bank (1993) *World Development Report: Investing in Health*, New York: Oxford University Press.

5
Three Decades of Community Development in Botswana: Is There Social Inclusion?

Morena J. Rankopo

Introduction

Botswana is a landlocked country situated at the centre of Southern Africa. It is surrounded by South Africa, Namibia, Angola, Zambia and Zimbabwe. It had a population of about 1.6 million in 2001. Botswana (formely Bechuanaland Protectorate) was a British colony from 1885 to 1965. At independence in 1966 Botswana adopted a Westminster type of democracy with general elections held every five years. Since then, only one party, the Botswana Democratic Party (BDP), has been returned to office in what has been declared free and fair elections by the international community. This party transformed Botswana from being the poorest country in the world to a miracle economy and success model of democratic leadership in Africa (Coclough and McCarthy 1980; Picard 1987). However, its significant gains in human development are being reversed by the HIV/AIDS pandemic (Republic of Botswana 2001).

This chapter examines community development practice in Botswana since independence in 1966 and the extent to which it has contributed towards social inclusion in the country. Until 1965 human needs were met informally through the family, household and community. Communitarianism was the dominant value that guided the provision of social welfare services and community development activities. These activities were based on mutual understanding and reciprocity in that everybody who benefited from these social provisions was also to play an active role in welfare activities at the household level. Missionaries played a very important role in the introduction of formal social welfare services. They helped establish primary schools and health clinics in the major villages. Efforts to systematically address human needs by way of social policy were neglected until after World War II when the Colonial Administration began to introduce remedial social welfare provisions due to nationalist political pressures for self-government in many colonies. Social welfare was introduced within the Department of Education in 1946 to replace the idea of mass education (Wass 1972). Botswana benefited from those political winds of change even though there was not much political activity in the colony to warrant immediate action.

The postcolonial state assumed office in 1966 and deliberately pursued economic policies geared towards addressing human needs using a mix of 'traditional' and modern institutions. This mix of 'tradition' with Western liberal democratic principles is said to be responsible for Botswana's economic miracle in Africa (Good 1992; Stedman 1993). The post-colonial state chartered a pragmatic approach best understood in contemporary terminology as 'the developmental state' (Edge 1998; Tsie 1996). Community development in Botswana was not founded on a specific policy but rather the four national principles of democracy, development, unity and self-reliance. It was used as a strategy for nation-building, development administration and rural development (Tsiane and Youngman 1985; Wass 1972). Methodologically, community development was premised on a Western positivist paradigm that encouraged a technical response rather than a humanistic response. Consequently, CD became part of a broader rural development strategy that was predominantly bureaucratised, centralised, top-down and programme-oriented. The future for community development lies in its ability to embrace indigenous approaches and other people-centred development models to help alleviate poverty, and improve the situation of marginalised populations.

The precolonial era

It is generally believed that Batswana chiefdoms had a tradition of democracy based on the *kgotla* [the chief's place, judiciary and general assembly] and *therisano* [consultation]. The *kgosi* (chief) was expected to rule in the best interests of his people (Ngcongco 1989; Tlou 1998). However, only the royals and commoners enjoyed the benefits of Tswana democracy. Settlers, ethnic minorities and women were not actively involved in *kgotla* debates (Inger 1985; Ngcongco 1989). Today, the BDP government uses a similar principle to project itself as *puso ya batho ka batho* (government of the people by the people) which is more inclusive in the sense that it promotes equality of all citizens as well as the right to democratic participation in development by all population groups including women and youth. However, there are still concerns that some aspects of the constitution are not ethnically neutral in that the constitution recognises 'principal tribes and minority tribes' when it comes to determining the composition of *Ntlo ya Dikgosi* (the House of Chiefs) (Balopi Commission 2000).

Communitarianism was the dominant discourse used to address human needs during the precolonial era. In a communal society, such as in the pre-colonial era, the extended family, neighbours, the ward and the chief all played an important role in addressing the human needs and concerns of community members within specific localities (Mwansa, Lucas and Osei-Hwedie 1998; Schapera 1955). The chief was the highest political authority and had the power to oversee development activities in his village.

The traditional social welfare system existed through informal social supports by village *mephato* (age regiments). Children, people with disabilities and the elderly were cared for by other members of the extended family (Mwansa, Lucas and Osei-Hwedie 1998; Schapera 1955). There were communal fields (*masotla*) that were cultivated by the villagers and the harvest stored in *difalana* (large granaries) at the chief's *kgotla* for distribution to the needy. The *mafisa* system, for example, was used to redistribute wealth to poorer families: those who had many cattle could give a small herd to a poorer family to tend (Tlou 1998). Thus there was a social net in place to cushion the needs of the underprivileged members of the tribe.

Community development during this era was a shared responsibility and therefore inclusive in a broader sense. Response to need was situated within the traditional tribal framework with the extended family playing a major role. It must be noted however, that the above discussion is not intended to suggest a golden era of a totally pluralistic democracy in Botswana. Women in traditional Tswana societies were confined to the home, while ethnic minorities were allowed to attend the *kgotla* as silent observers (Ngcongco 1989). This form of exclusion is still evident in some communities (Mompati and Prinsen 2000). Overall Botswana is doing well in terms of maintaining ethnic tolerance compared to many other countries (Carroll and Carroll 1997).

The colonial era: indirect rule and benign neglect of 'the barren land', 1885–1965

Throughout the colonial period, Botswana remained underdeveloped due to lack of visible economic opportunities within the country. Indicative of its lack of commitment to developing the country, Britain ruled Botswana indirectly by a Resident Commissioner based at Mafikeng in South Africa. General law and order was maintained through cooperation with the Batswana chiefs (Schapera 1955; Wass 1972). This was unlike many other African colonies where Britain had economic interests. However, Botswana was of strategic importance to British expansion to the North (Mwansa, Lucas and Osei-Hwedie 1998; Ramsay 1998).

Prior to World War II, formal social welfare provisions in the Bechuanaland Protectorate were found mainly in education: mass literacy classes. Adult literacy classes and missionary assisted schools were the main services available to Batswana (Wass 1972). The term community development was adopted following the Cambridge Conference of 1948 which sought to devise strategies for developing social welfare services in British colonies. However, it was not until the beginning of the 1960s that concrete action was initiated to implement community development programmes in the protectorate. Community development was piloted in a rural setting in 1965, and subsequently adopted as a strategy of development administration (Tsiane and Youngman 1985; Wass 1975). Colonial community development practice emphasised the role of the community, particularly the extended family in meeting the needs of people. This approach was later adopted by the ruling Botswana Democratic Party government. The few civic associations that existed were apolitical and focused more on the person's psychosocial development, for example, Boys Scout, Girl Guides and the Young Women's Christian Association (Wass 1972).

Formal community development education was established in the country in the early 1970s, and later replaced by social work in 1985. Community development theory and practice has tended to rely more on the American literature. The extension model of development was adopted by the mid-1970s (Youngman and Maruatona 1998) and this marked the decline of British influence in community development.

The post-colonial era: the developmental state 1966–1999

At the time of independence Botswana was not regarded as economically viable. It was one of the 25 poorest countries in the world. Although community development was introduced in the British colonies in 1948 it was formally launched in Botswana in 1965 and later adopted as a national planning principle. There was never a written policy on community development, a factor which has been recognised as a constraint in the practice of community development in Botswana (Republic of Botswana 1977). The introduction of community development coincided with the disastrous drought which continued up to the end of the 1960s. The new national government introduced a food-for-work scheme through which community development assistants distributed relief rations from the United Nations bodies and other donors. Food-for-work was the idea that villagers who participated in local self-help projects in their villages would be given food rations in exchange for their labour. This did not do justice to the philosophy of community development which emphasises that communities should control the development processes in their localities.

At independence the new government adopted the Transitional Plan for Social and Economic Development aimed at making Botswana economically viable within the shortest possible time. The state was placed at the centre of economic and social planning. It pursued a mixed economy approach until the 1990s when it began to consider the private sector as an engine of economic growth (Republic of Botswana 1970 and 1997). The discovery of diamonds in 1968 and other minerals in the early 1970s enabled government to play an active role in economic and social development as there was no private sector to spearhead development. Botswana's economic growth was among the highest in the world from 1965 to 1980. Growth rates between 14.2 per cent and 9.9 per cent were maintained between 1980 and 1990. While in 1965 Botswana's GDP per capita was US$60, by 1991 this figure had risen to US$2583 (Edge 1998, p. 337) resulting in perceptions that it was a model for success in Africa (Hartland-Thunberg 1978; Picard 1987). By the early 1990s Botswana was one of the few African countries to be classified by the World Bank as an 'upper middle income' country using the GNP factor (Duncan, Jefferis and Molutsi 1994). In 1997 Botswana was the 11th fastest growing economy in the world making it comparable to the 'Asian tigers', albeit for opposite reasons (Edge 1998; and cf. Chs 9 and 11 below).[1]

The main sources of income at independence were beef, subsistence agriculture and remittances from migrant labour working in South Africa (Hoppers 1986). The exploitation of minerals, especially diamonds, was the primary source of economic boom. The private sector remained the largest formal sector employer in 1995, and accounted for about 57 per cent of employment, followed by government at 37.1 per cent and parastatals at 5.9 per cent (Harvey 1992; Republic of Botswana 1997). Available data show that unemployment still remains high, though it has decreased from 21.6 per cent in 1994 to 19.6 per cent in 1998 (Central Statistics Office 1998) and 15.8 per cent in 2001

(Republic of Botswana 2001). While nearly half of all households were estimated to live below the poverty datum line in 1997 (BIDPA 1997), in 2001 the proportion was estimated to have reduced to about 36 per cent. Much needs to be done especially for the rural and urban poor, female-headed households, indigenous peoples and other underemployed persons.

Politically, Botswana provides an important lesson in the Commonwealth because it has successfully achieved its economic miracle in the context of a liberal democracy with free and fair general elections (Molomo 2000); not the authoritarianism characteristic of one-party socialist governments in African states (Molutsi 1998). The ruling Botswana Democratic Party has not articulated its political ideology, though some scholars assert that it favours a liberal democracy with an emphasis on free enterprise (Good 1992). Most expert opinion maintains that Botswana's economic and social development policies and programmes are driven by a pragmatic ideology (Stedman 1993; Tsie 1996). Ruling Democratic Party politicians like to argue that, unlike opposition parties, they do not have an ideology but respond pragmatically to development challenges.

Commenting on the nature of social policy in Botswana, Osei-Hwedie and Bar-On (1999) contend that most policies are community-based and pragmatic. Families continue to play a major role in caring for and supporting the sick, people living with disabilities and HIV/AIDS. Social welfare supports are means tested and provided only when the extended family is unable to assist. The government maintains that its pragmatic approach to development is guided by the national principles of democracy, development, unity, self reliance and *botho* (humanness). Collectively, these principles are believed to promote *kagisano* (social harmony) among the people (Republic of Botswana 1997). These principles are incorporated in all the six-year National Development Plans, and are the bases of social welfare and community development practice in Botswana.

Institutions for community development

After independence, a Department of Community Development headed by a commissioner was created at central government level to formulate policies and coordinate the implementation of community development projects throughout the country (Wass 1972). This agency was reorganised and renamed the Division of Social and Community Development in 1975 and more recently in 2001, the

Department of Social Services. A major criticism of this agency is that it was not able to develop a comprehensive national community development policy nor attain a lead role in terms of guiding national community development planning strategy (see Republic of Botswana 1979). Be that as it may, community participation has remained the guiding framework of Botswana's Rural Development Policy since 1973. A network of institutions was created to enable people to influence decision-making processes on social development matters at the local, district and national levels (Danevad 1993). Liberal democracy and indigenous communitarian principles were adopted by the government to promote free speech and self-reliance. The *kgotla* (traditional assembly) was strengthened to include ethnic minorities, women and youth as active participants in the deliberation of local and national development issues. This mix of 'tradition' and modern institutions has made Botswana a unique model in Commonwealth Africa (Good 1996; Odell 1985).

The notion of people's participation in community development was premised on the Setswana traditions of consultation (Rankopo 2001; Tsiane and Youngman 1985). The centrality of the *kgotla* in consultation processes cannot be over-emphasised and reflects the government's policy of social inclusion. In his assessment of the role of the bureaucracy in promoting community participation, Liphuko (1989) concludes that there is evidence to support the view that there is adequate consultation between people and the government. However, recent research seems to challenge this view. The bureaucracy is more powerful than politicians and other civil society groups. This leads it to dominate social policy debates in general (Charlton 1991; Somolekae 1993). This has led to a top-down approach to community development.

A recent Participatory Rural Appraisal (PRA) study commissioned by the government revealed that although extension workers view community participation as central to development planning, they do not believe that the community can meaningfully contribute to the resolution of their development needs (Youngman and Maruatona 1998; Prinsen et al. 1997). It is evident from this PRA study that a change of focus in community development approaches must be accompanied by changes in the way practitioners behave towards the people they seek to empower. In other words community development practitioners need to change negative attitudes inherited from their colonial education which privileged formal education over indigenous knowledge and professional expertise over community wisdom. The addition of *botho* (humanness), as the fifth national principle in 1997, is a deliberate effort by government to promote Batswana's shared value which emphasises compassionate caring, loving and respect for all people regardless of their ethnic or racial backgrounds (Republic of Botswana 1997 – Vision 2016). This principle is consistent with the new vision of participatory community development.

Community development towards the 21st century

The last decade of the 20th century has witnessed critical debates on the future of community development in Botswana. The rapid development of the country has presented new challenges, dilemmas and paradoxes that have a direct bearing on the workings of community development as a vehicle for rural improvement as well as for the implementation of national principles, particularly self-reliance. Since the 1990s the government has openly embraced a private sector-led, open market strategy. At the same time, it has introduced a number of reforms aimed at promoting community empowerment and capacity building. This emphasis on the community as the vehicle for meeting human needs has come during the decline of the rapid economic growth witnessed during the 1980s. The new rural development strategy underscores this shift of emphasis:

> The strategy seeks to introduce a more effective and sustainable approach to rural development by substantially increasing the role of community participation and community leadership in identifying their own economic needs and aspirations and formulating and implementing their own action plans to address these (Republic of Botswana/CBSRD 1997: v).

The above strategy seeks to reverse the dominant model of development which views the state as a provider of development. This philosophy of community development is consistent with current international CD literature which emphasises people-centred approaches to development with the state workers as facilitators and the government as partner and sponsor of community-based development initiatives. This is consistent with current thinking in international CD practice (see Campfens 1997) and Commonwealth practice in particular which has promoted good governance, transparency and accountability (Green 2001). Local community development education and training over the last five years have emphasised these principles.

Although the community-based strategy embraces many of the principles and values consistent with current community development discourses that promote participatory development and community control of local development initiatives, it does not embrace indigenous concepts such as *boipelego* (community development), *a re ipelegeng* (community self-determination), *therisanyo* (consultation), *tshwaragano* (cooperation) and *botho* (humility) that I believe are the cornerstone of an indigenous humanistic approach to community development in Botswana. It must be acknowledged, however, that the strategy recognises the important role played by civil society groups. As such it starts on a very good premise which is consistent with progressive international community development literature (see Campfens 1997). A major challenge for Botswana in that regard is that of enhancing the inclusion of civil society groups. However, indigenous principles need to be clearly articulated as they risk being taken for granted.

In Botswana, there exists a small civil society which is still maturing and trying to find its identity in a rapidly changing environment. Whilst both government and communities acknowledge the contribution of civil society in community development, academicians contend that they are generally weak and wanting as agents of participatory development (Molutsi and Holm 1990; Holm Molutsi and Somolekae 1996). Molutsi and Holm stated that:

> ...civil society lacks the capacity and initiative to organise itself...it does not have group political culture; few politically oriented groups exist; elected representatives rarely feel compelled to engage the public in policy discussion; private newspapers are weak; and the political parties do not reflect grassroots opinion on policy questions. (Molutsi and Holm 1990: 323)

The above observation may be better understood against the background of colonial governments' failure to develop civil society and the political conservatism of post-independent Botswana. Throughout colonial rule there were virtually no civil groups apart from missionary activity. The first generation civic associations that were formed in the 1960s supported the status quo. Their focus was leisure, sport and welfare. The second generation civic associations from 1980 onwards began to have a more explicit political agenda and openly challenged structural inequalities in the country. Their focus was ethnic equality, human rights, labour and women's rights issues. The women's movement has made significant contributions in challenging unfair cultural practices, political and legal barriers that exclude women from participating equally in development activities (Molomo 1998). Ethnic minorities also have organised associations which are beginning to play an important role in the areas of cultural development and ethnic equality advocacy. Currently, there are protests against the Government of Botswana's treatment of indigenous peoples (Basarwa or San) sponsored by the United Kingdom-based Survival International. Thus, these civil society groups need to be collectively recognised for their attempted contributions towards creating a socially inclusive Botswana society.

Civil society groups are not without constraints. When Botswana was upgraded to the list of middle-income category following its rapid economic growth many donors decided to leave the country and/or remove Botswana from their list of deserving countries[2]. Not much has been done to develop domestic funding sources – at least before the recent creation of the Botswana Coalition for Non-Governmental Organisations (BOCONGO) (Molutsi and Somolekae 1998). The Government has committed itself to formulating a national policy on NGOs which will outline how NGOs are to be assisted. BOCONGO holds the view that government funding should not constrain NGOs in ways that would make them little more than 'watchdogs' over marginalised populations (Molutsi and Somolekae 1998).

Conclusion

This chapter has demonstrated that good governance combined with prudent planning and financial management has been responsible for Botswana's good performance in social development. In the first two decades of independence the state made a strong social policy attempt to redistribute profits to promote equality and social cohesion especially in the rural areas. This mixed economy approach was a result of British influence which had sought to promote capitalism and liberal democracy through community development in the Commonwealth of Nations. Now there is a growing tension between economic and social policy imperatives arising from globalisation, which is pressuring the Government of Botswana to move away from subsidising social services towards free market purchasing.

While the British legacy has declined significantly in terms of community development theory and practice, the influence of the Commonwealth in Botswana, and Africa in general, is likely to continue in the area of social policy. The role of the Commonwealth in shaping the advancement in the social inclusion of women, girl-children, young people and Indigenous Peoples in Botswana has been significant. It has been shown in the case of Botswana that government adopts a pragmatic approach to development. It selects policy choices on the basis of what works within its context. Therefore, the Commonwealth will continue to be an important forum, amongst other multilateral bodies, for promoting social inclusion. Future social policy debates in Botswana must explore possibilities for the greater inclusion in the national development planning process especially of indigenous ethnic minorities, women, young people and the rural sector. Community development in Botswana needs to be a part of these processes and to learn from other nations.

Notes

1. The growth performance of the Asian Tigers was rated remarkable precisely because of their lack of natural mineral (or other) resources, set against their abundance of people.
2. Note the comparable sudden switch in the treatment afforded Hong Kong from the mid-1960s (Jones 1990: 170).

References

Balopi Commission, The (2000) *Presidential Commission on sections 77, 78 and 79 of the constitution of Botswana*, Gaborone: Government Printer.
Botswana Institute of Development Policy and Analysis (1997). *A study of poverty and poverty alleviation in Botswana*, Gaborone: BIDPA.
Campfens, H. (ed.) (1997) *Community development around the world: Practice, theory, research, training*, Toronto: University of Toronto Press.
Carroll, B.W. and Carroll, T. (1997) 'The state and ethnicity in Botswana and Mauritius: A democratic route to development?', *Development Studies*, 33 (4), pp. 464–486.
Central Statistics Office (1998) *1995/96 Labour Force Survey*, Gaborone: Ministry of Finance and Development Planning.
Charlton, R. (1991) 'Bureaucrats and politicians in Botswana's policy making process: A re-interpretation', *Commonwealth and Comparative Politics*, 29 (3), pp. 265–288.
Coclough, C. and McCarthy, S. (1980) *The political economy of Botswana: A study of growth and distribution*, Oxford: Oxford University Press.
Danevad, A. (1993) *Development planning and the importance of democratic institutions in Botswana*, Bergen, Norway: Chr. Michelsen Institute.
Duncan, T., Jefferis, K. and Molutsi, P. (1994) *Social development in Botswana: A retrospective analysis*, Gaborone: Government Printer.
Edge, W.A. (1998) Botswana: Developmental state. In W.A. Edge and M.H. Lekorwe (eds), *Botswana: Politics and Society*, Pretoria: J.L. van Schaik Publishers, pp. 333–348.
Good, K. (1992) Interpreting Botswana's exceptionality, *Journal of Modern African Studies*, 30 (1), pp. 69–95.

Good, K. (1996) 'Towards popular participation in Botswana', *Journal of Modern African Studies*, 34 (1), pp. 53–78.
Green, R. (ed.) (2000), *The Commonwealth Yearbook 2000*, London: Commonwealth Secretariat.
Hartland-Thunberg, P. (1978) *Botswana: An African growth economy*, Boulder: Westview.
Harvey, C. (1992) *Botswana: Is the economic miracle over?*, Discussion paper 298. Brighton, UK: Institute of Development Studies.
Holm, J. D., Molutsi, P.P. and Somolekae, G. (1996) The development of civil society in a democratic state: The Botswana model, *African Studies Review*, 26 (5), 22–28.
Hoppers, W. (1986) *After training what? Youth training and employment in Botswana and Zambia*, London: Commonwealth Secretariat.
Inger, D. (1985) A personal view of the constraints on effective participation in rural development in Botswana. In Tsiane and Youngman (eds), *The theory and practice of people's participation in rural development* (pp. 31–37), Gaborone: Government Printer.
Jones, C. (1990) *Promoting Prosperity: The Hong Kong Way of Social Policy*, Hong Kong: The Chinese University Press.
Liphuko, S.D. (1989) 'Civil service consultation: An examination of three cases'. In Molutsi, P.P. and Holm, J.D. (eds), *Democracy in Botswana*, Gaborone: Macmillan.
Molomo, M. (2000) 'Understanding government and political parties in Botswana', *Commonwealth and Comparative Politics*, 38(1), pp. 65–92.
Molomo, M.G. (1998) The roles and responsibilities of members of parliament in facilitating good governance and democracy, in W.A. Edge and M.H. Lekorwe (eds) *Botswana Politics and Society*, Pretoria: J.L. van Schaik Publishers, pp. 11–31.
Molutsi, P.P. and Holm, J.D. (1990) 'Developing democracy when civil society is weak: The case of Botswana', *African Affairs*, 89 (356), 323–340.
Molutsi, P. (1998) 'Politics and civil society in Botswana: Future scenarios'. In W.A. Edge and M.H. Lekorwe (eds), *Botswana: Politics and Society*, Pretoria: J.L. van Schaik Publishers, pp. 489–498.
Molutsi, P. and Somolekae, G. (1998) *The way forward for strengthening relationships and collaboration between the government, private sector and non-governmental organizations in Botswana*, Gaborone: Botswana Coalition for Non-governmental Organisations.
Mompati, T. and Prinsen, G. (2000) 'Ethnicity and participatory development in Botswana: Some participants are to be seen not heard', *Development in Practice*, 10 (5), pp. 625–637.
Mwansa, L.K., Lucas, T. and Osei-Hwedie, K. (1998) 'The practice of social policy in Botswana', *Journal of Social Development in Africa*, 13 (2), pp. 55–76.
Ngcongco, L.D. (1989) 'Tswana political tradition: how democratic?' In J. Holm and P. Molutsi (eds), *Democracy in Botswana*, pp. 42–47. Gaborone: Botswana Society.
Odell, M.J. (1985) 'Local Government: traditional and modern roles in the village *kgotla*'. In L. Picard (ed.), *The evolution of modern Botswana*, London: Rex Collings.
Osei-Hwedie, K. and Bar-On, A. (1999) 'Sub-Saharan Africa: Community-driven social policies'. In Morales-Gomez, D. (ed.), *Transformational social policies: The*

new development challenges of globalisation, Ottawa: International Development Research Centre.

Picard, L.A. (1987) *The politics of development: A model for success,* London: Lynne Reiner Publishers.

Prinsen, G. et al. (1997) *PRA: Contract and commitment for village development,* Ministry of Finance and Development Planning, Gaborone: Government Printer.

Ramsay, J. (1998) 'The establishment and consolidation of the Bechuanaland Protectorate, 1870–1910'. In W.A. Edge and M.H. Lekorwe (eds), *Botswana: Politics and Society,* Pretoria: J.L. van Schaik Publishers, pp. 62–98.

Rankopo, M.J. (2001) 'Towards an indigenous approach to community development in Botswana: A social work perspective', unpublished PhD thesis, the University of Queensland. Brisbane: Australia.

Republic of Botswana (1970) *National Development Plan 3 – 1970–1975,* Gaborone: Ministry of Finance and Development Planning.

Republic of Botswana (1977) *Report of Community Development Review Committee,* Gaborone: Ministry of Local Government and Lands.

Republic of Botswana (1997) *Community Based Programme Strategy for Rural Development,* Gaborone: Ministry of Finance and Development Planning.

Republic of Botswana (1997) *Vision 2016. Report of the Presidential Commission on the vision for Botswana in the twenty years between 1996–2016,* Gaborone: Office of the President.

Republic of Botswana (1997) *National Development Plan 8 – 1997–2003,* Gaborone: Ministry of Finance and Development Planning.

Republic of Botswana (2001) Budget Speech, 2001, Gaborone: Ministry of Finance and Development Planning.

Schapera, I. (1955) *A handbook of Tswana law and custom,* London: Oxford University Press.

Somolekae, G. (1993) 'Bureaucracy and democracy in Botswana: What type of a relationship?'. In J.S. Stedman (ed.), *Botswana: The political economy of democratic development,* USA: Lynne Rienner Publications.

Stedman, J.S. (ed.)(1993) *Botswana: The political economy of democratic development,* USA: Lynne Rienner Publications.

Tlou, T. (1998) 'The nature of Tswana states: Towards a theory of Batswana traditional government – the Batawana case'. In W.A. Edge and M.H. Lekorwe (eds), *Botswana: Politics and Society,* Pretoria: J.L. van Schaik Publishers, pp. 11–31.

Tsiane, B.D. and Youngman, F. (eds) (1985) *The theory and practice of people's Participation in rural development.* Proceedings of the RECC Workshop held in Kanye, 18–22 November, 1985. Gaborone: Government Printer.

Tsie, B. (1996) 'The political context of Botswana's development performance', *Journal of Southern African Studies,* 22 (4), pp. 599–619.

Wass, P. (1972) 'The history of community development in Botswana', *Botswana Notes and Records,* 4, 81–93.

Wass, P. (1975) Issues for development in Africa: Lessons from Botswana, *Community Development Journal,* 10 (1), pp. 14–23.

Youngman, F. and Maruatona, T. (1998) 'A departure from the past? Extension workers and participatory rural development – The case of Botswana', *International Journal of Lifelong Education,* 17 (4), pp. 236–246.

6
Social Welfare and Social Development in South Africa: Reshaping the Colonial and Apartheid Legacy for a Global Era

Leila Patel and James Midgley

Introduction

As in other Commonwealth nations and indeed, other regions of the world, the challenges of globalisation have placed new demands on South Africa's social welfare system. Although the government is faced with pressures to enhance the country's capacity to engage actively in the international economy, in view of its own ideological leanings and a very high poverty rate, it has rejected the argument that the country will only be internationally competitive if it avoids allocating substantial resources to social programmes. On the other hand, it is seeking to promote economic development and recognises that it can only do so if the country is internationally competitive.

When the Mandela government came to power during the immediate post-apartheid period in the mid-1990s, a concerted effort was made to formulate a developmental approach to social welfare that would abolish the racist heritage of the apartheid era, transcend the older colonial legacy with its residualist and paternalist elements, and offer a new and dynamic approach suited to the demands of the global era. Inspired by an expanding body of social development literature as well as the efforts of the United Nations to promote a social development perspective through its World Social Summit in 1995, the South African government in 1997 adopted an important policy document known as the *White Paper for Social Welfare*. This document established a new 'developmental' policy framework for social welfare in South Africa that it hoped would promote equity, participation and social investment.

The developmental approach offers the prospect of modernising South Africa's welfare system in ways that will enhance its ability to meet the challenges of the global era. While the discriminatory legacy of the past must be replaced, it is also desirable to formulate policies and programmes that will foster economic development without sacrificing the country's commitment to promote the social well being of all its people. Accordingly, while the South African experiment with developmental social welfare rejects the neo-liberal recipe, it does not deny the need for economic development. Instead, it contends that economic and social development goals can be harmonised within an ongoing process of progressive social change. By adopting a developmental approach to social welfare, the South African government hopes to harmonise economic development with social welfare, to invest in human capacities, and in this way to respond positively to the challenges of globalisation.

Colonialism and welfare in South Africa

The colonial era began when the Dutch East India Company established a trading and agricultural station at the Cape in 1652. Although Portugese and other European traders had anchored in Table Bay to replenish their ships, the Dutch decided to create a permanent settlement. Officials of the Company obtained land grants and began to settle after the Napoleonic Wars. When the British seized the Cape, the numbers of settlers increased. The indigenous Khoi people of the Cape were displaced and increasingly absorbed into agricultural servitude. Slaves from other African countries and the East Indies were imported. Racial conflicts became common, but there was also racial intermingling among the settlers, the Khoi and Africans. Conflict also developed as Africans and settlers competed for scare natural resources to support their herding societies (Katzen 1969).

Most people, including the settlers, were poor in that their incomes were low and living conditions were primitive. Education was limited and few people were literate. Life expectancy was also low and health services rudimentary. Various epidemics caused widespread illness and death and, in general, public health provisions were non-existent. Welfare was regarded by the community as a matter of individual and family responsibility, and generally, the family and kinship groups provided social support in times of need (MacKendrick 1990).

However, as in Europe, the Church provided aid to the destitute who had no relatives or other means of support. Widows, children and those with disabilities were regarded as deserving of help. Generally, these services were directed at people of European origin. Poor relief was provided by the Dutch Reformed Church and charitable institutions were constructed. Subsequently, legislation was passed to provide support to the children of the European settlers through the establishment of orphanages, and services for people with disabilities and poor relief were created (McKendrick 1990).

In the early 19th century, South Africa became a British colony and deep resentments developed between the new colonial administration and the original Dutch settlers who moved northwards. This led to further conflicts with the African tribes (Thompson 1969; Wilson 1969). Colonial rulers nurtured an exclusive group consciousness, which manifested itself in racial and social supremacy. The Dutch settlers' belief in predestination and of being the 'chosen people' gave religious sanction to their racial attitudes, while the social Darwinist belief that a natural hierarchy of races existed, provided a powerful justification for racial domination and segregation in all aspects of life including social welfare (De Villiers 1971). Education, health and social welfare provisions were segregated long before the advent of apartheid after the World War II. The foundations of racial discrimination, the denigration of indigenous people, welfare paternalism and the distorted nature of social welfare policies favouring whites as a welfare elite, were laid during colonial times (Patel 1992).

Social welfare under the apartheid regime

South Africa changed from an agrarian society to an industrial society following the discovery of minerals in 1860. The Dutch-speaking settlers who had left the Cape in the wake of British annexation in the early 19th century had established two republics, known as the Orange Free State and the South African Republic to the north of the Cape Colony, where they pursued their traditional agricultural interests. The discovery of huge reserves of diamonds and gold in these two republics attracted a significant number of European prospectors and, as conflicts between the newcomers and the original settlers escalated, Britain invaded. After the bitter and destructive Anglo-Boer war of 1899–1901, the two republics were integrated with the region's other British territories to form a union that, in 1910, became self-governing (Thompson 1971). Ironically, the new country's political elite now included the very Dutch-speaking settlers, now known as 'Afrikaaners', who had fought the British. Together with English-speaking settlers and the industrial and commercial interests they represented, the newly formed Union of South Africa experienced industrial transformation (Hobart Houghton 1971).

The way in which industrialisation occurred resulted in the pauperisation of blacks, and some whites, and laid the foundation for racial capitalism and racial differentiation in social welfare. The mining industry – the engine of industrialisation – required a large labour force and thousands of black workers were employed on the mines living under appalling conditions in the emerging cities. Industrialisation forced peasants and subsistence farmers into wage labour leading to increased rural poverty especially among women and children, the elderly and the disabled. Parallel to African poverty, poverty among the white population and especially the Afrikaaners also emerged as a major social and political concern in the first four decades of the 20th century and had a profound effect on the development of social welfare in South Africa (Hobart Houghton 1971; Patel 1992).

In 1929, the Carnegie Commission of Enquiry into the 'poor white problem' resulted in the creation of the first state welfare department in 1937, the professionalisation of social work and the adoption of the partnership between state, religious philanthropy and voluntary organisations. The main functions of state welfare were defined as 'rehabilitation of the socially maladjusted individual or family, the study and treatment of conditions giving rise to maladjustment and the co-ordination of services' (Brummer 1964, p. 20). White poverty was believed to be caused by social and economic underdevelopment and the powerlessness of the Afrikaaner working class. State intervention, the creation of employment opportunities and extensive supportive social services were considered to be essential in addressing poverty.

Race was a key element in South African politics and was most effectively manipulated by the National Party which had been formed by disaffected elements within the Afrikaaner elite who rejected the compromising relationship which had been forged with the English-speaking South Africans and the British imperialists. Their extreme form of Afrikaaner nationalism was rooted in the agrarian experience, slavery and Calvinism. The recreation of the earlier Afrikaaner republics became a key aspiration of the nationalist movement. Influenced by Nazi ideology which further legitimated their racist beliefs, these Afrikaaner elements were determined to use whatever means they could to obtain power.

The Nationalist Party won the 1948 election with strong support from white workers. The basic tenets of white supremacy found expression in its new ideology of apartheid, which had been formulated by the Party's ideologues and presented to the electorate and the wider world as a just and fair separation of racial groups on the ground of preserving ethnic and national identify. The new government also moved quickly to consolidate the political support of the white working class through both social and investment programmes and large-scale employment in the civil service. Welfare programmes were an integral component of its political agenda.

Apartheid enfranchised a white minority who participated in a Westminster-style parliamentary democracy. It was based on the notion of separate development and separate political participation through pseudo-democratic political institutions created for Africans and later for Indians and coloureds. Ten ethnic independent homelands and self-governing territories were created in economically underdeveloped rural reserves for Africans where they were expected to live and exercise their political rights. The homelands played an important role in labour supply and in the social reproduction of labour and provided a safety net for the unemployed, women and children, the old and the sick. Africans in urban areas were considered by the apartheid government to be temporary residents and had no political rights in urban areas. The urbanisation of Africans was restricted through pass controls, the restriction of residence rights in urban areas and a myriad of policies and statutes curtailing civil and human rights.

Capitalist development was achieved through this system. High profit levels were secured as labour costs were borne by the homeland reserves that subsidised the reproduction and supply of labour. Over the years, the subsistence economies declined and the reserves were no longer able to sustain the reproduction of labour and provide a safety net to those who had been marginalised by the system. Faced with a profitability crisis in the early 1970s, South African firms commenced the restructuring of production and African employment. This resulted in African unemployment and new patterns of labour supply and social reproduction of labour including the construction of a differentiated system of labour, made up of temporary migrants and permanent residents. The pass system was unsuccessfully modified to accommodate these changed conditions and failed to prevent the growth of a settled urban African population, which was to become a major force in the mass democratic movement against apartheid (Hindson 1987).

Access to welfare resources was also racially differentiated. A racial hierarchy between the different population groups namely whites,

Indians, coloureds (people of mixed race), and Africans, who constituted the majority of the population, was created. Whites received the greatest share of welfare resources while Africans benefited the least. In real terms, welfare spending on whites was at least six times more than on the poor black population (Terblanche 1987). Social services for whites were modeled on European style 'welfare state' policies. By contrast, social welfare provisions for blacks were residual or non-existent (Patel 1992; McKendrick and Dudas 1987).

The welfare model of the apartheid era was not only inequitable and discriminatory but relied on inappropriate methods of intervention, which were not suited to the local context. During the colonial period, residential facilities had been established and this tradition continued into the apartheid period. An over-reliance on remedial interventions dominated service delivery strategies to an unsustainable extent, and had limited impact on social needs. This trend was prevalent in many Third World countries, relying on the uncritical replication of welfare modalities from industrial societies, resulting in inappropriate social services (Midgley 1981; Midgley 1998). However, South African social policy had some positive aspects. A significant role was played by voluntary and religious philanthropic organisations in the delivery of social welfare services and a network was built up over many years gaining experience and expertise in the delivery of welfare services.

Another significant development was the emergence of statutory social security consisting of contributory and non-contributory benefits. Social assistance programmes for the elderly, disabled, war veterans and single women with children were provided. These programmes had their beginnings in the Old Age Pensions Act of 1928, which provided for non-contributory pensions to the elderly. The Blind Persons and Pensions Act was passed in 1936 and the first Disability grants were paid in terms of the Disability Grants Act of 1946. During the 1930s and 1940s, social insurance programmes such as Workmen's Compensation and Unemployment insurance were introduced (McKendrick and Dudas 1987).

Over the four decades of the Nationalist apartheid regime, the standard of living of whites became comparable to that of populations in advanced industrial societies while poverty and inequality rose among black South Africans. A downward trend in the apartheid economy commenced in the early 1970s due to the changing international economic conditions. A strong white labour movement emerged and the flaws in the grand apartheid design began to be apparent. The social contradictions intensified amid sustained international pressure and the rise of a mass democratic movement. A cycle of resistance, state reaction and repression followed throughout the 1980s.

These changes were also reflected in changing welfare policies and programmes. Non-contributory social pensions were gradually expanded for blacks (Ardington and Lund 1995; Ardington 1994); while welfare expenditure for Africans increased from 25 per cent of total expenditures in 1950 to 35 per cent in 1987. These expenditures excluded allocations received by the homeland authorities from the apartheid government for welfare programmes and social pensions for rural Africans. Expenditure for Indians and coloureds increased from 14 per cent of total expenditures in 1950 to 20 per cent in 1987 (Terblanche 1987). The latter groups were able to secure piecemeal reforms through their participation in separate but discredited political institutions. In short, in spite of the distorted development of the welfare system, a significant infrastructure of human resources, policy and legislative frameworks was being created in the apartheid years. Free and open elections were held for the first time in the nation's history in 1994. This resulted in the coming to office of a coalition government committed to South Africa's reconstruction. New opportunities to develop a welfare system which took account of the needs of all South Africans also emerged.

Developmental social welfare in the post-apartheid era

President Nelson Mandela's African National Congress-led government introduced the Reconstruction and Development Programme (RDP) which many regarded as a development manifesto for the nation (African National Congress 1994). Its goals were to meet basic needs, develop human resources, build the economy, and democratise the state and society. The RDP cut across line ministries, integrating a range of goals in the social, economic and governmental sectors. It advocated equitable, integrated, sustainable and people-driven development strategies and was predicated on the achievement of peace and security for all. Nation building was considered a necessity to overcome racial, income and gender inequality and divisions caused by apartheid and the racial character of capitalist development in South Africa.

The RDP proposed that economic growth be redistributive, sustainable and geared to maximising the productive capacity and human resources of the society. Targets were set for social and human development in a range of sectors; such as education, health, social security and social welfare, housing, infrastructure, land reform, job creation through public works and small business development. A leading role for the state was envisaged, in partnership with the private sector and civil society organisations. The financing of the RDP was to be achieved through the redirection of existing government spending rather than by increasing public expenditures. The new government inherited a large budget deficit and an economy faced with a structural crisis and negative economic growth rates. The RDP advocated the restructuring of the economy to place it on a high growth path – a 6 per cent growth rate was needed to begin to incrementally finance the development needs of the country.

The 1997 White Paper

A two-year consultative process culminated in a new national consensus on welfare signified by the adoption of the *White Paper for Social Welfare* in 1997 (South Africa 1997). The tension between reconciling fiscal constraints with rising social expectations posed a particular challenge. Social welfare expenditures in 1996 were considered to be high in comparison with other countries at the same level of development – nine per cent of total national government expenditure and three per cent of GDP. However, South Africa faced major problems such as structural unemployment, rising crime and violence, skills deficits, and a poor human development index. It is in this context that developmental approach to social welfare was adopted. It stressed the importance of productive policies and investments that empowered people to achieve their optimal capacities and maximise resources and opportunities. This drew on international social policy research (Midgley 1994, 1995, 1999; United Nations 1988); years of developmental social welfare experience in other countries; and the Copenhagen Declaration on Social Development adopted by the United Nations World Summit for Social Development in 1995 (United Nations 1996).

The *White Paper* was based upon the following elements:

- *The inter-relation between social and economic development:* Development accompanied by redistribution through social investments in key social sectors can make a significant contribution to human and social capital and can improve the human development status of the vast majority of the population.
- *Equitable allocation of resources to those in need:* Social interventions targeted at the poor and vulnerable and those with special needs are

emphasised. This selectivist approach differs from universalist European welfare models (Mishra 1999).
- *Social rights:* The right to social security and the rights of children were constitutionally safeguarded as part of a commitment to social and economic rights. This approach to rights resonates with current thinking about citizenship which is active and incorporates notions of care, civic virtue, relational reciprocity and interdependence between providers and recipients (Drover 2000).
- *Role of the state:* A proactive role for the state as the initiator and facilitator of social development in partnership with civil society is favoured. This approach recognises the contribution of voluntary organisations, the business community and others but also guarantees social rights as a part of citizenship rights.
- *Partnerships between the public, private, and voluntary sectors:* Collaboration is considered to be a national collective responsibility. This is critical when approximately 10,000 registered welfare and development organisations are engaged in development and social welfare activities.
- *Individual, family and community empowerment and development*: People-centered development strategies are stressed. These strategies place emphasis on citizen participation, community development and the delivery of community-based social services within an integrated and generalist model for social work and social development practice.

Implementing the *White Paper*

In 1996, the Growth and Redistribution Strategy (GEAR) was introduced. It was designed to accelerate economic growth and initiate structural reforms designed to manage the government's debt and budget deficit. Critics argue that the neo-liberal economic ideas reflected in the GEAR strategy will undermine the government's capacity to meet its social development commitments and address the legacy of the past. It is claimed that the slow progress in reaching the government's RDP targets is due to a preoccupation with debt reduction which has crowded out social development targets (May, J. 2001). However, the adoption of GEAR did not mean that the government had wholeheartedly abandoned its social commitments.

The federal social welfare agency, the Department of Welfare, was renamed the Department of Social Development. It has two main components: social security and welfare services and assistance. Social security amounts to 90.5 per cent of total social development expenditure (South Africa, National Treasury 2001). Welfare services include facilities and community services; individual, group and community development interventions, delivered by voluntary organisations subsidised by government, together with other statutory and protective services.

Social security is the post-apartheid government's most effective poverty alleviation programme reaching 3.9 million of the poorest 40 per cent of the population with a level of expenditure and coverage exceeding that of other middle income or poor countries (South Africa, National Treasury 2001; Ardington and Lund 1995). Non-contributory old age pensions are paid to 1,942,000 old people. These pensions have the highest uptake levels. Disability benefits are paid to 706,000 beneficiaries. Out of 3 million poor children targeted to receive child support benefits, 1.7 million have been registered since 1998. The government has phased out the old discriminatory income maintenance programme for single women with children and instituted a child support benefit that is more equitable and fiscally viable. Foster care grants are paid in respect of 93,357 children. To achieve racial equity, expenditures on social assistance increased rapidly in the 1990s (South Africa, National Treasury 2001). The challenge for the future is to explore active labour market policies to complement social assistance and create opportunities for productive employment of poor people through skills development, job-placement programmes, government financed public works programmes, community service and building the assets of the poor.

Achievements and challenges

The political and economic transition from apartheid to a non-racial democracy in a more integrated global world without violence on a major scale is a major achievement. However, the transition has been accompanied by ever rising social costs as evidenced by high unemployment, rising levels of crime including transnational crime and violence, especially domestic violence and child sexual offences. South Africa has also recorded an exponential growth in the numbers of people infected by HIV/AIDS. These are significant challenges for all South Africans and, of course, for the country's social welfare policies and programmes. It should be recognised that the *White Paper* provides a long-term perspective, a perspective which can only be realised incrementally.

There are some particular reform priorities. Close to 87 per cent of the welfare services budget is still being spent on residential institutions especially for elderly white people. Human resource capacity to implement the new social development approach must also be enhanced both to provide community-based services and within central administration. Voluntary agencies responsible for social welfare services have been under great pressure to realign their programmes and budgets with the new approaches outlined in the *White Paper*. Adequate financial incentives are needed and protocols for the contracting of services by government must still be developed. The division of responsibilities between government and its non-governmental partners and between national, provincial and local spheres of government responsibility also requires urgent attention.

Conclusion

South Africa has embarked on an ambitious programme of restructuring the welfare system it inherited from the colonial and apartheid periods. Success will depend very much upon the way the challenge of economic globalisation is handled. The government can hardly adopt isolationist policies that seek to protect the South African economy from external trade, investments and other influences. The apartheid regime's collapse was, in part, brought about by economic difficulties resulting from its enforced isolation from the world economy. On the other hand, the government can hardly embrace neo-liberalism. This would be contrary to its historical role as the champion of the oppressed and impoverished, and its commitment to address the racist capitalism which the apartheid regime had implemented. Instead, it is cautiously pursuing a middle path between excessive state economic control and excessive economic liberalisation (cf. references to the 'Third Way' elsewhere in this volume). Developmental social welfare is integral to this approach. By promoting social investment, and linking economic and social policies in a coherent way, the government hopes to respond effectively to the challenge of globalisation (Midgley 1999, 2000).

South Africa is also cooperating closely with other African countries and hoping to promote greater economic cooperation in the region. Economic cooperation may promote closer cooperation in social welfare as well. It is in this regard that the Commonwealth has potentially such a major contribution to make. First, though still evolving, the South African experience of developmental social welfare may provide important lessons for other Commonwealth nations seeking a reintegration of economic and social policy. Second, it will be recalled that the expulsion of South Africa from the Commonwealth was a significant factor in the eventual demise of apartheid. The problems of ethnic conflict and oppression in many countries of the Commonwealth and indeed the rest of the world remain a very serious barrier to social development. Here, the experience of South Africa's relatively peaceful transition from colonialism and release from decades of oppression under the apartheid regime is salutary.

References

African National Congress (1994) *The Reconstruction and Development Programme: A Policy Framework*, Johannesburg: Umanyano Publications.

Ardington, E.M. (1994) *Quantitative Analysis of Socio-economic Data from Five Thousand Households in Kwazulu*, Centre for Social Development Studies Research Report No. 4, Durban: University of Natal.

Ardington, E. and Lund, F.J. (1995) Pensions and Development: The Social Security System as a Complementary Track to Poverty Alleviation Programmes, Durban: University of Natal, Center for Social Development Studies.

Brummer, F. (1964) *The Structure and Policy of Welfare Services in South Africa with Particular Reference to the Role of the State*, Pretoria: The Government Printer.

De Villiers, R. (1971) 'Afrikaaner Nationalism'. In M. Wilson and L. Thompson (eds), *The Oxford History of South Africa, II South Africa 1870–1966*, London: Oxford University Press, pp. 365–423.

Drover, G. (2000) 'Redefining Social Citizenship in a Global Era', *Canadian Social Work*, 2 (1), 29–49.

Hindson, D. (1987) *Pass Controls and the Urban African Question*, Johannesburg: Ravan Press.

Hobart Houghton, D. (1971) 'Economic Development, 1865–1965'. In M. Wilson and L. Thompson (eds), *The Oxford History of South Africa, II South Africa 1870–1966*, London: Oxford University Press, pp. 1–48.

Katzen, M.P. (1969) 'White Settlers and the Origin of a New Society, 1652–1778'. In M. Wilson and L. Thompson (eds), *The Oxford History of South Africa, I South Africa to 1870*, pp. 187–232.

May, J. (2001) 'Meeting the Challenge? The Emerging Agenda for Poverty Reduction in Post-Apartheid South Africa'. In Wilson, F., Janji, N., Braathen, E. (eds), *Poverty Reduction. What role for the State in Today's Globalized Economy?*, London: Zed Books, pp. 302–326.

McKendrick, B.W. (ed.) (1990) *Introduction to Social Work in South Africa*, Pretoria: Haum Tertiary.

McKendrick, B.W. and Dudas, E. (1987) 'South Africa'. In Dixon, J. (ed.) (1987) *Social Welfare in Africa*, London: Croon Helm, pp. 184–217.

Midgley, J. (1981) *Professional Imperialism: Social Work in the Third World*, London: Heinemann.

Midgley, J. (1994) 'Defining social development: Historical trends and conceptual formulations', *Social Development Issues*, 16 (3), 3–19.

Midgley, J. (1995) *Social Development: The Developmental Perspective in Social Welfare*, London: Sage Publications.

Midgley, J. (1998) 'Colonialism and Welfare: A Post-Colonial Commentary'. *Journal of Progressive Human Services*, 9 (2), 31–48.

Midgley, J. (1999) 'Growth, Redistribution and Welfare: Towards Social Investment', *Social Service Review*, 77 (1): 3–2.

Midgley, J. (2000) 'Globalization, Capitalism and Social Welfare: A Social Development Perspective', *Canadian Social Work*, 2 (1) 13–28.

Mishra, R. (1999) *Globalization and the Welfare State*, UK: Edward Elgar.

Patel, L. (1992) *Restructuring Social Welfare Options for South Africa*, Johannesburg: Ravan Press.

South Africa, National Treasury (2001) *Intergovernmental Fiscal Review*, http://www.treasury.gov.za

South Africa, Department of Welfare (1997) *White Paper for Social Welfare*, Government Gazette Notice 1108 of 1997, Pretoria: Ministry for Welfare and Population Development.

Terblanche, S.J. (1987) *A New Fiscal Policy and Economic Philosophy for South Africa in Transition*, Stellenbosch: University of Stellenbosch, Department of Economics.

Thompson, L. (1969) 'Cooperation and Conflict: The High Veld'. In M. Wilson and L. Thompson (eds), *The Oxford History of South Africa, I South Africa to 1870*, pp. 391–446.

Thompson, L. (1971) 'Great Britain and the Afrikaaner Republics.' In M. Wilson and L. Thompson (eds), *The Oxford History of South Africa, II South Africa 1870–1966*, London: Oxford University Press, pp. 289–324.

United Nations (1988) *Guiding Principles for Developmental Social Welfare Policies and Programmes in the Near Future*, New York: United Nations.

United Nations (1996) *Report of the World Summit for Social Development: Copenhagen, 6–12 March 1995*, New York.

Wilson, M. (1969) 'Cooperation and Conflict: The Eastern Cape Frontier'. In M. Wilson and L. Thompson (eds), *The Oxford History of South Africa, I South Africa to 1870*, pp. 233–271.

7
Socially Inclusive Social Security in Rural Tamil Nadu, India[1]

Barbara Harriss-White

Introduction

The main preoccupation of Indian writers on social affairs during the colonial period was with the poverty *of* India. Only after Independence did the debates shift to poverty *within* India, and it was not until the late 1960s that an anti-poverty agenda began to take shape. Since the 1970s, the Indian Government has laid down layer upon layer of policies addressed to the needs of the poor, such as food subsidies, basic needs programmes (drinking water, education, health and sanitation), special agricultural programmes targeted on small and marginal farmers, more agricultural targets for drought-prone, desert and mountainous regions, minimum wages, development programmes for women and children, training for young people, nutritious noon meals for schoolchildren (and sometimes also for pre-schoolers and old people). By the early 1990s, such measures were consuming 38 per cent of India's public sector plan outlay (Guhan and Harriss 1992).

Universalistically 'anti-poverty' on paper and in intention, this humus of policy has nevertheless been compacted into the agrarian structure, the tessellation of caste and ethnicity, and the moulds of gender with – consequently – very modest redistributive results. It has also been re-interpreted as a form of *promotive* social security – reducing the need for help instead of providing help for those in need. Conspicuous by its absence is *protective* social security for the mass of the people of India.

During the colonial period and since, protective social security has been restricted to public sector employees and workers in the organised sector – at its highest 12 per cent of the total work force, and now down to 7 per cent. Within the organised sector, 'public employees are served best, or rather have ensured that they are best served' (Guhan 1992, p. 288). Those implementing anti-poverty policy-cum-promotive social security (from which a combination of fraud and rent-seeking leaches between 15 to 80 per cent of funds, according to region) are precisely those entitled to protective social security (Corbridge and Harriss 2000). Their retirement age is five years lower than the minimum threshold at which old age pensions can be provided for destitute agricultural labourers. The latter's life expectation lags behind that of civil servants by several decades.

The great majority of India's population was and remains effectively excluded; thereby rendering the very concept of social exclusion, in its original European incarnation, inappropriate (cf. Chs 2 and 3 above). Even for the protected elite, access to social security for workers in the organised industrial sector is notoriously defective, not the least because of employers' widespread evasion of their obligations. Furthermore, state insurance benefits (e.g. survivor benefit and old age pensions) are often inadequate, illiberal in their qualifying criteria and delayed in their implementation.

In this chapter, the case for a more 'socially inclusive' policy on social security is examined both in theory and in practice – the latter with reference to three villages in South India. As will become clear, this is not the anachronistic exercise it might seem at first sight.

State mediated protective social security

Protective social security (in this case social assistance), as implemented in contemporary India, covers the territories of medical care, sickness and maternity benefit, family benefit, injury benefit, invalidity and disability benefits, old age pensions and survivor benefit – together with unemployment benefit on an insurance basis. It is the responsibility of each of the constituent states of India and the extent or otherwise of its operation is entirely a matter of state discretion .

The state of Uttar Pradesh introduced a means-tested old age pension scheme as early as 1957, but it was not until the 1980s that this idea had reached all the states. In some of them there are now also provisions for destitute widows and severely physically disabled people; and – in a few – survivor benefits in respect of death from specified occupational hazards. In short, a patchwork of social security arrangements has been evolving in the same piecemeal fashion as has anti-poverty policy as a whole (Guhan 2001). Nationally, old age pension coverage for those below the poverty line – quantitatively the most important provision – is under 20 per cent of those notionally eligible, though there are significant variations in coverage between the states (Jhabvala and Subrahmanya 2000).

While a decline in social welfare expenditure had been expected as a result of 'liberalisation', the 1990s should have seen an *increase* in expenditure on protective social security for the poor, had equity been high on the development agenda. But India's cautious consensus on social security legislation merely stressed the development of entitlements in the organised sector, dependant on the discharge of employers' liabilities.

To be sure, in the unorganised or 'informal' sector, institutions for the payment of premia for insurance protection against risks of occupational disease were ripe for development. Mutual benefit societies, trades unions and workers' co-operatives have started to claim and campaign for appropriate social protection (Jhabvala and Subrahmanya 2000). Currently, an arbitrary subset of occupations, with a range of modes and rates of tax, are entitled to benefits focussed on health, housing and education – viz. workers in mining, *beedi*-rolling[2], cinema, dock and construction work – all being subsectors where such 'tax' collection is most feasible. Even here, however, the social security provision is exiguous; home-based workers and agricultural workers proving almost impossible to reach (See Jhabvala and Subrahmanya 2000). So a bedrock of *protective social assistance* remains essential, especially for the contingencies of old age and death.

Far from being exorbitant, the costs of a minimalist protective programme for income-poor households could be quite modest. The Working Group on Social Security of the Economic Reforms Commission in 1984 proposed a package of OAP and survivorship benefit which would amount to one per cent of GNP and less than four per cent of combined central and state revenue (Guhan 1992). Furthermore, on the advice of S. Guhan (a former member of the elite Indian Administrative Service and by then a scholar activist), the Government of Tamil Nadu initiated a set of social assistance schemes in 1989 – including pensions for old people, widows, deserted wives, and the physically handicapped; maternity assistance; marriage grants and accident relief – amounting to 1.5 per cent of state revenue expenditure and administered through pre-existing channels. So long as the trade-offs between maximum feasibility and minimum benefit prove politically manageable, the benefits can be of a mass nature (Guhan 1994).

In its 1995–96 central government budget, the Congress Party, appreciating the vote-pulling potential of such benefits – largely as a result of the experience in Tamil Nadu – set in place enabling laws for a National Social Assistance enabling programme, whereby states could increase their social security coverage with central government support, albeit at the cost of central government 'interference'. The programme consisted of a Rs 75 per month pension for destitute people over the age of 65[3], a national maternity benefit fund disbursing Rs 300 to poor women for their first two live births and a national family benefit fund giving Rs 5,000 to poor households on the death of their primary bread winner, if within the age-band 18 to 64. The central government's financial obligation was to be capped at a sum equal to the proportion in each state below the 1987–88 poverty line, with reference to the proportion of the population estimated as being over 65 in the 1995 Sample Registration Survey projection (Narayanan 1996). This paltry pension has since been hoisted to Rs 125 per month (£1.60) and the age threshold lowered to 60 for wage workers. Nevertheless the uptake by states remains patchy, access is rationed and the age threshold serves to screen out exactly those workers who most need the pension – those whose life expectancy is lowest.

Social security and structural adjustment in Tamil Nadu

In 1989, as already remarked and before India embarked on its slow process of economic liberalisation, Tamil Nadu established a system of pensions for the poor, covering old age, disability and widowhood. Following this, the state – without consulting Central Government and with no detailed thought as to its financing – was quick off the block in 1992–93 to protect its high profile spending priorities and to counter the anticipated adverse effects of structural adjustment on the poor. The Finance Minister announced 'highest priority in safeguarding the position of the poor and underprivileged. We have organised a comprehensive safety net which will ensure that no person in Tamil Nadu suffers from want and deprivation'.

Tamil Nadu's version of 'market socialist' development (widely regarded as a form of competitive populism between the two local Tamil nationalist parties) has involved the creation and piecemeal embellishment of a rudimentary welfare state. In 1993–94, expenditure on social services amounted to 41 per cent of total state expenditure (Narayanan 1996, p. 32). Before and throughout the era of market liberalisation Tamil Nadu has had the highest outlay on social security of any state in India – which has contributed to its growing revenue deficit.

This safety net is comprehensive, for it involves food security and nutrition; public health, drinking water; housing, shelter and employment; and special programmes for those in special need (Narayanan 1996, p. 31). Social security is only a small component – about 10 per cent – of this 'safety net'; with pensions as its main element. Yet it is no more than the post hoc re-labelling of a set of policies on which Tamil Nadu has long placed emphasis.[4]

The number of pensioners covered in Tamil Nadu increased from 392,600 in its first year of operation in 1989 to 602,100 in 1995 (Narayanan 1996, p. 39). The pension had indeed been protected, meagre as it was (Rs 50 per month, increased to Rs 75 in 1992 and Rs 100 in 1995). But with a 50 per cent increase in coverage, even this small component has proved difficult to maintain and is under pressure from efforts to reduce state expenditure.

In this situation, the significance of the Government of India's enabling scheme is threefold.

- First it is an endorsement of Tamil Nadu's approach;
- Second it is a declared central government obligation;
- Third, the central government will contribute to its funding: though such funding of the social sector has been criticised by the National Development Council as an illegitimate encroachment on state sovereignty.

Social assistance in three villages

Pensions and other social security benefits are sanctioned at the level of the *taluk* (a district subdivision of about 100 villages) by the revenue inspector (RI) based on applications certified as 'verified' by village administrative officers (VAOs). The cash element is then sent monthly by post as a money order. But in Tamil Nadu pensions also have had an important, additional, discretionary 'in-kind' element: pensioners being entitled to the Noon Meal cooked at the local school – or else 4 kgs of rice supplied monthly, free of charge, from the local Fair Price Shop – together with two pieces of clothing per year supplied free at festivals. A variety of encounters with the state (village and local revenue officials, postmen, fair price shopkeepers and noon meal cooks) is thus involved in the access by the poorest rural people to social assistance. This interface is subject to temptations of patronage and rent seeking.

In what follows, our evidence comes from three sources: first censuses of three villages[5] in northern Tamil Nadu, canvassed in 1993, in which beneficiaries identified themselves; second, a more detailed survey of beneficiaries in 1995; third, official data on beneficiaries in each village. There are discrepancies between the three sources of evidence. Table 7.1 includes the official record of coverage while Table 7.2 shows the actual population of elderly in the villages.

With an official record of 26 pensioners in Nesal (a large, accessible, developed village), seven in Vinayagapuram (a remote but agriculturally developed village) and two in Veerasambanur (a small, remote and poor village), 7, 13[6] and 2, respectively, were caught in our sample. With extremely few exceptions, their pensions date from 1989, the period of establishment of the social security scheme targeted at poor people. The sources of their information about rights (village officers, the panchayat president, teachers, postmen and political party workers) were all local. The time taken to arrange the posting of pensions varied hugely: from 3–18 months in Nesal; from one to 12 months in Vinayagapuram and from two weeks to 12 months in Veerasambanur. There were very few cases which did not need bribes: to VAOs, revenue inspectors, the

Table 7.1 Estimated Coverage of Old Age Pensions (Three Villages in Tamil Nadu)

	Total population	65+ population	65+ population in needy and neediest categories	65+ population in neediest categories	OAP cases (in official records)
1. Nesal	1551	94	56	34	26
Proportion of OAP cases (%)	1.7	27.7	46.4	76.5	
2. Vinayagapuram	1153	63	37	19	7
Proportion of OAP cases (%)	0.6	11.1	18.9	36.8	
3. Veerasambanur	578	25	21	14	2
Proportion of OAP cases (%)	0.3	8.0	9.5	14.3	
4. All three villages	3282	182	114	67	35
Proportion of OAP cases (%)	1.1	19.2	30.7	52.2	

Source: Survey data, 1995.

Table 7.2 Demographic Position of the 65+

Village	Male population	Female population	Total population
Nesal	764	787	1551
of whom 65+	47	47	94
proportion of 65+ (%)	6.2	6.0	6.1
Vinayagapuram	584	569	1153
of whom 65+	34	29	63
proportion of 65+ (%)	5.8	5.1	5.5
Veerasambanur	284	294	578
of whom 65+	14	11	25
proportion of 65+ (%)	4.9	3.7	4.3

Source: Village Census Schedules, 1993–4.

talukdar, primary health centre doctors (and, later on, universal Rs 3 tips to the postmen who deliver the pension). Bribes and other initial transactions costs could amount to as much as three months' pension payments. Pensions, once agreed, were normally delivered in a timely and regular fashion; though there had been one case of a two-month hitch in 1995, because of the parlous condition of state-finances, about which everyone complained. Despite their economic vulnerability, none of their pensions had been diverted to others, since all beneficiaries live alone (except the plainly fraudulent).

While the Sample Registration Survey tables for 1992 gave Tamil Nadu's proportion of over-65s as 4.2 per cent for men and 4.3 per cent for women (see Table 7.2), those declared for Nesal (6.2 per cent men and 6 per cent women) and Vinayagapuram (5.8 per cent and 5.1 per cent) are unusually high, while Veerasambanur's (4.9 per cent men and 3.2 per cent women) is closer to the state average but more gender-biased against women. It is possible that the first two villages were further advanced in their demographic transition than the average for the state. But it is also just possible that age was exaggerated in the expectation of entitlements from the impact of our research.

Eligible and non-eligible beneficiaries

In Nesal six out of the seven pensioners are not strictly eligible (three being disqualified by age and three by having income), but their situations are still ones of intense poverty. Other sources of income vary from Rs 900 per year (from agricultural labour) to Rs 2,520 (from trade in *dosas* [rice pancakes]). There was one case of outright fraud, in which the Vice-President of the Ambedkar Iyakkam (a local NGO for scheduled castes) had procured a pension for his father-in-law who lived in a household of seven people with two incomes and his own income of Rs 5,700.

In Vinayagapuram by 1995, 13 people had pensions, while seven were off-record; and nine were being evaluated. Eight of the latter were strictly ineligible. Meanwhile, in three cases of destitution – and complete dependence on the pension and on charity – the age criterion was being flouted. In five pensioner households, the family income ranges from Rs 1,440 from agricultural labour to Rs 2,264 (from another household member's job as a Noon Meals cook).

Of the two successful receipts of pensions in Veerasambanur, one is eligible: a deaf and blind man aged 75 living alone, for whom the pension is his sole income. The other is not technically needy, being the village barber whose wife is the village midwife. Together they have a subsistence income of paddy provided collectively by the village.

Eligible non-beneficiaries

In Nesal there are 10 destitute people, some of them disabled, who have extremely low incomes, in receipt of meagre support (at best) from sons. They exist in acute poverty, unable to afford the bribe to render them officially eligible for pensions. In Vinayagapuram, three otherwise eligible non-beneficiaries sell milk, work in the fields and get family support of a meagre Rs 500 to Rs 2,520 per year. In Veerasambanur each case of three eligible non-beneficiaries gets family support of up to Rs 600 per year.

Clearly the official definition of eligibility is highly restrictive, and local interpretations of neediness prevail more often than not. Since the criteria of eligibility, one aspect of targeting, is not set in tablets of stone, it is worth examining 'need' more carefully.

Need can be proxied by an income threshold since the census data for village households contain estimates for private incomes. On the basis of an already restrictive subsistence poverty line of Rs 150 per adult in 1993–94[7] and half – Rs 75 – per dependent child, an annual private 'subsistence income estimate' (SIE) has been calculated for each household with at least one member aged 65 or over on the basis of the household size and composition given in the village census schedules. People over 65 in households above the SIE are classed as 'not needy' (though the threshold is conservative and though there is no knowing the 'fairness' of individual allocations). Those in households between 0.5 and 1.0 SIE are classed as 'needy' and those in households under 0.5 SIE are 'neediest' (Table 7.3). Within the latter category there are two kinds of household. One is 'collapsed' or shattered, consisting of old individuals or couples – these are *prima facie* the most deprived and destitute – and the other contains old people living with younger relatives.

In Nesal some 60 per cent of households with old people are under the SIE and 37 per cent (30 households, with 36 per cent of the elderly) are in the neediest category. Of the latter, one third are collapsed households close to destitution. The three old couples are in each case supported from agricultural labouring by the wife which brings in annual incomes in the region of Rs 900 to Rs 960. Of the individuated

Table 7.3   Household Composition and Extreme Poverty

	\multicolumn{4}{c}{Number of households (% in brackets)}
	Not needy	Needy	Neediest	Total
Nesal				
All households (%)	157	116	72	345
	(45.5)	(33.6)	(20.9)	(100.0)
HHs with 65+	32	19	30	81
	(39.5)	(23.5)	(37.0)	(100.0)
HHs with children under 5	61	39	24	124
	(49.1)	(31.5)	(19.4)	(100.0)
Vinayagapuram				
All households (%)	149	70	43	262
	(56.9)	(26.7)	(16.4)	(100.0)
HHs with 65+	23	16	17	56
	(41.1)	(28.6)	(30.3)	(100.0)
HHs with children under 5	60	28	10	98
	(61.2)	(28.6)	(10.2)	(100.0)
Veerasambanur				
All households (%)	60	37	40	137
	(43.8)	(27.0)	(29.2)	(100.0)
HHs with 65+	4	7	13	24
	(16.6)	(29.2)	(54.2)	(100.0)
HHs with children under 5	22	16	11	49
	(44.9)	(32.7)	(22.4)	(100.0)
All three villages				
All households (%)	366	223	155	744
	(49.2)	(30.0)	(20.8)	(100.0)
HHs with 65+	59	42	60	161
	(36.6)	(26.1)	(37.3)	(100.0)
HHs with children under 5	143	83	45	271
	(52.8)	(30.6)	(16.6)	(100.0)

households, that of the scheduled caste male aged 85 depends on his light casual work: uprooting paddy seedlings plus family support totalling Rs 600 a year from two sons who are agricultural labourers. The other six neediest elderly people are single women. The kind of work they are able to do includes collecting and drying cow dung and gleaning. They subsist on petty remittances from relatives and on local charity. Only three of the 13 most destitute households receive a pension. In one case where a husband has a pension, his wife is also eligible but excluded. Eight people would be ineligible even though extremely needy because of meagre transfers of money within their families. Indeed, in two cases their applications for pensions had been rejected on these grounds. In a further case, an eligible person cannot afford the bribe and transactions costs of Rs 300 necessary to gain access to the pension.

In Vinayagapuram, 59 per cent of both the households and the population over 65 are beneath the SIE and 30 per cent (17 households) are in the neediest category in which four are individuated or are elderly couples. Two of these destitute households receive, and depend utterly on, their pensions. The other two receive petty support from sons and small localised acts of charity. In Veerasambanur as many as 84 per cent of households contain old people and are below the SIE and 55 per cent (13 households) are among the neediest. In five households elderly people live alone, two are above the level of need. But levels of support in the other three – in the absence of the pension – amount to Rs 600 per year (Table 7.4).

Those receiving old age pensions are 19.2 per cent of the population above the age of 65. Pensioners are 31 per cent of the total in the 'needy' category and 52 per cent of those who are the neediest. The number of pensions would need to be doubled to cover the total population of neediest and trebled to cover them together with the merely needy.

Table 7.4 Old Age and Poverty

Category	Nesal HH	Nesal People	Vinayagapuram HH	Vinayagapuram People	Veerasambanur HH	Veerasambanur People
Not needy	32	38	23	26	4	4
Needy	19	22	16	18	7	7
Neediest	30	34	17	19	13	14

Source: Village Census Schedules, 1993.

If strictly applied, the official eligibility criterion is very restrictive (Tables 7.5, 7.6). People over the age of 65 are ineligible if they have any relatives bound by custom or usage to support them, regardless of the actual availability, extent and regularity of such support or however meagre their own earnings. As actually applied, 20 per cent of Old Age pensions have leaked out of both the age and eligibility criteria and 60 per cent of actual pensioners are ineligible on one or other count. Age is being interpreted in an elastic way. Support is being interpreted in terms of its quantitative availability and not in terms of legal eligibility.

Widows' pensions

Some scheduled caste widows came to know about the existence of a pension and their rights to it via the Ambedkar Iyakkam (an organisation

Table 7.5 Analysis of Cases of Old Age Pension

Village	Eligible cases	Ineligible	Ineligible cases On account of age	On account of income	On account of both age and income
1. Nesal	1	6	3	3	2
2. Vinayagapuram	1	8	4	4	–
3. Veerasambanur	1	1	1	1	1
4. All three villages	3	15	8	10	3

Source: Survey Data, 1995.

Table 7.6 Analysis of Old Age Pension Cases According to Eligibility and Need

	Not needy	Needy	Neediest	Total
Eligible				
(all three villages)	–	–	3	3
1. Nesal	–	–	1	1
2. Vinayagapuram	–	–	1	1
3. Veerasambanur	–	–	1	1
Ineligible				
(all three villages)	1	3	11	15
1 Nesal	1	1	4	6
2. Vinayagapuram	–	1	7	8
3. Veerasambanur	–	1	–	1

Source: Survey Data, 1995.

of the lowest castes), others through the president of the Panchayat (the lowest unit of local government covering about 10 villages) and village officers. The access lag was six months on average. Bribes of Rs 1–300 were involved in over four-fifths of cases. Once in receipt of pensions, all recipients had control over its disposition.

In Nesal, of the 12 beneficiaries sampled, only two are eligible, a woman living alone aged 70 and a disabled, scheduled caste widow aged 40, also living alone. Nine however are not strictly eligible according to official criteria because they receive support or earn income. Examples: (i) a 12-year-old son who brings in Rs 1,200 a year as a weaving assistant; (ii) incomes from agricultural labouring of Rs 400 to Rs 1,800 a year; (iii) the collection and sale of firewood amounting to Rs 3,260 a year. There is one case of a pension fraudulently obtained, through the Ambedkar Iyakkam, for a woman whose husband is still living. In Vinayagapuram there is one widow-pensioner, aged 30, with 0.1 acre of land who needed a bribe of Rs 100 and a six-month wait to obtain her pension. In Veerasambanur, one of the two pensioners is actually ineligible on grounds of family support. The other, a widow aged 60, also gets Rs 1,400 as an agricultural labourer.

Thus of the 15 widow pensioners, only two are strictly eligible yet, except for the one case of fraud, all the rest have gone to people under the SIE (subsistence income estimate).

Social Assistance: being gently politicised?

The scheme was brought in under the DMK Government and when we studied it was being administered by the AIADMK. In the set of recipients willing to state their affiliation, 80 per cent of the pensions had been distributed to open supporters of the ruling party (Table 7.7).

Table 7.7 Political Affiliation of Beneficiaries

Party	Nesal	Vinayagapuram	Veerasambanur
Old Age Pensions			
AIADMK	4	9	1
DMK	–	1	2
No allegiance	3	2	1
Widow's Pension			
AIDMK	6		
No allegiance	6		

Conclusions

For Tamil Nadu – and other states in India?

Tamil Nadu's 'social safety net' is being implemented in terms of *need* rather than that of strict *eligibility* in these villages (Table 7.6). Fourteen of the 18 pensions have gone to the neediest (those in households with under half a very conservative SIE) and a further three more to needy people (with 0.5 to 1.0 the SIE). But of the 24 elderly people who live alone (36 per cent of the total elderly) 22 of whom are needy, only seven are eligible and only five (21 per cent) get the pension.

Entitlements are not well known. Wide and sustained publicity is necessary to increase knowledge of the existence of such schemes. Procedures need to be as simple as possible and the application forms more widely available.

The rationale for screening by 'destitution' rests:

- *first* on the evidence of state budgets that are deteriorating;
- *second* on the argument that the pension should supplement and not displace informal social security from the family;
- *third* that broader targeting may increase leakages and capture by those at the upper end of the distribution of those entitled.

Nevertheless it is clear that current eligibility criteria are excessively restrictive. An affordable, pro-active and rational selection procedure for pensions could involve:

- reducing the age threshold for manual workers;
- targeting all single member households and couples aged over the age threshold which are living alone on income from all sources of less than the equivalent of Rs 600 in the mid 1990s (so that the SIE would be reached using transfers or earnings plus the pension);
- targeting all the neediest first: i.e. households with income of less than half the SIE. If this still threatens state budgetary resources, then those within this category with the highest dependency ratios could be targeted first.

The amount of the pension is extremely low. Many recipients, when their opinions were canvassed in our survey, wanted it increased to Rs 200 per month (£3 in the mid-1990s). But in the absence of an increase in the state budget, there has to be a trade-off between coverage and adequacy. Yet, at the very least, the pension needs to keep track with inflation.

Other problems lie with the administration of social assistance. While the official norm for approval of applications is three months, most instances here took six to 18 months. Further, the transactions costs (including travel, a photograph and the dominant element, bribes) amounted to 3–4 months' benefit, with significant monthly tips thereafter to the postmen who delivered it. That such 'retail' corruption is going to be corrected by punitive action on corrupt low-level officials by those further up the system, is not likely – save to be further translated into extortion. In its absence, pressure from below can only be applied by the Panchayat or by local NGOs where they exist. But NGOs are not particularly superior either as intermediaries or as publicisers of rights. The Ambedkar Iyakkam, in Nesal has been instrumental in getting benefits for scheduled castes, but has not eliminated the need for bribes and has even acted as facilitators in cases of gross errors of ineligibility.

For the Commonwealth?

Can the experience of one Indian state and of the needy people of three villages within it, have any relevance for the wider Commonwealth? It may be so. First, this account has demonstrated the need for rich members of the Commonwealth to support the attempts of now heavily indebted states like Tamil Nadu to implement their 'welfare states' for poor people. Second, Tamil Nadu's social security system, while being no model of best practice in terms of its administrative effectiveness (being as embedded in social relations of patronage, caste, gender and party politics as any other aspect of its development) does demonstrate that a skeletal system to serve poor people is *possible* to implement and that it need not be exorbitantly costly. Other cash-strapped Commonwealth countries may even see its experience as an example.

Meanwhile rich Commonwealth members could help to facilitate frank and critical exchanges of experience between themselves and developing Commonwealth countries. For the Commonwealth to be distinguished by its collective prowess over protective social security would be a signal achievement indeed.

Notes

1. The evidence on which this chapter is based was collected as part of the DFID-funded project (Adjustment and Development: Agrarian Change,

Markets and Social Welfare 1972–93) directed by Dr S. Janakarajan of the Madras Institute of Development Studies and the author. The chapter does not reflect the official views of the funders. The empirical part of the chapter adheres closely to 'Social Assistance in the Three Villages' a set of comprehensive notes and tables from the social security field schedules compiled under this project by the late S. Guhan (1996) at the Madras Institute of Development Studies, Chennai. Guhan also made extensive comments on social security (incorporated here) at a workshop on this project at the Madras Institute of Development Studies in 1996, as did A. Dayal and N. Narayanan to both of whom the present author is grateful.
2. The *beedi* is a local cigarette.
3. Rs 60 to the pound sterling in the mid 1990s, Rs 75 to the pound sterling in 2002.
4. The revenue deficit increased from 11.2 per cent in 1989–90 to 15.7 per cent in 1994–5 (Narayanan 1996).
5. These villages are the basis of a book on economy and social welfare (Harriss-White and Janakarajan, 2004).
6. Our field investigator found many more pensioners in fact than there are on the record.
7. Based in turn on the official poverty line of Rs 118 per adult in 1987–8, assuming 5 per cent inflation, then rounding down from Rs 158 to Rs 150 (and assuming half the cost for a dependent child is Rs 75 [Guhan 1996])

References

Corbridge, S. and J. Harriss (2000) *Reinventing India: liberalization, Hindu nationalism and popular democracy*, Cambridge: Polity Press.

Guhan, S. (1992) 'Social Security in India: Looking one Step Ahead', in B. Harriss, S. Guhan and R. Cassen (eds), *Poverty in India: Research and Policy*, New Delhi: Oxford University Press.

Guhan, S. (1994) 'Social Security Options for Developing Countries', *International Labour Review*, Vol. 133, No. 1, pp. 35–53.

Guhan, S. (1996) 'Social Assistance in the Three Villages'. Paper to the Conference on 'Adjustment and Development' at the Madras Institute of Development Studies, Chennai.

Guhan S. (2001) 'Social Security for the Poor in the Unorganised Sector' pp. 50–86 in S. Subramanian (ed.) *India's Development Experience: Selected Writings of S. Guhan*, New Delhi: Oxford University Press.

Guhan S. and Harriss B. (1992) Introduction in B. Harriss, S. Guhan and R. Cassen (eds), *Povery in India: Research and Policy*, New Delhi: Oxford University Press, pp. 1–23

Harriss-White, B. and Janakarajan, S. (2004) *Rural India Facing the Twenty First Century*, London: Anthem.

Jhabvala, R. and Subrahmanya, R.K.A. (2000) *The Unorganized Sector: Work Security and Social Protection*, New Delhi, Sage.

Narayanan, N. (1996) 'The Social Safety Net in Tamil Nadu during the Structural Adjustment Process', paper to the Workshop on 'Adjustment and Development', Madras Institute of Development Studies, Madras.

8
Social Policy and the Sri Lankan Welfare State: The British Colonial Legacy

Laksiri Jayasuriya

Introduction

Sri Lanka has the unusual record of having evolved a 'welfare state' in a non-industrialised Third World country. Admittedly, from the late 1970s, Sri Lanka underwent a political and economic crisis which coincided with the decline of the social democratic state and the welfare state. Nevertheless, for a country with a poor per capita Gross National Product (GNP), Sri Lanka's achievement, relative to comparable countries, remains remarkable (UNDP 1990–6; Osmani 1994; Jayasuriya 2001).

This paper[1] will argue that the development of social policy, without discounting domestic social and cultural influences, is largely a legacy of Sri Lanka's British colonial past.

Social policy and the early colonial state (1833–1931)

This first phase of social policy development was heavily influenced by a major constitutional reform document, the Report of the Colebrooke-Cameron Commission of 1833 (Mendis 1956, 1957; de Silva 1965, 1981). The thinking of Colebrooke and Cameron was markedly influenced by the utilitarianism[2] of the era in Britain, especially by the writings of Jeremy Bentham (in the case of Cameron) and James Mill (in the case of Colebrooke) (Stokes 1959). But whereas Colebrooke's contribution was geared to establishing an efficient unified system of public administration, Cameron was primarily concerned with introducing a liberal political culture based on the rule of law and a new system of judicial administration (Mendis 1956).

Colebrooke's reforms sought to incorporate, in an alien colonial context, British liberal and utilitarian values, such as the merit principle and equality of treatment. Thus Colebrooke made a strong case for the inclusion of Ceylonese (i.e. local inhabitants) in the higher echelons of the public service, hitherto confined to British civil servants drawn from élite universities in Britain. Similarly, he argued strongly for a competitive system of examinations as the basis of entry to the Civil Service – an idea borrowed from the Northcote-Trevelyan reforms of the Civil Service in Britain (Warnapala 1974; Goldthorpe 1964; Sleeman 1973; Evans 1978).

Utilitarian ideas were also evident in another Colebrooke-inspired reform proposal: the abolition of the semi-feudal traditional practice of compulsory service (*rajakariya*), whereby high status persons had the right to extract forced labour from lower caste ordinary workers and peasants. Such reforms helped create an atmosphere conducive to private enterprise. A free wage labour force working in the plantation economy was also conducive to 'the development of individualism ... a potent feature in the proposals of Colebrooke for economic reform' (Samaraweera 1973: 86; Snodgrass 1966).

Meanwhile the rest of the economy, based on traditional peasant agriculture, remained relatively neglected. (Snodgrass 1966; Bandarage 1983). In effect, there emerged a 'dual economy': one 'highly organised, foreign-owned, capitalist plantation economy [alongside] a tradition-bound, primitive, self-sufficing subsistence peasant economy' (Ponnambalam 1980: 8). The new colonial export economy helped generate a significant commercial entrepreneurial culture, which in turn helped create a local capitalist class (Bandarage 1983; Jayasuriya 2001). This new local bourgeoisie was destined to play a vital role in shaping subsequent political and social developments, especially in the campaigns for political reform and self-rule.

Meanwhile, no less significant for social policy development were the far-reaching judicial reforms proposed by Cameron (Samaraweera 1973: 87). The *Charter of Justice* introduced a uniform system of judicial administration and helped establish an independent judiciary as the basis of good government. These reforms were intended to serve as an effective check on the abuse of executive powers. More significantly for the longterm, they laid the basis for the rule of law and the protection of the equal rights of all individuals within an open and accountable judicial system. Contrary to customary practices, the administration of justice was henceforth to be without distinction of race, creed or social status.

Yet another major influence on social policy development was the impact of Evangelical Christian missionary enterprise on the British Colonial Office and its colonial administrators (Stokes 1959; Dicey 1996; also cf. Ch. 2, p. 15 in this volume). The reformist zeal and 'civilising mission' of Christian missionaries was reflected in such as the action taken to mark the end of polyandrous marriage, the abolition of slavery, and the non-recognition of caste in all areas of public policy. Nevertheless, during this early period, Christian missionaries were mostly seen as auxiliaries of government for tackling social problems; themselves being regarded as representatives of the 'government religion'.

One final, lasting consequence of the 1833 reforms was that education, understood as the promotion of English education, had become a cornerstone of colonial social policy (Jayaweera 1969). To be sure, access to English education was confined to the urban middle class and made available mainly through state-assisted missionary secondary schools. Direct *state* involvement in education occurred only towards the latter part of the 19th century, and was mainly confined to the provision of primary education (mostly in the rural sector) where the medium of instruction was in the vernacular (Sinhalese or Tamil).

It was the secondary-school-led 'Christianisation' which helped colonial administrators sever traditional links with pre-colonial religion. At the same time, it marked the beginning of a two–tiered educational system which was to reinforce the social and cultural differentiation between an urban-centred English-educated middle class and a rural indigenous/vernacular-educated peasantry. In the long run, of course, the revolt against the Christianisation of the state was to be a key feature of the Buddhist religious and nationalistic revivals fuelling the opposition to colonial rule (Houtart 1974) (see below).

All political and social developments during this early phase of colonial rule were guided by two main factors: the need for stable, efficient and orderly government and the cost-effective use of public money in the management of the colonial economy. A characteristic feature of British colonial rule was the manner by which the British sought allies within each colonised territory as 'a class of collaborators' (Mamdani 1976: 42). Hence the doctrine of 'indirect rule' based on a partnership with local élites.

Inevitably, questions of social development proved secondary to questions of governance and economic growth. Colonial administrators endeavoured to promote social welfare measures only in so far as these were likely to strengthen British rule by gaining the goodwill of, in this case, Sri Lanka's inhabitants. Achievements in the health sector, mostly in curative services, were widely acclaimed by the British Colonial Office which took pride in the Sri Lankan hospital system as a much publicised model of efficiency (Mair 1944; Uragoda 1987). Nevertheless the underlying objectives of the Colonial Office remained as pragmatic as they were humanitarian (Jones 2002).

Certainly, one of the distinctive features of 19th century imperial policy relates, in this case, to the treatment of indentured labour, recruited from India for employment in the plantation sector on a contract basis. To be sure, much of the pioneering social legislation introduced during this period, e.g., health care for Indian labour on particular estates, plus minimum wages, was intended to facilitate the continued recruitment of such immigrant Indian labour (Pieris 1967; Wickramaratne 1977). Nevertheless improved sanitary conditions in the plantations did result in a marked reduction 'in the estate crude death rate from 35.2 per 1,000 in 1924 to 21.1 per 1,000 in 1934' (Pieris 1999: 17).

More significantly, the special treatment afforded indentured Indian labour at work in the plantations was instrumental in ensuring a more general system of government intervention in industrial relations in Ceylon. The beginnings of trade unionism in Ceylon were apparently greatly assisted by the British trade union movement and the Labour Party (Jayawardena 1972), for all that it was not until the early 1930s that organised labour began to make any direct impact on social and economic policy developments within Sri Lanka (Kearney 1971; Jayawardena 1972).

Social policy in the late colonial state (1931–1948)

The first three decades of the 20th century was a period marked by agitation for a greater degree of self-rule, as manifested by the Ceylonisation of the administration, the politicisation of the urban working class, and the growth of a strong nationalist movement (Kearney 1971; Jupp 1998). The nationalist movement spearheaded agitation for constitutional reform and succeeded in persuading the Colonial Office to appoint a Reform Commission in 1927. Implementation of the Reform proposals emanating from this Donoughmore Commission was to be the responsibility of Lord Passfield (the redoubtable Sidney Webb), Secretary of State for the Colonies in the Ramsay MacDonald Labour government (Russell 1982).

The commission 'found that in many provinces poverty and ill health were the lot of many villages ... many sections of the people had not even decent housing or adequate facilities for primary education ... no poor law system for relieving destitution, no system of compensation for injured workmen, no up to date system of factory legislation and no control over hours and wages in sweated trades' (Mendis 1957: 118).

Confronted by these facts, the Commissioners wanted to make the elected representatives of government more accountable and responsive to the needs of the people. Government so far, they argued, had been more of 'an oligarchy or plutocracy, not a democracy' (Jeffries 1962: 33). Addressing the neglect of social welfare policies and legislation by the previous administration, the Commission went on to recommend a unique form of government for Ceylon (modeled on the then London County Council): a semi-autonomous system of government (1931–1948), with a deal of power to exercise legislative and executive responsibilities; in effect a halfway house between colonial office delegation and complete self-rule.

In reality, however, the Commission's recommendations ushered in a period of power without responsibility. Financial responsibility remained with the non-elected Officers of the Crown, all of whom were British civil servants. Hence one outcome of democratisation and of the new structures of government was the passage of much social legislation, without any indication of how such measures were to be financed and implemented (Jayasuriya, Fernando and Allbrook 1985). Nevertheless, social legislation once placed on the statute book tended to acquire a momentum of its own. Just so did this extensive process of social legislation (1931–1948) help create a political culture of welfarism which was later to be adduced (and accepted) as an argument for political independence.

The welfare politics of this late colonial state were focused mainly on education and health. Education reforms were associated with the nationalist and religious movements of this period, being directed towards a greater measure of educational equality through free education and compulsory schooling; together with the ending of the dominant role of the Christian Church in state-assisted secondary education (Jayasuriya 1969; Houtart 1974). These radical changes required a dramatic increase in public expenditure and, not surprisingly (in retrospect), led to an intensification of social and political conflict.

Meanwhile the field of health care also gained salience, not least a result of the need to mitigate the social effects of the Great Depression of the 1930s, the severe drought of the mid-1930s and recurrent malaria epidemics (Jones 2000). Health policies were enhanced by an increase in medical facilities for neglected rural areas. Several indicators, such as rates of infant mortality and crude death rate, bore witness to the effectiveness of such health care policies, and in particular, to the increased utilisation of health services by the rural population (Perera 1985; Gunatilleke 1985). Above all, the systematic programme of malaria eradication ranks as one of the main social achievements of this period (Pieris 1999; Jones 2000; Gunatilleke 1985).

Social policies relating to public welfare (e.g. unemployment relief, food subsidy) and social infrastructure (mainly housing, and public utilities) proved less pressing as issues for competitive politics, but the welfare politics of the late colonial state were also heavily influenced by the social and economic consequences of the Depression. The response of successive governments was similar in tone to earlier official and unofficial reports emanating from Britain (see Newnham 1936). It was the first systematic attempt in Sri Lanka to quantify problems of poverty and unemployment and to prescribe remedial measures; yet the state-sponsored relief measures adopted were reminiscent of the British Poor Law of the 1920s (Jayasuriya et al. 1985).

By contrast, the food subsidy[3] (rice, wheat flour and sugar), introduced during World War II as an emergency welfare measure available to all without a means test, was destined to continue as an unprecedented, 'home grown' institutionalised welfare measure for nearly three decades (Gavin and Chandrasekera 1979). After all, as Beveridge had remarked: 'If for warfare, why not for welfare'? (Bruce 1961).

The consolidation of welfarism (1948–1970)

With its achievement of political independence in 1948, the ensuing Sri Lankan welfare state was built around three major social documents (the first two inherited from the pre-independence era): the Kannagara Report 1943 (resulting in the *Education Act of 1945*); and the Jennings Report 1947 (leading to the establishment of the *Department of Social Services* in 1948); the Cumpston Report 1950 (leading to the *Health Act of 1953*). Arguably, therefore, the foundations of the Sri Lankan welfare state bear some comparison with the 'three pillars' of the British welfare state (Marshall 1973). Certainly the principle of collective provision for common human and social needs through state intervention was firmly established. Hence it was, perhaps, that during the first two decades of independence (1948–68), social expenditure relating to education, health, transport, food subsidisation, and public welfare assistance, hovered at around 40 per cent of total public expenditure or 10–12 per cent of Gross Domestic Product (GDP) (Marga Institute 1974; Jayasuriya et al. 1985; Osmani 1994; Alailama 1995).

The Kannagara Report recommended a system of *universal, compulsory* free education from kindergarten to university. Its objectives struck some (e.g. Dr Perera, a student of Harold Laski at the LSE) as 'amazing revolutionary', for all that they were more characteristic of Fabian than Marxist revolutionary socialism. They included:

> the prevention of unemployment, the raising of the standard of living of the masses, increased production, a more equitable system of distribution, social security of co-operative enterprise, etc.... [none of which] can be fully realized without mass education. We are of the opinion that free education must come first and foremost (Perera 1944: 5).

The 'dominant motivation was the egalitarian ideology of removing inequalities' (Jayasuriya 1969: 91).

The next pillar of the Sri Lankan welfare state, the Report on Social Services (1947), could be termed the Sri Lankan equivalent of Britain's Beveridge Report. Its main focus was on social security, with regard to unemployment, old age, disability and destitution. However, while the Commission gave serious consideration to the thinking underlying British social policy,[4] it did not actually recommend adopting Beveridge-style policies for Sri Lanka. The Jennings Report (as it came to be known) maintained that its intention was to formulate policy responses relevant and appropriate to Sri Lankan social and economic conditions.

One of its main concerns was to develop a financially viable plan for social security for wage earners in the public and commercial sectors. Hence the establishment (1958) of an Employers Provident Fund (EPF) (cf. the reference to EPFs in chapters 9 and 10 below), covering all private firms and public bodies. This apart, however, the import of the Jennings Report would seem to have been more academic than practical. Its blueprints did not necessarily get translated into programmes and services, nor did the report itself elicit much political interest (Savy 1972; Jayasuriya 2000).

The third pillar of the Sri Lankan welfare – the Cumpston Report – resulted in the Health Services Act of 1952. This Report's most significant recommendation, reflecting the egalitarian ideology of welfarism, was the abolition of private practice for doctors in the public sector, on the grounds that:

> no government [can] justify the expenditure of public funds to provide a subsidy to a select group of doctors so that they can provide a private medical service to the exclusive group in a position to pay a (sometimes large) fee   (Cumpston Report 1950: 9).

This policy recommendation was regarded as central to the establishment of a state-funded, equitable system of national health care. This later led to the progressive introduction of Western medical services (Gunatilleke 1985). Admittedly, the bulk of these services were located in the urban areas. Nevertheless this rapid expansion existed alongside a well-developed system of indigenous medicine which was mainly responsible for catering to the health care needs of a sizable section of the rural population (Pieris 1999). Again, this 'medical pluralism' reflected the socio-structural realities of Sri Lanka's 'dual society' (Jayaweera 1969: 8).

As a result, the *welfare politics* of this period, structured around a loose political alliance of nationalists and the radical Left, resulted in the consolidation in the 1960s of the patchwork of welfare policies constituting the Sri Lanka 'welfare state' (Government of Ceylon 1963). A distinctive feature of the period was the systematic attempt to develop a complementary package of rural policies which – quite apart from their economic rationale – were critical to the consolidation of the Sri Lankan welfare state. The same rural policies helped create an influential rural middle class whose aspirations were eventually to challenge the hegemonic power of the urban English-educated middle class (Jayasuriya 2000).

These rural policies played a significant role in containing the *ethnic politics* of this period. They had special significance for the Tamil people, who were mostly concentrated in their traditional homeland in the north of Sri Lanka and greatly dependent on agriculture for their livelihood. In short, the Tamil people received considerable economic benefits from the rural policies of the state, which in turn helped offset the economic losses suffered when they were deprived of their hitherto main source of livelihood, which had been in public sector employment.

This deprivation had been a direct result of the educational reforms introduced in the post-1956 era, making Sinhalese the official language, and leading to what was termed the 'Sinhalisat&ion of the state' (Moore

1985). The regional impact of these controversial policies was reflected, for instance, in changes to the pattern of university admissions as a result of the introduction of district quotas, and the standardisation of marks[5] according to language medium – Sinhalese or Tamil – in 1974/75. These educational policies – all of which served to disadvantage Tamil people in the labour market – had been intended to 'neutralise the superior performance of Tamil medium students' (de Silva 1979), and their hitherto privileged position in the labour market.

The rural social policies of the welfare state had offered the Tamil people at least a degree of monetary compensation for these economic losses (Tambiah 1986). However, with the fall in market demand for minor food crops, following the removal of agricultural subsidies and other forms of protection, agricultural production in the Tamil areas (the Jaffna district) fell sharply and caused severe economic hardship (Moore 1985). This in turn exacerbated latent ethnic tensions, destroying the earlier politics of ethnic accommodation, which had to a large extent been held together by the Sri Lankan welfare state (Gunasinghe 1984).

The 'Post Colonial' era: 1970s–1990s

The 1970s and 1980s witnessed the transformation of the Sri Lankan polity from *welfare* to *warfare*.[6] The *political* ethos which emerged in the cultural milieu of the post-1970s needs to be seen in the light of the far reaching impact of the militant youth revolt of 1971 (Halliday 1971; Obeysekera 1974; Keerawella 1989). This landmark event, associated with a radical nationalism, heralded the death knell of many centuries of colonisation and marked the beginnings of the search for a new cultural ideology, a sense of national identity and the experimentation with new social and political ideas and institutions.

But this search was constrained by adverse economic circumstances, by the ethnic tensions of the 1980s and by the subsequent civil war (Tambiah 1986; Watson and Gamage 1999). The authoritarian state (1977–94) replaced the earlier social democratic state. The background to the social policy strategies of the conservative, neo-liberal governments of 1977–94 is to be partly found in the collapse of the growth strategies pursued in the earlier period of welfarism, which had been heavily reliant on the surplus from the plantation sector, in an undiversified economy. The welfare state became paralysed by economic stagnation, growing budget deficits, and a draining of foreign exchange reserves (Kelegama 1987).

In the post-1977 era, Sri Lanka departed sharply from its past welfare ethos, adopting the policies and practices of a neo-liberal market economy. The country became open to full-scale development with foreign aid and private capital. As the late Mr J.R. Jayawardene, President of Sri Lanka (1977–83) declared, in one of his grand utterances, the conservative governments of the post-1977 era 'Let the Robber Barons in'! The policies of economic liberalisation and a free market were also assisted by the constitutional reforms of 1977, introducing a completely new, Executive Presidential model of government and administration, in place of the previous Westminster style.

The universalistic policies of the previous era were abandoned in favour of a residualist welfarism based on a 'safety-net' strategy directed primarily to relieving absolute poverty. The new policy mix of economic growth and welfare also sought to encourage the delivery of welfare, including health and education services, via the private sector. State sponsored social welfare schemes (*Janasaviya* and later, *Samurdhi*) were conceded only as a matter of pragmatic political convenience, as a transitional or provisional measure and, importantly, linked to productive enterprises conducive to income and employment generation (Gunatilleke 1999; Sanderatne 2000).

The overall strategy was to exchange the previous policy of growth with welfare for one based on market oriented growth with 'safety nets'. This policy shift required a drastic curtailment of public expenditure in key areas of social policy, such as education and health (most of which was redirected to defence expenditure).[7] Furthermore, these policies were based on an anticipation of the benefits of 'trickle down' with the objective of promoting self-reliance as against welfare dependency.

Manifestly, the changes in all aspects of political, economic and social life introduced by the neo-liberal/conservative regimes of 1977–94, were exacerbated by escalating ethnic conflict. The fracturing of the social justice rationale of the welfare state, coupled with the replacement of its Westminster-style political institutions and the cultural alienation of the disempowered indigenous élite, highlighted deep-seated social and political tensions surrounding the collapse of the politics of welfarism.

In this regard, Sri Lanka runs the risk of emulating the Brazil of the 1970s, which witnessed a prosperity favouring the middle class, but left large sections of the poor untouched. Mindful of this possibility, a Centre Left Coalition government eventually came into power in 1994, pledged to pursue a more disciplined, transparent approach to economic growth, but one which was also more equitable. With its political rhetoric of 'structural adjustment with a human face', or the desire to 'humanise capitalism', the government claimed that it was committed to the pursuit of the goals of distributive justice and greater social equality.

Back to social democracy?

The Centre-Left Coalition government of 1994–2001, despite its superficial success in restoring the trappings of a social democratic state, failed to resolve the dilemmas and contradictions of electoral politics that has dominated Sri Lanka for the last 50 years, in a manner suited to the needs of the new global economy. The election of President Wickremesinghe, in December 2001, precipitated a fragile peace agreement with the Tamil rebels (signed in Oslo in February 2002), followed by a power-sharing deal (December 2002) designed to give the rebels regional autonomy. What this can possibly signify for the future of the Sri Lankan welfare state it is obviously too early to say.

Conclusion

In the absence of a coherent social philosophy, the social policy and welfare reforms of the past two decades in Sri Lanka have been driven by the constraints of an economy on a war footing, the dictates of international agencies, and vested interests, especially the influential corporate sector.

In this regard, the essential ideas for a new social democracy for Sri Lanka may well be found in various forms of revisionist social democracy that have recently emerged in Europe and elsewhere (Jayasuriya, K. 1999). Britain's 'third way' eschews the extremes of the new right and the socialist orthodoxy of the old Left – the two dominant philosophies of the post war period – and aims to reconcile the realities of the international economy, global capitalism and market efficiency with issues of social justice – 'the cornerstone of the social democratic project' (Giddens 1998; Jayasuriya, K. 1999; note also the numerous references to the Third Way elsewhere in this volume). Accordingly, a distinctive feature of 'third way' politics in Europe, has been the endeavour to demonstrate how the idea of the welfare state, based on equality, can be reconciled with market forces which are by nature inegalitarian (Giddens 1998).

This new thinking requires, first and foremost, a defence of the principles and values of the welfare state against its philosophical rejection by neo-liberal conservative governments; the essence of the argument being that the re-articulation of social democracy in Sri Lanka needs to be built around a version of communitarian citizenship that incorporates the ethnic pluralism of Sri Lankan society as well as the social rights dimension – so pivotal to Marshall's understanding of citizenship (Jayasuriya 1993; Jayasuriya 2000).

Above all, in Sri Lanka, as elsewhere, the future of the welfare state depends on the ability to distinguish *economic liberalism*, the operation of market forces, from *political liberalism* embodying the rights of political and social citizenship. Historically, this has not been an easy task but this should not deter 'ethical liberals', or social democrats from detaching market assumptions of capitalism from the principle and value of social democracy and integrating them into a truly democratic vision of 'participatory citizenship' (Phillips 1992b) incorporated within 'market socialism' (Jayasuriya 2000: Ch. 6). In forging this linkage between *capitalism* and *welfarism*, and charting a new political agenda for social democracy, Sri Lanka may once again acquire a pathfinding role as a model social democratic state for the rapidly transforming market economies of developing countries.

Admittedly, the return of a social democratic regime reminiscent of the earlier form of liberal political culture in 1996 (Jayasuriya 2000) witnessed cosmetic changes to these conservative social policies. But the future remains again uncertain, after the return of a more conservative Centre-Right government in 2001.

Notes

1. This is in part a revised and edited version of a paper first published in the *Journal of the Royal Asiatic Society of Sri Lanka* (see Jayasuriya 2003).
2. 'The spirit of utilitarianism sought to justify actions on the basis of contributions towards increasing human satisfactions and decreasing dissatisfactions' (Sleeman 1973: 14). Utilitarians encouraged purposive social institutions, e.g. anti-slavery, factory legislation, improving public health, etc., where the greatest good of the greatest number would be provided.
3. Sen (1981) identifies the food subsidy as an example of the concept of 'entitlements', in particular, as a method of universal support of non-exclusion guaranteeing the 'right to food' and being effective in famine prevention.
4. Jones (1993: 30–32), for instance, has observed that the wartime appeal of the Beveridge Report, and the deference shown it by Allied governments, proved no guarantee that the great man's proposals were actually to be copied in detail anywhere else.

5. Standardization of marks was designed to correct examiner variability between the language media. The intention was 'to arrive at a uniform scale so that in the end the number qualifying from each medium would be proportionate to the number sitting the examination in each medium' (de Silva 1978).
6. See Dunham and Jayasuriya (2000), Sanderatne (2000), and Laksham and Tisdell (1999) for an extended discussion of economic and social development in the post 1970 period. Gamage and Watson (2001) provide a succinct account of ethnic conflicts in this period; see also Jayasuriya (2001).
7. Comparing social expenditure and defence expenditure since 1970, it is evident that whereas social expenditure, as a percentage of GDP, declined from eight per cent in 1970 to approximately six per cent in 1996, defence expenditure increased from a mere two per cent to about six per cent in 1996 – a threefold increase.

References

Alailama, P. (1995) *Post-Independence Evolution of Social Policy and Expenditure in Sri Lanka*, Colombo: Centre for Women's Research.
Bandarage, A. (1983) *Colonialism in Sri Lanka*, Amsterdam: Mouton.
Bruce, M. (1961) *The Coming of the Welfare State*, London: Batsford.
de Silva, C.R. (1978) 'The politics of university admissions: a review of some aspects of the admissions policy in Sri Lanka 1971–78', *Sri Lanka Journal of Social Sciences* 1 (2).
de Silva, C.R. (1979) 'The impact of nationalism on education: the schools take over (1961) and the university admissions crisis 1970–75', M. Roberts (ed.), *Collective Identities, Nationalisms and Protest in Modern Sri Lanka*, Colombo: Marga Institute.
de Silva, K.M. (1981) *A History of Sri Lanka*, London: Oxford University Press.
de Silva, K.M. (1965) *Social Policy and Missionary Organisation in Ceylon 1840–55*, London: Royal Commonwealth Society.
Dicey, A.V. (1996) *Lectures on the Relation Between Law and Public Opinion in England during the Nineteenth Century*, Homes Beach: Gaunt.
Dunham, D. and S. Jayasuriya (2000) 'Equity growth and the insurrection: Liberalization and the welfare debate in contemporary Sri Lanka', *Oxford Development Studies* 28(1): 97–110.
Evans, E.J. (1978) *Social Policy 1830–1914*, London: Routledge.
Gavin, J.D. and Chandrasekera, S. (1979) 'The impact of public food, grain distribution and food consumption and welfare in Sri Lanka', *Research Report No 13*, Washington DC: International Food Policy Research Institute.
Giddens, A. (1998) *The Third Way – the Renewal of Social Democracy*, London: Polity Press.
Goldthorpe, J.H. (1964) 'The development of social policy in England 1800–1914', Transactions of the Fifth World Congress of Sociology 4(4): 41–56.
Government of Ceylon, Ministry of Finance (1963) *Economic and Social Progress 1956–62*, Supplement to Budget Speech, Colombo: Government Press.
Gunasinghe, N. (1984) 'The open economy and its impact on ethnic relations in Sri Lanka'. In: *Committee for Rational Development (CRD), Sri Lanka: The Ethnic Conflict*, New Delhi, Navarang.

Gunatilleke, G. (1985) 'Health and development in Sri Lanka: An overview'. In: S.B. Halstead et al. (eds), *Good Health at Low Cost*, New York: Rockerfeller.

Gunatilleke, G. (1999) 'Development Policy Regimes'. In W.D. Lakshman and C.A. Tisdell (eds), *Facets of Development of Sri Lanka since Independence: Socio-Political, Economic, Scientific, and Cultural*, Brisbane: University of Queensland Press.

Halliday, F. (1971) 'The Ceylonese Insurrection', *New Left Review* 69.

Houtart, F. (1974) *Religion and Ideology in Sri Lanka*, Colombo: Hansa.

Jayasuriya, J.E. (1969) *Education in Ceylon before and After Independence 1939–68*, Colombo: Educational Publishers.

Jayasuriya, K. (1999) 'Revisionist social democracy', *Australian Quarterly* (AQ) 71 (May–June).

Jayasuriya, K. (2001) Review Essay: 'The making of the Sri Lankan bourgeoisie'. Review of K. Jayawardane (2000) *From Nobodies to Somebodies: The Rise of the Colonial Bourgeoisie Sri Lanka*. Social Scientists' Association, and Sanjiva Books, Colombo, Sri Lanka, *Sri Lanka Economic Journal* 2(1): 168–175.

Jayasuriya, L. (1993) 'Citizenship and welfare: rediscovering Marshall'. In P. Saunders and S. Graham (eds), *Beyond Economic Rationalism: Alternative Futures for Social Policy*, Sydney: Centre for Social Policy, University of New South Wales.

Jayasuriya, L. (2000) *Welfarism and Politics in Sri Lanka*, Perth, School of Social Work and Social Policy, University of Western Australia.

Jayasuriya, L. (2001) 'Rethinking social development: towards an equitable future for Sri Lanka', *South Asian Economic Journal* 2(1): 105–121.

Jayasuriya, L. (2003) 'The Evolution of Social Policy in Sri Lanka, 1933–1970', *Journal of Royal Asiatic Society of Sri Lanka*, Vol. XLVI.

Jayasuriya, L., Fernando, G. and Allbrook, M. (1985) 'Sri Lankan social welfare'. In J. Dixon and H.S. Kim (eds), Social welfare, London: Croom Helm.

Jayawardena, K. (1972) *The Rise of the Labour Movement in Ceylon*, Durham, North Carolina: Duke University Press.

Jayaweera, S. (1969) 'Development of secondary education'. In *Education in Ceylon*, Part II. Colombo: Ministry of Education.

Jeffries, C. (1962) *The Path to Independence*, London: Pall Mall Press.

Jones, M. (2000) 'The Ceylon malaria epidemic of 1934–35: A case study in colonial medicine, *Social History of Medicine* 13 (1).

Jones, M. (2002) 'Infant and maternal health services in Ceylon 1900–1948: imperialism or welfare?' *Social History of Medicine* 15 (2).

Jupp, J. (1978) *Sri Lanka: Third World Democracy*, London: Frank Cass.

Kearney, R.N. (1971) *Trade Unions and Politics in Ceylon*, New Delhi, University of California Press.

Keerawella, G.B. (1989) 'The Janatha Vimukthi Peramuna (JVP) and the 1971 uprising', *Social Science Review*, Vol. 2.

Kelegama, S. (1987) 'Growth and equity – A review of the Sri Lankan experience', *Sri Lanka Economic Journal* 2 (1).

Lakshman, W.D and C.A Tisdell (1999) (eds), *Facets of Development of Sri Lanka since Independence: Socio-Political, Economic, Scientific, and Cultural*, Brisbane: University of Queensland Press.

Mair, L. (1944) *Welfare in British Colonies*, London: Royal Institute of International Affairs.

Mamdani, M. (1976) *Politics and Class Formation in Uganda*, London: Heinemann.
Marga Institute (1974) *Welfare and Growth in Sri Lanka*, Colombo: Marga.
Marshall, T.H. (1973) 'Citizenship and social Class'. In T.H. Marshall (ed.), *Class, Citizenship and Social Development*, Connecticut: Greenwood.
Mendis, G.C. (1957) *Ceylon Today and Yesterday*, Colombo: ANCL.
Mendis, G.C. (ed.) (1956) *The Colebrooke–Cameron Papers* (2 Vols), Cambridge: Cambridge University Press.
Moore, M. (1985) *The State and Peasant Politics in Sri Lanka*, Cambridge: Cambridge University Press.
Obeysekera, G. (1974) 'Some comments on the social background of the April 1971 insurgencies in Sri Lanka', *Journal of Asian Studies* Vol. 33.
Osmani, S.R. (1994) 'Is there a conflict between growth and welfarism? The significance of the Sri Lankan debate', *Development and Change*, 25 (2): 387–421.
Perera, N.M. (1944) *The Case for Free Education*, Colombo: Ola Book Company.
Perera, P.D.A. (1985) 'Health care system in Sri Lanka'. In S.B. Halstead et al. (eds), *Good Health at Low Cost*, New York: Rockerfeller.
Phillips, A. (1992b) 'Citizenship and feminist politics'. In G. Andrew (ed.), *Citizenship*, London: Lawrence and Wishart.
Pieris, R. (1967) The role of government in labour relations in Ceylon, in *Labour Relations in the Asian Countries*, Tokyo: Japan Institute of labour.
Pieris, I. (1999) *Disease, Treatment and Health Behaviour in Sri Lanka*, Sydney: Oxford University Press.
Russell, J. (1982) *Communal Politics under the Donoughmore Constitution (1931–47)*, Colombo: Tisara Prakasakayo.
Samarawera, V. (1973) 'The Colebrooke–Cameron reforms'. In: K.M. de Silva (ed.), *History of Ceylon* (Vol. 3), Colombo: University of Ceylon.
Sanderatne, N. (2000) *Economic Growth and Social Transformations*, Colombo: Tamarind.
Savy, R. (1972) *Social Security in Agriculture*, Geneva: ILO.
Sen, A. (1981) *Poverty and Famines: an Essay on Entitlements and Deprivations*, Clarendon: Oxford University Press.
Sleeman, J.F. (1973) *The Welfare State: Its Aims, Benefits and Costs*, London: Allen and Unwin.
Snodgrass, D.R. (1966) *Ceylon: An Export Economy in Transition*, Homewood: Illinois University Press.
Stokes, E. (1959) *English Utilitarians and India*, Oxford: Oxford University Press.
Tambiah, S.J. (1986) *Sri Lanka: Ethnic Fratricide and the Dismantling of Democracy*, London: Tauris.
UNDP (1990–6) *Human Development Reports*, New York: Oxford University Press.
Uragoda, C. (1987) *A History of Medicine of Sri Lanka*, Colombo: Sri Lankan Medical Association.
Warnapala, W.A. (1974) *Civil Service Administration in Ceylon*, Colombo: Department of Cultural Affairs, Government of Sri Lanka.
Watson, I.B. and S. Gamage (eds) (1999) *Conflict and Community in Contemporary Sri Lanka: Pearl of the East of Island of Tears*, New Delhi: Sage.
Wickramaratne, L.A. (1977) 'Peasant agriculture'. In K.M. de Silva (ed.), *Sri Lanka: Problems of Governance*, Colombo: International Centre for Ethnic Studies.

Reports

Colebrooke–Cameron Commission Report (1833).
Newnham Report (1936) *Relief of Distress due to Sickness and Shortage of Food*, Sessional Paper No. V. Colombo: Ceylon Government Press.
Jennings Report (1947) *Report of the Commission on Social Services*, Sessional Paper No. VII. Colombo: Ceylon Government Press.
Cumpston Report (1950) *Report on the Medical and Public Health Organizations of Ceylon*, Sessional Paper No. III. Colombo: Ceylon Government Press.
Hamlin Report (1957) *Report on Children's Services*, Sessional Paper No. VII Colombo: Ceylon Government Press.

9
Balancing State Welfarism and Individual Responsibility: Singapore's CPF Model

Tan Ern Ser

Introduction

Welfare provisions are not without economic costs. In other words, the ability to provide welfare hinges on the creation and maintenance of a viable economy which motivates and rewards productive members, yet shoulders the responsibility of supporting its weaker members. What then is the basis of a viable economy? Can it be socially responsible as well? According to Wright (1996: 139), 'Markets have all the dynamic merits that make them the most expedient way of organizing economic life; but they sometimes want to go where they should not, having an intrinsic and irresponsible blindness to the outcomes of their operation.' Among other reasons, this inherent blindness explains why socialism has not gone out of fashion, despite the so-called triumph of capitalism and the fall of communism in the late 20th century. Wright (1996: 137) quoted Leon Blum, a French socialist leader, to say that 'It is on the foundation of socialist principles that societies, whether consciously or not, are everywhere being reconstituted.'

But, as alluded to above, the brand of socialism, as widely practiced at the turn of the new millennium, is not geared towards total decommodification, but one which 'embraces the market ... consumers and consumerism ... emphasizing ... commitment to production (caring was not enough, unless you could pay for it) and competent economic management' (Wright 1996: 133), while upholding 'an ethic of community and mutual responsibility' (Wright 1996: 136). This mutual relationship involves linking 'the responsibilities of the state to do all it can to provide the opportunities for full citizenship with the responsibilities of individuals, groups, organizations to respond to those opportunities' (Wright 1996: 147).

I have cited extensively from Wright (1996) because his book entitled 'Socialisms: old and new', while dealing with Britain in particular, and Europe in general, captures rather succinctly the essence of 'Asian socialism' (Smyth 2000: 25) and state welfarism in post-independence Singapore. The 'Asian model' – more particularly, the 'Singapore model' – constitutes a third model, an approach best captured by Holliday's (2000: 708) 'productivist welfare capitalism', where 'social policy is strictly subordinate to the overriding policy objective of economic growth.'

This model is reflected in the welfare ideology of the ruling People's Action Party (PAP), the political party holding the reins of state power in Singapore since 1959. The PAP's welfare ideology in turn bears the mark of Lee Kuan Yew, founder and prime minister of modern Singapore from 1959–1990 and currently senior minister. For this reason, a good knowledge of Lee Kuan Yew's philosophy on welfare provides a handle for understanding the character of state welfarism and, more specifically, the compulsory savings scheme, known as the Central Provident Fund (CPF), which serves as the cornerstone of Singapore's welfare system.

State welfarism-Singapore style: the ideology

While the term 'welfarism' is used in this essay, it is not one that sits comfortably within the official vocabulary of the Singapore government. Indeed, Lee Kuan Yew (2000: 116), in the second volume of his recently published memoir described Singapore as a 'fair, not welfare society'. This discomfort with welfarism perhaps explains why an official publication from the Ministry of Information and the Arts (1996), while dealing with what may be easily understood as welfare programmes and services, was given the title 'Sharing Success'. The pamphlet uses the phrase 'levelling up' to describe what the government has done for 'lower-income', not poor, families. This is the essence of welfarism – and socialism – Singapore-style.

Lee Kuan Yew (2000: 116) defines socialism as a fair society, as opposed to a market society of 'winners take all'. It is important to note that socialism-Singapore style aims at achieving a 'fair' society, not an egalitarian or classless society. This 'fair' society is premised upon the equalizing of opportunities, not rewards or outcomes. Indeed, capitalist, free-market competition, with its consequent inequality, is unashamedly encouraged in Singapore. The rationale being that it will provide the incentives for people to give their best performance, thereby producing a vibrant economy capable of generating wealth and a high standard of living.

However, in Lee's views, the wealth must not be seen as going only to the winners, because a 'winners take all' system will create social tension; hence, the need to 'redistribute the national income through subsidies on things that improve the earning power of citizens, such as education' (Lee 2000: 116), housing, and health care. He is not inclined towards subsidizing consumption and providing unemployment benefits, arguing that these would dampen self-reliance and work incentive, thereby encouraging a 'handout-' or crutch-mentality. At the same time, while he sees the importance of providing health care services, he is ever mindful that medical benefits are more at risk of wasteful consumption. (cf. The reference to Blair's part-Singapore-inspired 'Third Way in Ch. 2, p. 24 above.)

State welfarism-Singapore style in practice

State welfarism is predicated upon people having paid jobs, thereby possessing the means to support themselves and their dependents. Welfare is therefore not about giving handouts, but about providing people with the opportunities to train for skills and credentials, thereby improving productivity and wages. At the same time, welfare is also about generating sufficient well-paying jobs capable of absorbing labour market participants equipped with value-adding skills and knowledge. Where highly skilled people get well-paying jobs, they would be in a position to look after their own welfare and that of their dependents, while setting aside sufficient savings for retirement and health care costs.

However, people do lose their jobs, for reasons that are structural rather than individual, or because of circumstances not within their control. For instance, there could be a mismatch between job vacancies and skills availability. This gap between vacancies and skills may be bridged by skills retraining or upgrading, but it increasingly entails the creation of sufficient decent-paying jobs, a condition which is not easily achieved in a recession, or, worse, amid the structural changes characteristic of the new economy. There are obviously limits to a welfare approach confined to 'job creation and skills upgrading', and good justifications for supporting the provision of unemployment benefits; but doing so would undermine the principle of self-reliance that constitutes the backbone of the PAP's welfare ideology.

Nevertheless, the state recognizes that, even in a buoyant economy, there will always be a small minority who cannot take care of themselves and who do not have families who are obliged – or could be legally required – to look after them. For people in this category, social assistance can be extended as a matter of philanthropy, but not of citizenship rights. The government prefers to channel the assistance through non-government welfare agencies or programmes supported by private donations and government grants, though it does provide direct monetary grants to people who have no means of financial support and to those in low-income families. The rationale for preferring indirect assistance, as opposed to giving out cash, is the fear that the latter approach would inculcate a 'handout' mentality, or a long-term dependence on the state, whether on the grounds of charity or, worse, of citizenship rights (cf. the provision of public assistance in colonial Hong Kong).

As alluded to earlier, the state does extend financial assistance to the 'truly needy' and to 'low-income' families with monthly household income below S$1,500 (http://www.familytown.gov.sg). The difference between the 'truly needy' and 'low-income' is that while the former are unable to work – due to old age, illness, disability, or unfavourable family circumstances – and have no means and no one to depend on, the latter refers to people who work full-time, but are in low-paying jobs. It should be noted that while the government is unable to reduce the proportion of those currently in the 'truly needy' category, it has taken various measures to ensure that the size and proportion of future 'truly needy' people will be kept small. Such measures include encouraging singles to get married; married couples to reproduce above replacement levels, if they can afford it, with some help from the so-called 'baby bonus' scheme; all citizens to keep healthy; and elderly persons to stay employed or, if not in employment, to return to the labour market.

What can be observed is that state welfarism-Singapore style has, as its starting point, individual self-reliance made possible through life-long learning, skills acquisition and upgrading, personal health maintenance. Where the person is unable to look after himself or herself, the second line of defence is the family. Marriage and family formation are therefore very much a part of the welfare approach in Singapore. For the hopefully small minority who can neither be self-reliant, nor have family support, the third line of defence is the 'community', defined as non-government or government-sponsored welfare agencies or programmes who could deliver financial assistance and medical benefits, without involving the government directly in the delivery of welfare services and financial aids. Given the various lines of defence, the welfare system-Singapore style is seemingly all-inclusive.

Thus far, we have dealt with those who have fallen through the cracks of the 'self-reliant' welfare approach. The majority of citizens are expected to be in the self-reliant category, capable of looking after themselves and their dependents. Somewhat paradoxically, the state is most inclined to help these people help themselves. One of the key instruments of welfare provision for the able is the Central Provident Fund (CPF) Scheme, together with generous subsidies for housing, education, and health care, while retirement and unemployment benefits remain outside of the purview of state subsidies, except for the 'truly needy'.

However, the government is currently faced with the prospect of having to provide financial assistance to employed or erstwhile employed persons suffering from or at risk of experiencing relatively long-term unemployment, wage cuts, or wage restraints, a situation made worse by the terrorist attacks on the United States on September 11, 2001. A *Straits Times* poll (September 29, 2001) indicated that many want the government's help package to go beyond training and creating jobs, to providing direct aid in the form of food vouchers, as well as financial assistance for education and health care costs. One ruling party MP was quoted as saying that 'the emphasis of the help package should be on providing immediate relief on bread-and-butter issues', while another MP suggests allowing retrenched workers to 'borrow from their own CPF accounts and repaying the loan when they get a job'. The latter suggestion not only has important implication for a possible role for the CPF Scheme in regard to unemployment benefits, but also reflects some hesitancy towards the provision of direct assistance in cash handouts to help pay for consumption.

The current economic downturn has posed a challenge to the fundamentals of Singapore's welfare ideology. However, while there is unlikely to be any fundamental change to the welfare ideology, the economic downturn and restructuring has focused public attention on those questions relevant to the politics of social inclusion in a vibrant, but vulnerable economy: 'How big will the (welfare) umbrella be? Who will be sheltered? And will it stay open long enough for the weather to get better?' (*Straits Times*, September 29, 2001). Inevitably, much attention will be paid to the CPF, a key cornerstone of state welfarism-Singapore style.

The colonial legacy

The CPF Scheme, as originally conceived, was established by the British colonial government in 1955, four years before the PAP came into power in 1959, and 10 years before Singapore became an independent nation in 1965 (cf. references to other versions of CPF in Chs 8 and 10 of this volume). It began with a then seemingly rather modest objective, which was to provide financial security for employees on retirement or upon 'premature involuntary withdrawal from the labor force'.

The CPF Scheme almost became a non-starter (CPF Board 2000: 7). It can be traced back to a CPF Bill tabled in the Legislative Council in 1951 and later sent to a Colony Select Committee. This Committee considered representations from employers (The Federation of Industrialists and Traders) and employees (The Singapore Trades Union Congress), as well as the Retirement Benefits Commission appointed by the British colonial government. Both the employer and employee federations preferred a provident fund scheme, while the Commission recommended a pension scheme that would pay retirees a small monthly sum for life. The latter preferred the pension approach as it 'could provide full benefits within a few years of operation', whereas 'a provident fund would not provide adequate retirement benefits until about 1970 (or 15 years from 1955)' (Low and Aw 1997: 14). The Select Committee eventually proposed the provident fund approach to the Legislative Council as it felt that the general sentiments were against a pension scheme (Singapore Association 1955: 2). The CPF bill was adopted in May 1955. Subsequently, there were two recommendations for a social insurance pooling scheme. These were rejected by the British colonial government, which continued to favor the provident fund approach.

It is interesting to note that while Britain itself had two forms of pension scheme at that time (the Beveridge 'universal', flat rate National Insurance pension, together with a growing spread of non-statutory *occupational* pensions for those in secure employment), the Colonial Office preferred using the provident fund approach for the colonies (Lim 1986). Low and Aw (1997: 19–20) argued that 'the British government had simply been quite firm in making a political decision not to be financially burdened with the social security plans of the colonies.' In contrast, Vasoo and Lee (2001: 278) attributed the British government's preference for the provident fund alternative to 'lack of resources'.

But as it turned out, the British colonial government had left behind an important legacy and viable retirement benefits system to Singapore. Had the legacy been a pension scheme, the successor government would have been saddled with a very costly and difficult to maintain welfare state, requiring future generations to support earlier generations through high taxes. In contrast, the provident fund approach is based on a self-financing principle. It operates as a compulsory savings scheme with mandated contributions from both employees and employers. During the last decade, the PAP Government has on several occasions even contributed to CPF accounts from its budgetary surpluses. One observes that the PAP has inherited a model that does not put any demands on public revenues, yet allows the government enough resources and flexibility to develop a comprehensive, viable welfare system compatible with its philosophy of promoting market economy and individual responsibility.

The CPF scheme

The basic concept of the CPF Scheme has in many ways remained unchanged since its inception. It operated – and still operates – as a broad-based, self-financing savings scheme with compulsory contributions from the employee and his or her employer. However, its role has, by design, expanded over the last three decades to cater to an increasingly more affluent population, thereby becoming a cornerstone of the PAP's brand of state welfarism particularly after 1968. Understandably, the CPF Scheme has undergone various changes, and is still being modified in response to demographic and economic changes, such as the graying population, growing proportion of singles, and the various economic downturns (1985–86, 1997–98, and late 2000 to present).

As with any welfare system, the bottom-line always matters, whether the funds come from national reserves, budgetary surpluses, taxes, or savings of individuals. Given that the CPF Scheme has been put to multiple uses over the years, it is essential that contributors deposit a substantial part of their earnings into the scheme. The main contributions come from employees and their employers. At its inception in 1955, the employee and employer each contributed five per cent of the employee's monthly wages or salary. The rates reached a peak in 1984, with employees and employers contributing 25 per cent each (up to a fixed income ceiling), which meant an individual's compulsory monthly savings could be as high as

50 per cent of his or her monthly wages. CPF contributions also earned relatively high interest rates, compared to ordinary savings placed in commercial banks.

During the 1985–86 recession, the employer's contribution was reduced to 10 per cent, which effectively meant a wage cut of 15 per cent. Such a drastic wage cut would be unheard of in most developed countries. As the economy improved after 1986, the rates leveled off at 20 per cent each in 1994. This meant that employees received a five per cent increase in take-home pay, even as they saved 20 per cent of their monthly wages, together with another 20 per cent contributed by their employers.

The economy again experienced a recession in 1997–98, which led to a CPF cut of 10 per cent from the employers' component. With economic recovery in 2000, the employers' contribution rate was raised to 16 per cent. Unfortunately, even as employees were anticipating the restoration of the 'balanced' 4 per cent, the economy was again hit with yet another recession, made worse by the 9/11 terrorist attacks on the United States. At the present time of writing (2003), the economy is experiencing some noticeable recovery, but while younger workers can expect a restoration of the earlier CPF cut, older workers will remain with the lower CPF rates even when the economy is deemed to have recovered. The rationale for not restoring the CPF rates of older workers is to enhance their chances of remaining employed. But with many citizens using their CPF funds to pay for housing mortgages, adopting the CPF-cut approach may have political costs for the PAP government, particularly if the unemployment level remains high or even rises over a sustained period of time.

Housing

As mentioned earlier, the CPF Scheme has been put to many uses, the major one being home ownership. In 1968, the Public Housing Scheme was introduced to allow citizens and permanent residents to use their CPF savings to pay for subsidized housing built by the Housing and Development Board (HDB). In 1981, the home-ownership scheme was extended to allow for the use of CPF savings to purchase private residential properties. With these arrangements, the proportion of 'home owners' has increased to 92 per cent by 2000 (MITA 2001: 21). While this makes an impressive picture, it is also predicated upon 'home-owners' having sufficient funds – and a job – to pay their monthly mortgages. While it has been argued in the past that CPF cuts are superior to wage cuts in that wage-earners do not experience a drop in their disposable incomes, the situation in more recent years is quite different (Tan 1997). Now, in so far as 'home-owners' are expected to dip into their other savings to meet mortgage payments, the situation has been made worse by retrenchments and the possibility of long-term unemployment.

Health care

Apart from home-ownership, CPF savings could be used to meet health care costs. At present, the '36-percent of monthly wages' contribution is apportioned as follows: 26 per cent goes into the 'Ordinary Account', four per cent into the 'Special Account' (see below), and six per cent into the 'Medisave' Account. It should be pointed out that employees above 55 years of age, the previous mandatory retirement age, contribute a lower proportion of their monthly wages than their younger counterparts (18.5 per cent for those above 55 up to 60; 11 per cent for those above 60 up to 65; and 8.5 per cent for those above 65), but a higher percentage of their contribution goes to the Medisave Account (e.g., 8.5 per cent for those above 65, as compared to 6 per cent for those 35 years or younger).

The savings in the Medisave Account could be used to pay for hospital charges and the medical treatment of members as well as those of their immediate family members. Together with MediShield, an optional insurance to cover the costs of catastrophic illnesses, the Medisave Account seeks to ensure that members have sufficient funds to co-pay for subsidized health care. The rationale for the co-payment approach was to prevent the kind of abuse, wastage, and long waiting time for surgical operations characteristic of the free medical services approach (Lee 2000: 122).

Nevertheless, it was recognized that, with a co-payment scheme, the issue is less about wastage than about inability to pay. In 1993, the Medifund was established with money from government revenue to cover citizens who have exhausted all means – personal savings, personal CPF savings, and CPF savings of immediate family members – to co-pay their medical bills. More recently, in June 2002, the ElderShield, an insurance scheme, was introduced to help pay for the medical and home care costs of citizens, aged 40 to 69 years, who become severely disabled. For those above the age of 70 years who are from low-income households and who are not eligible to be covered under ElderShield, the government has put in place the Interim Disability Assistance Programme for the Elderly (IDAPE).

Education

Besides housing and health care, CPF savings could also be used for members' or their own children's tertiary education in local institutions, in response to the importance that Singaporeans place on acquiring a university degree. However, the amount withdrawn is considered a loan, which means that a member or member's dependent using the scheme would have to return the loan plus interest within a certain time-frame – 10 years. The rationale for the loan approach is that the CPF's key objective remains 'saving for retirement' (CPF 2000: 8), despite the growing number of uses it has been assigned over the years.

Retirement

The CPF, as originally conceived, was intended to be a retirement fund. With the growing list of uses added to the CPF Scheme as originally conceived, there is a high probability that one could be left with very little CPF savings at retirement. While the government supplies HDB apartments, which can be purchased by citizens at subsidized prices, the amount required for mortgage payments could be quite substantial, relative to the amount deposited into one's CPF account. To ensure that members will have sufficient CPF savings to provide a 'subsistence allowance upon retirement', the Special Account component of the CPF savings was set up, together with the Minimum Sum Scheme. This minimum sum can either be invested in a life annuity or deposited with a bank, giving the CPF member a 'subsistence' monthly income for life or another 20 years, respectively (CPF 2000: 6). More recently, effective from September 1, 2002, the government has instituted certain measures relating to the use of CPF to dampen over-investment in property acquisitions.

Investment

Another feature of the CPF Scheme is to allow the savings to be used for investment purposes. The rationale for this feature, as spelt out by Ngiam Tong Dow (2001), CPF Chairman, is to encourage members to 'take greater personal responsibility for their old-age financial security'. The investment scheme was first introduced in 1978, permitting members to purchase shares in the main public transport company, the Singapore Bus Service (SBS). Various modifications were added over the years: 1986, 1993, 1997, and 2001. The response to the investment scheme has been substantial. Lee Kuan Yew (2000: 125) observed that by 1997, '1.5 million CPF members had invested in stocks and shares, mostly blue chips on the main board of the Stock Exchange of Singapore.'

A third contributor

Thus far, we note that the two main contributors to the CPF accounts are employees and their employers. There is a third contributor – the government. The government has been distributing CPF 'top-ups' out of its budgetary surplus since 1993. The booklet accompanying the Prime Minister's National Day Rally Speech 2001 reported that, as at the end of financial year 2000, the government has deposited a total of S$1.68 billion into CPF accounts (MITA 2001: 27). A large portion of these 'top-ups' were channeled into the Medisave component of CPF accounts, primarily to encourage members to purchase medical insurance in preparation for future medical needs. The CPF 'top-ups' have also been given as cash grants to help adult Singaporeans purchase shares (MITA 1996: 24).

Conclusion and implications

The Singapore CPF Scheme, together with other measures, such as the recession 'rescue' packages, suggests how welfare provisions, in general, and social security and pension funds, in particular, do not necessarily entail imposing high tax rates and borrowing from future generations. More importantly, it reflects an effective balancing of state welfarism and individual responsibility, which thereby enhances the probability that the individual will give his or her best in production, and use only what he or she needs in terms of services. It also balances the market economy with an inclusive community which takes care of the needy while ensuring that the majority of citizens are able to respond to opportunities provided by the market economy and the state.

However, as with other welfare approaches, the viability of the CPF Scheme hinges on preserving a vibrant economy with high employment levels. A key issue to consider is whether the CPF can remain buoyant and meet the challenges of the 'new insecurities' (cf. Byrne 1999) brought about by globalization. The state will face its greatest challenge should any recession hit the middle class in terms of not only long-term unemployment but also falling property and stock prices wiping out a substantial portion of individual life-time savings. Nevertheless, because it is easier to cut CPF contributions than wages or pensions, the CPF system has, with the help of a strong government, acquired a rather flexible quality over the years. Furthermore,

CPF benefits are portable, not tied to any particular employer. This flexibility can therefore help the economy and individuals adjust to fluctuations brought about by globalization (Aspalter 2002: 183).

All in all, there is clearly much that can be learned from the Singapore CPF model. Nevertheless, given that the British had also bequeathed this legacy to its other colonies – now Commonwealth countries – in Asia and Africa, it would be instructive to compare how the provident fund approach has evolved in the Commonwealth over the last half a century. Such a comparative study and exchange of information under the auspices of the Commonwealth can facilitate the learning of best practices, as no one country can claim to have an absolute monopoly on how to create a more viable, more socially inclusive, more adaptable welfare system.

Indeed, while Singapore's CPF approach is widely acclaimed as a welfare model for the new millennium (Vasoo and Lee 2001; Aspalter 2002), it possesses some inherent problems. Thus, as both Asher (1995 and 2002) and Ramesh (2000 and 2001) have pointed out: not only are those in informal employment and non-employed persons not covered by the CPF Scheme, but the apparently high individual CPF savings are also inadequate to provide financial security in retirement and old-age. Presumably, part of the solution to this problem could involve the use of 'tax-finance redistributive' measures and 'increasing the share of financing through government surplus', steps which could in turn entail 'a paradigm shift in the philosophy of social security' in Singapore (Asher 2002: 116).

References

Asher, Mukul G. (1995) 'Compulsory Savings in Singapore: An Alternative to the Welfare State', NCPA Policy Report No. 198, Dallas: National Center for Policy Analysis.
—— (2002) 'Pension reform in an affluent and rapidly ageing society: The Singapore case', *Hitotsubashi Journal of Economics*, 43: 2.
Aspalter, Christian, (ed.) (2002) Discovering the Welfare State in East Asia, Westport, CN: Praeger.
Byrne, David (1999) *Social Exclusion*, Buckingham: Open University Press.
Central Provident Fund (CPF) Board (2000) *A People's Wealth, A Nation's Health: The CPF Story*, Singapore: CPF.
Holliday, Ian (2000) 'Productivist Welfare Capitalism: Social Policy in East Asia', *Political Studies*, 48: 4, pp. 706–723.
Lee, Kuan Yew (2000) *From Third World to First: The Singapore Story 1965–2000*, Singapore: Times Edition.
Lim Chong Yah, and Associates (1986) *Report of the Central Provident Fund Study Group*. Unpublished report, Singapore: Department of Economics and Statistics, National University of Singapore.

Low, Linda and Aw, T.C. (1997) *Housing a Healthy, Educated and Wealthy Nation through the CPF*, Singapore: Times Academic Press/Institute of Policy Studies.

Ministry of Information and the Arts (MITA) (1996) *Sharing Success: government programmes 1990–1995*, Singapore: MITA.

Ministry of Information and the Arts (MITA) (2001) *Singapore: The last 10 years (supplement to Prime Minister Goh Chok Tong's National Day Rally Speech 2001)*, Singapore: MITA.

Ngiam Tong Dow (2001) 'CPF Board Annual Report 2000: Chairman's Statement' News Releases August 24, 2001.

Ramesh, M. (with M. Asher) (2000) Welfare Capitalism in Southeast Asia: Social Security, Health, and Education Policies, London: MacMillan.

—— (2001) (1992) 'Social Security in Singapore: Redrawing the Public-Private Boundary' in Garry Rodan (ed.), *Singapore*, Aldershot: Ashgate.

Singapore Association (1955) *Pensions, Provident Fund or Insurance? An examination of the means of providing for old age in Singapore*, Singapore: Straits Times Press.

Smyth, Paul (2000) 'The Economic State and the Welfare State: Australia and Singapore 1955–1975' *CAS Research paper No. 23*, Singapore: Centre for Advanced Studies, National University of Singapore.

Straits Times, various issues in 2001 and 2001.

Tan, Ern Ser (1997) 'Theorising the dynamics of industrial relations and trade unionism: lessons from the Singapore case' in Ong J.H., Tong C.K., and Tan E.S. (eds.) *Understanding Singapore Society*, Singapore: Times Academic.

Vasoo, S. and James Lee (2001) 'Singapore: social development, housing and the Central Provident Fund', International Journal of Social Welfare, 10: 276–283.

Wright, Tony (1996) *Socialisms: old and new*, London: Routledge.

Many other radical communal experiments have foundered in the bedrock of sexual differences, and it is probably no accident that the monastic orders of Christianity, Buddhism, and other religions, which have been among the most successful and enduring of communal living groups, have been monosexual. They have solved the problem of relations between men and women by eliminating them altogether. As a fringe benefit, they have not had to worry about child care, unless they chose to specialize in caring for other people's children (orphanages, schools), thereby giving themselves a widely acceptable and this-worldly *raison d'être*, and providing themselves with an alternative mode of self-perpetuation. By drawing recruits from among their wards and pupils, monastic orders developed a nonsexual mode of reproduction for themselves and freed the women of the propertied classes of some of the onus of child rearing.

More recently, the bitter disenchantment of many radical women with bisexual communal living groups and with male-dominated radical political groups, and their strident insistence on sexual separatism (to the extent of advocating lesbianism or at least discouraging emotional involvement with men) point also to the great difficulty of trying to ignore the biologically-based gender differences. Although it remains a moot question whether the source of the difficulty is entirely sociogenic, or partly biological and partly social, experience strongly suggests that the androgynous ideal is unattainable.

The basic mechanism insuring a high degree of sex role conformity is, of course, early socialization. Long before an infant is capable of performing the roles ascribed to either sex, he or she is already strongly channelled along sex lines. The process of sex identification is usually well set in the second year of life. The indomitable human spirit occasionally rebels against this brainwashing. Not all little girls want to play with dolls and serve tea with miniature porcelain sets; some little boys like to knit or to help cook dinner. Most societies find ways of accommodating such deviants, but almost always with some degree of stigmatization. The aggressive woman is a "bitch"; the sensitive man is a "sissy."

Two phenomena of interest here are transvestism and homosexuality; though often linked in Western societies, the two are clearly distinct, sharing only a common deviance from ascribed sex roles.[2] The *transvestite* is a person who expresses

---

[2]Part of the confusion is semantic. Unfortunately, we use the same word in English to refer to gender and to erotic and reproductive behavior. Transvestism has to do with sex-gender; homosexuality is in the realm of sex-eroticism. Obviously, our central concern in this book is with sex-gender, and we are interested in sex-eroticism only insofar as it relates to sex-gender.

a general preference for the role ascribed to the sex opposite to his or her own, and thus frequently dresses and behaves accordingly. Such persons may or may not be homosexuals. *Homosexuals* are persons erotically attracted to members of the same sex; some seek to emulate members of the opposite sex by playing the opposite sex role in a homosexual relationship, but many assume their own sex role and despise the opposite sex. The homosexual frequently deviates from his ascribed sex role only in the choice of sexual partners, while the transvestite has generally rebelled against gender-role ascription.

The range of cultural responses is wide, but, from our fragmentary cross-cultural evidence, it seems that transvestism is more widely stigmatized than homosexuality. In a number of societies, such as ancient Greece, Arab countries, some Melanesian groups (Davenport, 1965), and the Nyakyusa of Tanzania (Wilson, 1951), homosexual behavior is matter-of-factly accepted as either a substitute for or a supplement to heterosexuality. The same is often true in the sex-segregated institutions (such as boarding schools and prisons) of societies that otherwise condemn homosexuality. Homosexuality and bisexuality do not threaten sex role differentiation.

Even in the limited and private sphere of choice of sexual partners, homosexual behavior in many societies that tolerate it does not deviate from gender-role ascription. In a number of these societies, bisexuality is the norm, and homosexuality is a substitute for heterosexuality. Davenport (1965), for example, reports a Melanesian group that tolerates homosexual relations, including anal intercourse between adult male friends (or even brothers), or between adult males and boys aged seven to eleven, but which completely lacks any conception of the exclusive homosexual as a person assigned a special social role. Similarly, Evans-Pritchard (1970) reports acceptance of the custom of "boy marriage" among Zande warriors. Extensive polygyny among the nobility creates a scarcity of marriageable women for young warriors, who have to postpone marriage until their late twenties or thirties, and thus resort to socially accepted pederasty as an alternate sexual outlet. The Western notion of exclusive homosexuality as a form of sexual deviation is probably far less common than matter-of-fact recognition and tolerance of bisexuality.

Social response to transvestism, on the contrary, is almost invariably negative, ranging from ridicule and loss of status to death. Some North American Indian societies institutionalized the role of *berdache* or male transvestite, but in a very marginal way. In ancient Greece and Japan, male actors played female roles in their classical theater, but these are hardly cases of generalized tolerance of transvestism. In Western societies, the stigma has typically been strong. One of the charges that led Joan of Arc to the stake was that she behaved "immodestly." Although her judges unsuccessfully tried to ascribe sexual promiscuity to her, it was evident that she had the audacity of dressing like a man. Her pleas that this was simply a matter of convenience were rejected. Her "immodesty" was one of status, not of eroticism—she did not accept her lowly place as a woman. Even in contemporary Western societies, as indeed in all but the most revolutionary ones (such as Communist China) bent on abolishing sex inequalities, the symbolic importance of sex-linked clothing styles is still apparent. We speak metaphorically of "wearing the pants" to mean "wielding power."

It seems that virtually all societies, not content with the moderate amount of sexual dimorphism with which we are born, further stress sex role differentiation through highly visible social means. Clothing styles stand out most obviously, but even in societies in which nudity or near-nudity is the rule, gender differences are visibly expressed through body adornment such as tatooing, scarification, jewelry, tooth mutilation, and the like.

Interestingly, similar differences in dress and body adornment are also widely used to mark differences in rank or social status. They are then known as "sumptuary regulations." Nevertheless, the widest use of visible symbols of status differences have been applied to sex and to age as the two most widespread bases of social differentiation. Seen in that light, transvestism is clearly a form of social protest, whereas homosexuality is either a last resort, or the expression of a personal penchant. An interesting hypothesis worth testing cross-culturally is that male transvestites are less stigmatized than female ones because the former merely "demote" themselves to female status, whereas the latter challenge male domination and thus threaten the power structure. Indeed, it seems that most cases of institutionalized transvestism, such as the ones mentioned earlier, have involved males playing female roles.[3]

Beyond differences in dress and body adornment, sex roles are also symbolically differentiated in most societies through a combination of rituals, taboos (for example, menstrual or postpartum), spatial segregation (separate sleeping quarters, men's clubs), and rules of etiquette (for instance, "chivalry"

---

[3]Similar phenomena exist in racial caste societies. For instance, in South Africa, a "white" person can much more easily "demote" himself to "colored" status than vice versa. Some whites living maritally with blacks, a punishable crime in South Africa, have opted for racial demotion as a solution to avoid prosecution, and their petitions for reclassification have sometimes been granted.

and "gallantry" in the Western tradition). All these mechanisms are basically means of entrenching a *status hierarchy*, and are also widely used to differentiate invidiously on bases other than sex. Some authors (Tiger, 1969; Tiger & Fox, 1971) have suggested that the organization of males in sex-segregated groups is biologically rooted in the evolutionary history of man as a hunter, but, as groups choose also to segregate themselves on the basis of age, education, class, occupation, ethnicity, "race," and many other invidious distinctions, the sociogenic hypothesis is more plausible. More convincing is the argument by Tiger and Fox (1971) that sex and dominance are closely linked in primates; thus, the tendency of men to organize in sex-segregated and exclusive groups would become an expression of male dominance over females and the young. Male seclusion, like other forms of exclusiveness, would seem to be more the expression of a negative desire to exclude than of a positive bond among men.

So far, we have established the following generalizations about sex role differentiation:
1. It is present in all societies.
2. It is instilled very early in the socialization process, typically in infancy, long before either adult role is to be assumed.
3. It is symbolically expressed through sharply distinct styles of dress and body adornment, and frequently also through rituals, taboos, spatial segregation, and etiquette.
4. It is functionally expressed through a sex-based division of labor in which a few social roles for which the biological advantages of either sex are obvious (war, infant care) are universally or nearly universally ascribed to the same sex.
5. The sexual division of labor is invariably elaborated well beyond the biologically based limitations, each society ascribing most of its occupations solely or overwhelmingly to a single sex.
6. As might be expected, when the sexual division is not rooted in biology, there is little cross-cultural consistency in the ascription of given occupations to either sex.
7. Deviations from socially ascribed sex roles are typically stigmatized by means ranging from ridicule and lowered status to ostracism and death.
8. Although individual women may outrank individual men, men as a group invariably wield more power and status than do women.
9. The degree of disparity between the status of men and women in a given society ranges from near equality to full-blown male tyranny.

10
After *The Malay Dilemma*: Colonial Heritage and Ethnic Exclusion in Malaysia

Souchou Yao

Introduction

Malaysia's relationship with the British Commonwealth can be best described as 'circumspect'. Since national independence in 1957, Malaysia's state policies of ethnic exclusion[1] have not received tough censure from the British Commonwealth in the way some 'rogue member states' like former South Africa, Fiji and Zimbabwe have done. To the disappointment of local progressive forces,[2] the British Commonwealth has been largely silent on the state violation of human rights such as the arrest and imprisonment of activists and politicians like opposition leaders Lim Kit Siang, and the ex-Deputy Prime Minister Anwar Ibrahim. In the eyes of the Commonwealth and the international community, Malaysia is not an 'undemocratic state' in the same way as Myanmar or Colombia. Malaysia has, in all appearances, parliamentary rule in the Westminster model; she is also a rising star among the NIEs (Newly Industrialized Economies) and actively courted, even in the post-1997 Asian financial crisis, by foreign investment and multinational corporations. Malaysia's economic success and international standing has helped to deflect criticism by international bodies like the Commonwealth.

This brief survey obviously over-simplifies the institutional and multilateral relations between Malaysia and the British Commonwealth. However, this chapter will be empirically judicious and focus on an aspect of 'British influence' on Malaysian social policy which has had a major and lasting influence: the policy of ethnic exclusion. More particularly, we highlight the central role of colonialism in giving credence to the idea of Malays as the 'original race' deserving social protection.

138

Over the years there can be no doubt that this *bumiputra* policy has consolidated the wealth and political power of the Malay elite in the apex of UMNO (United Malay National Organization) – the major Malay political organisation and dominant partner in the ruling coalition government. UMNO is the heartland of Malay nationalism and thus the pulse of Malaysian politics. In the UMNO General Assembly in June 2002, the Malaysian Prime Minister Dr Mahathir famously cried out of a feeling of helplessness in pulling his own people out of a culture of dependency on government handouts. Dr Mahathir's tears may well be read as signalling the tragic outcome of a redistributive social policy strategy built upon racialism and ethnic monopoly of rights and benefits. In this regard, a point needs to be made about the effects on the intended beneficiaries themselves. In Malaysia today, it is global forces like modern capitalism rather than transnational institutions like the British Commonwealth which bring the cosmopolitan pressure. Echoing the 'great transformation' in Marx's vision of capitalism (Marx and Engels 1959), these forces have the potential of breaking up the ethnic self-obsession of different communities, not the least among the Malays.

Colonialism and Malay cultural identity

As the shaper of national politics, and a source of inter-ethnic conflict, the so-called *bumiputra* ('Sons of the Soil') policy grants special privileges to Malays in the areas of education, state and national politics, the military, national culture and the economy. Officially, the pillars of Malay identity are recognised as *bahasa, raja dan agama* or language, the royalty and religion (Islam) (Shamsul 1999: 18); they form the powerful ideology of *ketuanan Melayu* or Malay Ascendancy. Historically, the key markers of 'Malayness' emerged out of the understanding of colonial writers and administrators like Stamford Raffles and William Marsden who often 'fostered special feelings of friendship' for Malays (Shamsul 2001: 75). Colonial texts helped to bring the term 'Malay' to common usage. Raffles, for instance, rendered the title of the major Malay text *Peraturan Segala Raja-Raja* into, more simply, *Sejarah Melayu* and in English, 'Malay Annals'. Similarly, Marsden (1811) in his *History of Sumatra* described the peninsula east of Sumatra as the place of origin of Malays, and gave it the name 'Malay Peninsula' – the precursor of the Malay term *Tanah Melayu* or literally 'Malay-land'. From these ideas about Malays as the 'first and original inhabitants' was developed the intractable notion of 'Malay race'.

The special relationship with colonialism thus nurtured a distinct primordiality in a Malayness which was previously open and pluralistic. In the 1840s, *bangsa Melayu* or 'Malay race' was used by Malay writers and began to find its place in the public arena. By 1891 'Malay' as a racial category – together with 'Chinese' and 'Tamils' – began to enter the colonial population census (Shamsul 2001: 76). Over the following decades uncertainty surrounded the British unique treatment of Malays until 1928 when the parliamentary undersecretary of state W.G.A. Ormsby-Gore confirmed that 'the primary object of our share in the administration ... must always be the progress of the indigenous Malay inhabitants ... (Ormsby-Gore 1928: 17–18; in Smith 1974: 259).

The British preservation of Malay political sovereignty was not without an economic motive. By a mixture of political/military intervention and indirect rule via the feudal Malay elite, the colonial power hoped to rationalise and settle the political and administrative troubles among the Malay states which had threatened British and Chinese investment in rubber and tin (Palmers 1974: 252). However there was also concern over the 'culture' of Malays which many British officials felt was in danger of being destroyed by the 'powerful and materialistic influences (represented by Chinese and Indian residents) which accompanied British rule.' (Palmers 1974: 258)

In any case, the colonial idea was seized upon by Malay nationalists. Malay nationalism racialised the cultural condition of *kemunduran* (backwardness), so that Malays become a people with distinct culture and tradition and under threat by 'other races'. For these historical reasons, in contemporary Malaysia, the idea of 'Malay deprivation' is a far more complex notion than simply the 'reality' of Chinese economic domination. For the Malay subject, the Chinese Other has become a means of self-definition. As a figure of self-inscription and one who helps to deflect the Malay subject's vulnerability, *alterity* ('otherness') quite simply 'incites' the regime of *exclusion* and *inclusion* in the ethnic social politics of Malaysia. The foundational idea of the state policy relies on the construction of *bangsa Melayu* as the 'first people' besieged and marginalised by the 'immigrant races'. Over the years, 'Malay's special positions' continues to provide the original point of reference for the state pro-Malay social policies, and no less so for Malay identity formation.

The Malay Dilemma and the making of *alterity*

The relationship between 'indigenous Malays' and 'immigrant races' points to the fluidity in the construction of alterity in order to give

Bangsa Melayu both substance and urgency. After independence, the post-colonial state took over wholesale the idea of *Bangsa Melayu* based on European racist discourse. The master text that so keenly achieves this is undoubtedly retired Prime Minister Dr Mahathir's *The Malay Dilemma* (1970).

When he published the book in 1970, Mahathir was still in the political wilderness. As a medical doctor, he drew on laws of hereditary science and applied them to Malay cultural practices. What emerged was a fusion of crude biologism and bad sociology, both relentlessly placing Malays in a *cul de sac* of social disadvantage and stunted biological development when compared with other immigrant communities. The origin of the problem, Mahathir argued, lay in the natural fecundity of the tropics in which Malays had traditionally founded their settlements. Here, in the richness of the tropics, even the weak and feeble-minded could survive and propagate. Natural abundance had ironically become an evolutionary trap by protecting Malays from the strenuous logic of natural selection.

At the same time the formulation silently but surely drew attention to the 'Chinese endowment'. The point is therefore famously made. The 'survival of the weak' among Malays is serious problem when placed in the context of a multiethnic society, where the 'immigrant communities' are already toughened by the environment of their home countries. The rural Malays are not a hardy and resourceful people. They are also presented as burdened with a form of Islam that is distinctively anti-modern and that sanctions, among other things, endogamy and thus 'the Malay partiality towards in-breeding' (Mahathir 1970: 24).

Mahathir's construction of the Chinese endowment thus 'fixes' an originary site from which he is able to reflect his understanding of backwardness and the genetic faultline of the 'Malay race'. On this site is laid the ethical cornerstone of contemporary pro-Malay *bumiputra* policy. For Mahathir and other Malay nationalists, such policy achieves its moral primacy and natural justice by countering Nature's work, by restoring Malays to the positions they deserve – vis-a-vis the immigrant communities.

The rise of the Melayu Baru

With regard to the British colonial heritage, the 'special position of Malays' suggests two crucial points. In the first place, there is no doubt that the central ideas underpinning *The Malay Dilemma* were already circulating in the colonial understanding of the racial characters of the peoples under its rule. For instance, opinions regarding Chinese commercial talent and propensity for hard work, and the Malay 'lack' of precisely these same qualities, were much in currency at the time (cf. Yao 1999, Alatas 1977). Such understanding is related to the pragmatics of 'divide and rule'; the purpose was to foster a kind of cultural – and economic – specialisation in order to slot Malays, Chinese and other 'races' in the colonial order.

Further, the idea of 'Malay disadvantage' constructs the Chinese Other as a figure of ambivalence. For the Malay subject, the Chinese Other is a figure deserving denunciation on the one hand, and inviting cultural emulation on the other. And out of this, the Chinese Other offers the final standards against which Malay achievement will be measured. This may well be the more elegiac Malay dilemma: in the construction of the Other, the idea of 'Malay special position' also becomes the source of Malay subjects' own infantalisation. This, I believe, is the more enduring – and psychologically graver – consequence of the British colonial view of the racial characteristics of the colonised peoples. All these have a special relevance in contemporary Malaysia. The pro-Malay *bumiputra* policy, despite Dr Mahathir's rhetoric, carries fateful consequences for its beneficiaries. For under pressure of capitalist modernity and transnational forces, key elements of the Malay professional elite – the so-called *Melayu Baru* or New Malays – are beginning to examine critically many aspects of state policy. And they do this precisely by questioning its universal benefit for Malays.

The growth of the Malay middle classes has to be seen in the context of the New Economic Policy (NEP) and other pro-Malay initiatives which have, especially during the Mahathir administration, nurtured *bumiputra* capitalists and professionals as a key objective. The constitutional reform to curtail the prerogatives and prestige of the Sultans, for instance, says much about the changing class structure among the Malay political elite over the Mahathir years. At the same time, scholarship schemes for *bumiputra* students, the massive state intervention in the economic sphere as well the corporate ownership of the ruling UMNO – what Joel Kahn calls 'party capitalism' (1992: 97) – have produced middle classes lodged between the Royal, with its traditional feudal allegiances, and the rural and urban poor. The so-called *Melayu Baru* range from the corporate 'wheelers and dealers' closely associated with the UMNO power base, the core of those organised around Keadilan who make up the Anwar supporters, to professionals and academics of uncertain allegiance, and even to Malay professionals working overseas. They can be modern, progressive, piously Islamic, corrupt, urban, hedonist and more. In regard to the *Melayu Baru*, the problem facing us is how to avoid imposing a formal coherence and unifying ideology that they do not have, yet to bring forth the subtle and imperceptible 'cultural convergence' existing among the group amidst their contrasting ambitions and political interests.

Analytically, quite a lot is at stake. For students of Malaysian society, the *Melayu Baru* signal a new epoch in which political divisions can no longer be drawn along the traditional Malay/non-Malay lines; an epoch when the most virulent criticisms against the state are coming from Malays themselves – both inside and outside UMNO. If the New Malays do not make a class, they are nonetheless seemingly animated by a common concern, by an anxiety about the social and psychological effects of the *bumiputra* policy. So it is in this sense that *Melayu Baru* have a point of convergence, just as they have a position in the changing social and economic conditions of the last decades.

To find a mediating category between wider social formation, and the values and emotions embodied in the Malay middle classes, we can most usefully deploy a concept like Raymond Williams' 'structure of feeling' (1965: 48–78). Anyone who knows about the social complexity of the *Melayu Baru* without being seduced by the formalism of a class analysis will find sympathy with his 'approach to culture':

> For we find here a particular sense of life, a particular community of experience hardly need expression, through which the characteristics of our way of life that an external analyst could described are in some way passed, giving them a particular and characteristic colour. We are most aware of this ... when we read an account of our lives by someone from outside the community, or watch the small differences in style, of speech or behaviour, in someone who has learned our way yet was not bred in them. *Almost any formal description would be too crude to express this nevertheless quite distinct/ of a particular and native style* (Williams 1965: 48; emphasis added).

If Raymond Williams's concept comes closest to describing the subtle 'cultural convergence' among the *Melayu Baru*, we still need to know something of the grounding from which they select, interpret and reinvent their ways of being in the world in what we call 'the making of culture'. The answer, I suggests, rests on the 'special position of Malays' nurtured by British colonialism, and brought to its flowering by the postcolonial state via the *bumiputra* policies and key texts like *The Malay Dilemma*. What drives the structure of feeling of the *Melayu Baru* is, in fact, the very ambivalence of the *bumiputra* policy, the contradiction and moral costs of which are, 30 years after its first implementation, increasingly coming to the fore.

Melayu Baru: contradiction and subversion

These contradiction and costs are articulated in two major arenas: Islam and the economy. Right from the colonial days, Malay nationalism had yoked its economic agenda onto cultural and political ones. 'The idiom of the Malay nationalist struggle was always put in terms of 'repossessing' (*merampas kembali*) or reclaiming political and economic dominance from the British and the immigrant population.' (Shamsul 1999: 95) As the pace of Malay economic ownership grows, Islam is being brought to bear on the economic; as indicated, for instance, by Islamic banking. At any rate, the question for the state is essentially about how to make wealth accumulation and economic drive sit comfortably with Islamic piety.

At the same time, with regard to the Malay middle classes, what is notable is their ambivalence towards the cultural effects of the pro-Malay NEP. Malaysian commentators have tended to dismiss such an ambivalence as nothing more than an internal squabble among Malay corporate elites over, say, the distribution of governmental contracts and other benefits. Badrul Hisham, for example, regards the *Melayu Baru* as nothing more than 'swashbuckling mavericks, macho men, armed with their portable hand phone, Giorgio Armani suits and Mont Blanc pens … (and drive) around Kuala Lumpur with their expensive German cars' (1998). For many Chinese, the questioning of Mahathir's administration by some quarters of the Malay elite is seen, to use the colourful phrase of an informant, like 'dogs fighting over the same piece of bone.'

Such scepticism, however, ignores many voices that ardently engage with the NEP and its effects on the Malays generally. Mokhzaqni Rahim, former professor of Economics at the University of Malaya, and managing Director of Inovest which holds the Kentucky Fried Chicken franchise, has suggested that

> *bumiputra* should get rid of the idea of owning 30 per cent of every venture … Instead of being constrained by the 'old idea of corporate ownership', … *bumiputra* (should) go for growth and the creation of

new industries which bring employment opportunities; restructuring would follow upon this   (Khoo 1992: 62)

The remark was made during a time of recession primarily to highlight the negative impact of the NEP on the national economy. The pro-Malay *bumiputra* policy, it is argued, distorts the working of the market and stifles competition, thus hindering growth and industrial efficiency of the national economy.

To these criticisms, Malay academic Abdul Rahman Embong would add UMNO leaders' obsession with 'pecuniary gains' which has led many of the 'Islamic-inclined Malay rural populace' to turn to Pas (Party Islam Malaysia) (Embong 2000: 2). Others query the moral authority of a state which has been unable to eradicate rural poverty while simultaneously nurturing a group of powerful Malays as corrupt, parasitic rentier capitalists. At the same time, interesting voices are being heard which interrogate the role of the state in installing 'the obedient and subservient Malay' through the promotion of Malay traditional 'cultural roots', according to a Malay academic interviewed. Malays need to undergo a 'mental revolution', he argues, in order to change their allegiance to the political elites, the Royalty, Islamic orthodoxy, and colonial influences.

The end of Malay ethnic self-possession?

On the whole, two major points can be inferred from these diverse criticisms. First is the professionalism of Malay capitalists, academics and technocrats who now seek to have a greater role in the society and especially in the industrial economy. Among its diverse practical effects, such professionalism suggests a propensity of some Malay middle classes to perceive their positions beyond immediate communal concerns.

Second, the overall critique reassesses the consequences of the state pro-Malay initiative, emphasising the structural dependency it has created. As usual Dr Mahathir has much to say on the issue. Repeating his frequent reminder that Malay businesses have to be competitive, he has over the recent years expressed his misgivings of the ways in which Malay entrepreneurs have become too reliant on the state, treating it like 'an open-ended opportunity machine' (Khoo 1992: 76). Whatever Mahathir's deeper political intentions, Malay businesses' inability to be competitive seems like an echo of the Malay cultural weaknesses that so moved him *in The Malay Dilemma*. His most passionate denunciation was reserved for the annual gathering of Malay leadership and rank and file during the June 2002 UMNO General Assembly in Kuala Lumpur. There he had accused Malays for having a 'stone-age mentality in IT age' and for being impatient to 'get rich quick'. On expressing his shame at the situation, his counsel perhaps carries little surprise:

> Learn from the Chinese. Remember when we sell licenses, contracts and other things to them, their cost of doing business increase. We do not have to carry the cost of buying licenses or contracts. But even though the cost of Chinese businessmen is higher, they can still make profits... .

The Commonwealth and 'National Cosmopolitanism'

It is hard not to detect here a genuine concern in Mahathir's decrying of the uncertain future of Malays in the new economy and society of the 21st century. It says much about Mahathir's charismatic personality and consummate political skill that he is able to make such an 'attack' of the NEP within the ranks of UMNO. His tearful performance before the UMNO audience urges the rewriting of *The Malay Dilemma* in the contemporary time. It is in the condition of globalisation, economic rationalisation and increasing competition, and not only in relation to the Chinese, that Malays have to find their place in the world.

In this sense, Mahathir adds his voice to the various critiques of the *bumiputra* policy by the Malay professionals and capitalists. I would like to suggest that the overall 'structure of feeling', to return to an earlier issue, constitutes a form of 'cosmopolitanism' *within the nation*; we shall call it 'national cosmopolitanism'. What justifies the use of the phrase is the rupture of the obsessive communalism that had traditionally defined Malay nationalism. There is a realisation that the ethnic binary of Malay versus Chinese no longer serves, in these times, to express the understanding of their new social and economic positions. Sceptics have viewed the self-critique of the *Melayu Baru* as nothing more than attempt to negotiate deals for themselves in the new configuration of economic and political opportunities. Nonetheless, speaking of Mahathir, it is hard not to think that what he has in mind is a new, more market savvy, modern, Malay subject. As he told the audience in a symposium on 'Malay Resilience in the 21st Century': 'The new breed of Malays are not alcoholics, gamblers, womanisers, nor one who rejects Islam and Malay customs like what is being attempted to be portrayed by those who wish to see the Malays continue to be backward and incapable of dealing with the modern day challenges'. In his vision, Islam and other traditional virtues and customs should not be the obstacle to economic progress, but instruments for 'dealing with the modern day challenges.' The cosmopolitanism of the *Melayu Baru* is similarly circumscribed.

The term 'cosmopolitanism' normally denotes a commitment to universal humanism,[3] or in the words of Bruce Robbins, to 'independence' and 'detachment from the bonds, commitments, and affiliations that constraint ordinary nation-bound lives' (Robbins and Cheah 1998: 1). However we can also think of cosmopolitanism as located, and entrenched in and arising from specified national and regional concerns. Those who embody this kind of cosmopolitanism do not necessarily look towards the universal, or anything like 'global citizenship', but apply themselves squarely to the local.[4] What this means is that, among other things, 'national cosmopolitanism' can be seen as a specific strategy of the local to manage and absorb new transnational and other universal experiences. In our case, the cosmopolitanism of the *Melayu Baru* is 'national' because the new structure of feeling it embodies encompasses national and cross-ethnic concerns in the social and economic arena 'within the nation'.

We are a long way from British colonial heritage and the state regime of ethnic exclusion. Yet considerations of these issues eventually lead to the present point. For all their convoluted desires and aspirations, the *Melayu Baru* are compelled to engage with that anxiety at the core of Malay subjectivity so powerfully inscribed by *The Malay Dilemma*. While in the past this anxiety was founded on the aggressive and commercially astute 'immigrant communities', what marks the new Malay sensibility is the realisation that the rehabilitative *bumiputra* policy is in fact weakening Malay self-initiative. After three decades of the NEP, Malay 'underdevelopment' can no longer be blamed on the fecundity of the tropics or on the culture of hard work and genetic endowment of the Chinese; rather it is now being attributed to a policy devised specifically to 'advance the Malays' in the first place.

With regard to the *Melayu Baru*, their 'national cosmopolitanism' thus implies two related processes. These are: an active response to the rationalistic ethos of capitalist modernity and professionalisation; and a suspicion of the Malay identity founded on the ethnic discriminatory policies of the state. The Mahathir administration has done a great deal in aligning the *bumiputra* policy to the aim of capitalist industrial growth. This means not only the nurturing of Malay middle class and capitalists, but also the active accommodation of foreign capital and transnational forces. The strategy, as Mahathir has famously argued, is to confine these exchanges to trade, finance and the diplomatic realm, while creating immunity against the cultural effects of 'Westoxication' (Yao 2001). In this sense, transnationalisation and global capitalism become localised, shaping national aspirations and industrial aims. 'Localisation' thus suggests that we need to understand transnational and cosmopolitan forces as having their particular cultural logics, articulating not merely sweeping secular and rationalistic forces, but new 'subjective forming' experiences as well.

The new cosmopolitan sensibility of Malays thus questions the pro-Malay policies and their cultural assumptions. These assumptions, in reproducing the discourse of the relative deprivation of Malays, creates what I have called the infantalisation of the Malay subject. This is really what is implicitly argued in the different interrogations of the NEP. The term infantalisation may be a trifle emotive, but it nonetheless encapsulates that significant ambivalence in the current reassessment of the *bumiputra* policy. If nothing else, 'infantalisation' helps to cut to the bone Mahathir's statement quoted earlier about Malay contractors, lawyers and businessmen whose survival depends on the government. But it also brings to mind British colonialism's view of Malays as gentle, childlike people living their simple life in innocent contentment. Mahathir's eager rally of Malays to 'catch up the Chinese', and colonial racialist discourse about Malays and their culture may well be underlined by a common discernment. Both thwart Malay aspirations by narrowing the horizon of hope. Both set the Malay social and economic attainment to no more than what the Chinese Other has already achieved – even in the postmodern conditions of global exchange and transnational cultural flow.

Afterward

The aim of this chapter has been to show the colonial influence on the formation of Malay subjectivity and on the ethnic exclusion policy of the state. In the making of the pro-Malay *bumiputra* policy, the British legacy became inextricably woven with national priorities and, not the least, the Malay elite's own need to maintain power and harness economic wealth. The situation is now increasingly being brought to question by the emergent cosmopolitanism of the Melayu Baru. The fact that a radical critique of ethnic exclusion has *not* come from liberal progressives, the non-Malay communities or international bodies like the Commonwealth, is highly suggestive. For one thing, it highlights the poor, underdeveloped civil society and the public sphere in the country.[5] Even so, writing as a Malaysian Chinese, I cannot but be moved by a certain optimism. For if the *Melayu Baru* can be seen as given over to a new structure of feeling, they show a propensity to see through the blind-spot of the ethnic binary and the claim to comprehensive benefits of a pro-Malay policy. The recognition of the social and moral costs of ethnic exclusion, I would like to propose, may well articulate a different vision of national politics in which advancement of 'Malay interests' has to accommodate, to a degree, a non-exclusivist approach, more in line with ideals of modern citizenship.

Notes

1. Some of the ideas of this chapter were explored in a paper presented at the Third International Malaysian Studies Conference (MSC3), Bangi, Malaysia, 6–8 August 2001. I would like to thank Anna Yeatman who directed me to the concept of 'cosmopolitanism', and Shamsul A.B. and Sumit Mandal who guided me through the evolving political landscape in Malaysia. I am however responsible for the analysis that ensues.
2. Some have expressed that the opening of virtual space by Internet has not substantially resulted in greater freedom of expression in Malaysia, see Gan (2001).
3. For Asad, cosmopolitanism is associated with a fluid and progressive sensibility eager to strike against established relations and cultural norms, one that impels a person 'to move, to change, and to invent'. (1993: 11)
4. Cosmopolitanism implies an empathy with others, and recognition of 'difference'. In the context of Western imperialism, this empathy has opened up a space in which the native/other – its culture, labour and economic resources – can be studied and appropriated. See Said 1995.
5. In interviews for this study, informants have stressed the role of Anwar Ibrahim in contributing to the situation. When as Deputy Prime Minister he had not moved towards reforming the draconian state measures under which he is now imprisoned.

References

Alatas, Hussein Syed (1977) *The myth of the lazy native: a study of the image of the Malays, Filipinos and Javanese from the 16th to the 20th century and its function in the ideology of colonial capitalism*, London: F. Cass, 1977.

Asad, T. (1993) *Genealogies of religion: discipline and reasons of power in Christianity and Islam*, Baltimore: Johns Hopkins University Press.

Embong, A.R. (2000) 'Umno and the changing political culture', http://phuakl.tripod.com/pssm/UMNO/html, accessed 3/4/2001.

Gan, Steven (2001) 'Malaysia's virtual democracy'. In Uwe Johannen and James Gomez (eds), *Democratic Transitions in Asia*, Bangkok: Friedrich Naumann Foundation.

Kahn, J.S., K.W. Loh, et al. (1992) *Fragmented vision: culture and politics in contemporary Malaysia*, Sydney: Asian Studies Association of Australia in association with Allen & Unwin.

Khoo, J.K. (1992) 'The General Vision: Mahathir and Modernization' in J.S. Kahn and F.K.W. Loh (eds), *Fragmented Vision: Culture and Politics in Contemporary Malaysia*. Sydney: Asian Studies Association of Australian/Allen & Unwin.

Mahathir bin, M. (1970) *The Malay Dilemma*, Singapore: Donald Moore.

Marsden, W. (1811) *History of Sumatra*, London: Longman.

Marx, K. and F. Engels (1959) *The Communist Manifesto*, New York: New York Labour News Co.

Ormsby-Gore, W.G.A. (1928) 'Report of His Visit to Malaya' [December 1928). In Roger M. Smith (ed.), *Southeast Asia: Documents of Political Development and Change*, Ithaca and London: Cornell University Press.

Palmer, J. Normal (1974) 'Malaysia and Singapore'. In *Southeast Asia: Documents of Political Development and Change*, Roger M. Smith (ed.), Ithaca and London: Cornell University Press.

Raffles, S. (1810 (1809)) 'On the Melayu nation, with a translation of its maritime institution', *Asian Researches* 12.

Robbins, R. and Cheah, P. (1998) *Cosmopolitans: Thinking and feeling beyond the nation*, Minneapolis: University of Minnesota Press.

Said, Edward (1995) *Orientalism: Western conceptions of the Orient*, London: Penguin.

Shamsul, A.B. (1999) 'Consuming Islam and containing the crisis: religion, ethnicity and the economy in Malaysia'. *Southeast Asian-Centred Economies or Economics?* M.C. Haodley. Copenhagen: Nordic Institute of Asian Studies.

Shamsul, A.B. (2001) 'Malay' and 'Malayness' in Malaysia Reconsidered: A critical Review.' *Communal/Plural: J of Transnational & Crosscultural Studies* 9(1).

Williams, R. (1965) *The Long Revolution*, Harmondsworth, Middlesex: Penguin.

Yao Souchou (1999) 'Social virtue as cultural text: colonial desire and the Chinese in 19th Century Singapore'. In Reading Culture: Textual Practices in Singapore, Phyllis G.L. Chew and Anneliese Kramer-Dahl edited. Singapore: Times Academic Press.

Yao Souchou (2001) 'Modernity and Mahathir's Rage: theorizing state discourse of the mass media in Southeast Asia', Yao Souchou (ed.), in *House of Glass: Culture, Modernity and the State in Southeast Asia*, Singapore: Institute of Southeast Studies.

11
The Tyranny of Home Ownership: Housing Policy and Social Exclusion in Colonial and Post-Colonial Hong Kong

James Lee

Introduction

Social policy in Hong Kong has generally been regarded as an example of the much talked-of East Asian social welfare model (Goodman et al. 1998; Gough 2000; Hort and Kuhnle 2000; Tang 2000; Holliday 2000; Ramesh and Asher 2000; Gough 2001; Aspalter 2002). This paper adopts a more cautious approach. The Asian financial crisis has exposed fundamental weaknesses in such a model. Simply emphasising Confucius values, work ethics, family obligations and supportive/directive state institutions (Tang 2000; Chen 2000; Ramesh and Asher 2000) cannot ameliorate social ills, particularly during an acute economic downturn.

Since 1997, Hong Kong has seen rapidly rising unemployment, widespread income and wealth contraction, and negative equities for those who had spent their life savings on their first home. The existing social welfare network is incapable of meeting social needs, as evidenced by the rising number of family breakdowns and families-at-risk. The number of new cases of public assistance has reached an historic high, at the very time government is seeking ways to cap social expenditure. A consistent pattern of welfare service retrenchment (Yu and Cheung 2003), coupled with parallel processes of social exclusion, is now underway. This paper demonstrates that one sector of social policy – housing and home ownership – has been of special import for the downward trajectory of socio-economic well-being in Hong Kong. The 'concluding' colonial government's housing policy, which placed home ownership at the core of its economic strategy, has contributed significantly to the destabilisation of the housing system; inaugurating an acute process of social exclusion whereby many households are facing multiple deprivation as a result of being trapped or lured into home ownership.

East Asian economies and housing policy models: the primacy of housing as a source of growth

Housing in East Asia is not seen – as in the west – either as a commodity for exchange or as a merit good for distribution. Housing is always regarded as a mixture of both. Nevertheless, housing policy in East Asia could be classified into three broad models: the *liberal-market*, the *socialist-market* and the *corporatist market* (Doling 1999). All three models place emphasis on a growth-oriented economy and engage market criteria as an important consideration for the delivery of housing. Their differences lie not so much in whether a market-oriented strategy is used, but rather how it is used (Table 11.1).

The *liberal-market* model is characterised by a housing system that uses the private housing market as the major distributor of housing. The government provides a small number of public rental housing units to cater for the needs of the poor while the private market is dominated by a large owner-occupation sector, complemented by a relatively small private rental sector. Public housing under this model is largely considered a form of residual welfare. An example of this model of housing policy can be found in Taiwan, where the public housing sector accounts for only five per cent of the total stock of accommodation. A similar situation also applies in South Korea, where the public housing sector accounts for only 8 per cent of total housing stock.

The *socialist-market* model is characterised by a great degree of state intervention via public housing. However the main difference between a pure socialist and a *socialist-market* model has been the progressive adoption of market strategies in the production and distribution of such housing. Traces of this model could be found in the Hong Kong of the 1970s, when government was building mass social housing for rent, accounting for nearly 40 per cent of the housing system. Today perhaps the socialist market model finds its greatest demonstration in China's current housing system (Lee 1999).

The third model – *corporatist market* – is characterised by the domination of institutional arrangements to facilitate mediation between competing housing interests. The assumption is that, under conditions of

Table 11.1 Three Models of Housing Policy in East Asia

	Liberal-market	Socialist-market	Corporatist-market
Basic housing system	• A combination of private and social housing, with the latter usually playing a supplementary role (e.g. Taiwan and Japan)	• A large social housing sector characterised by a high degree of producer subsidies • A small private housing sector (e.g. China, pre-1987 Hong Kong)	• A major part of the housing sector is provided through corporatist market arrangements; the distinction between market and state is blurred (e.g. Singapore)
Relationship between the public and the private housing sector	• The market acts as the major distributor of housing; public housing is essentially complementary and supplementary	• The state as the major distributor of housing; private housing only plays a minor role	• The distinction between private and public housing is blurred as the housing system is dominated by corporatist arrangements
Tenure structure	• Mainly private sector home ownership, supplemented by a small public rental/ownership sector	• Mainly public rental housing, supplemented by a small private ownership sector	• Mainly state-subsidised home ownership, supplemented by a small private housing market
The nature of housing	• Housing is essentially seen more as an asset with potential for a high exchange value	• Housing is essentially seen as a merit good	• Housing is seen as essentially both an asset and a privilege

Table 11.1 Three Models of Housing Policy in East Asia – continued

	Liberal-market	Socialist-market	Corporatist-market
Housing finance	• State subsidy is minimal and mean tested; housings are largely financed by the individual household through the market	• High level of state subsidies through subsidised rent, house price and tax relief	• Housing finance is mainly a combination of state subsidies and individual savings (e.g. the Singapore CPF)
Role of the State	• Plays only a minimal role except housing for the urban poor • Policy assumption – that the free market is the best way to distribute housing resources	• high level of state intervention in the production and provision of housing • Policy assumption – accepts that housing is a universal public good	• high level of state intervention in the provision of housing, but not necessarily direct production • Policy assumption – accepts there is market failure & that the state needs to regulate housing allocation

extreme constraint – for example in a situation of absolute scarcity in urban land supply – the market might not be the best way to allocate housing resources. In order to ensure an adequate supply of affordable housing the state needs to orchestrate an optimal level of coordination between various competing interests: namely the developers, the construction sector, and potential consumers. Under appropriate conditions, the state might even act as a competitive producer of affordable housing, as in the case of Singapore, where the Housing Development Board (HDB) produces and distributes 86 per cent of home ownership flats for sale. Housing is practically monopolised by the state in this case, with pricing controlled by an affordability index.

These three conceptual models are of course highly abstract. Nonetheless, the most important element that underpins them all is the salience of the housing sector to the economy. By this frame of reference, Hong Kong housing policy has veered between *liberalist market* (in the post-war years), to a more *socialist-market* mode in 60s–70s (with the launch of a mass public housing programme, not least by a progressive colonial governor)[1]; only to swing back to a revised *liberalist-market* model, with the privatisation policies heralded by the 1987 *Long-term Housing Strategy*. This last prevented Hong Kong from advancing into a corporatist market mode of public housing – one which might better have balanced competing housing interests (cf. Ch. 9 above, with regard to Singapore's housing strategy).

The implications of all this are twofold. First, housing interests continue to be concentrated in the real estate sector and within the sphere of government bureaucracy; with the interests of the wider public not being equally represented or protected in the decision-making process. Second, the domination of the real estate sector has legitimised the centrality of housing to economic development (Chan 2000). In consequence, Hong Kong's economic growth over the last three decades has developed a great dependence on revenues generated from land sales and from tax revenues related to real estate transactions. In economic terms, the annual value of new buildings put in place accounts for roughly five per cent of total GDP. The real estate and construction sector share of total stock market capitalisation was estimated at 45 per cent in 1997, whereas in US it was five per cent and in UK, under 10 per cent (Renaud, Pretorius and Pasadilla 1997). Over 35 per cent of bank lending belongs to real estate and construction businesses while, in any one year before 1997, over one-third of all government revenues came from real estate and construction-related transactions (Renaud, Pretorius and Pasadilla 1997). It is this particular emphasis which has provided a special place for the real estate sector in Hong Kong and special power for the developers to assert their influence.

From social housing to home ownership: the British colonial legacy

Post-war and post-Chinese Revolution, the colonial government's public housing policies – in the wake of the notorious Shep Kip Mei squatter fire of 1953 – were intentionally residual. The object was not so much to provide housing for needy families as to clear squatters from off the roofs of high density, highly vulnerable urban centres – and to site them ideally within reach of suitable (i.e. labour-hungry) areas of industrial development. The accommodation provided was primitive. Nonetheless, such was the shortage of affordable housing in Hong Kong, these public rental units soon came to be valued as a social benefit in themselves, which potential occupants wished to have access to and to see improved on – by, for instance, the addition of lifts and private cooking and toilet facilities. The successive upgrading of public housing standards throughout the 1960–1970s, together with a constant broadening of the criteria for tenant eligibility, resulted in this public sector's becoming a highly sought-after 'bargain' commodity – never lightly to be relinquished – in tight-packed, expensive Hong Kong (Jones 1990). It was a classic case of incremental, unplanned, unintended (in this case *socialist market*) policy development.

From the early 70s, the government worked to

- streamline the Hong Kong Housing Authority and render it more autonomous from the main government bureaucracy;
- launch the Home Ownership Scheme (HOS) in an effort to cope with the demand for private home ownership.

From the early 1970s to the late 1990s, there was a more than fourfold increase in the rate of owner occupation (from 12.7 per cent in 1971 to 53 per cent in 2001) (Figure 11.1).

The preference for owner occupation had been growing rapidly – partly as a result of lack of housing alternatives, but mostly as a result of homebuyers' strong anticipation that house prices would rise still further (Lee 1999, 2002). People saw home buying as the best investment in the 1980s and 1990s (Lee 1992). Whether this represented a cultural predisposition of the Chinese people to prefer property ownership remains open to question. Property owning had certainly proved an inflation-resistant investment – and an effective vehicle for wealth-accumulation – over the decade 1987–97, when property values increased five-fold.

The late colonial government's move to boost popular interest in home ownership, 'Singapore-style' (cf. Ch. 9 above), was designed not merely to counteract the problem of long-stay, increasingly well-off families continuing to 'block-off' public rental flats by refusing to move from this bargain accommodation; but as part of a more general effort to 'root' the Hong Kong people in their territory. Hence the deliberate attempt to limit the expansion of the public housing (rental) sector from the late 1970s and the complementary effort to promote private home ownership from 1987.

According to Figure 11.1 below, owner-occupation is the only form of tenure in Hong Kong to have risen sharply. By contrast, the production of public rental housing has been falling over the past five years. Finally, the increase in home ownership has been accompanied by a decline in private renting. The only buoyant market for private renting is concentrated at the upper end of the sector – the managerial staff of international companies. Private renting for both the working and middle classes remains of poor quality and small quantity (La Grange and Pretorius 2002).

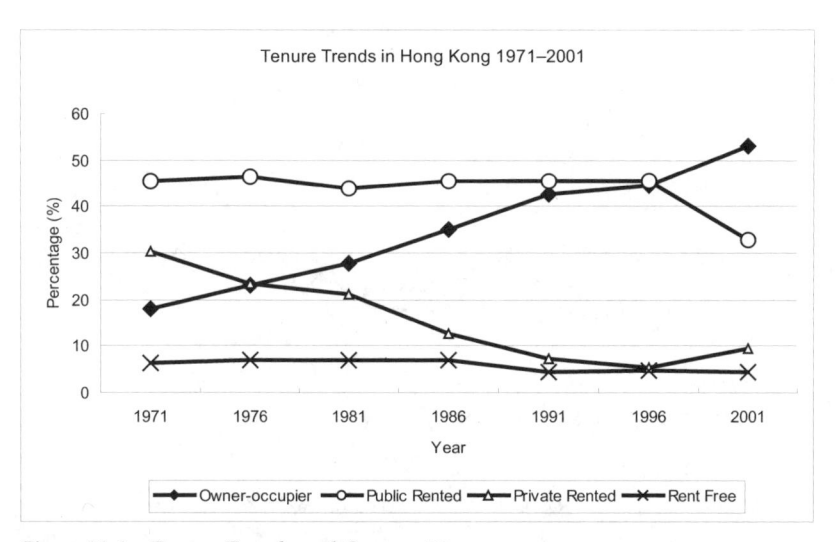

Figure 11.1 Tenure Trends and Composition
Source: Various years of Rating & Valuation Department Annual Reports and various Census Reports.

Market failure and house price inflation

House prices increased six-fold in real terms from 1973 to 1997 (Figure 11.2), an equivalent of 7.4 per cent real annual growth over a period of 25 years. Despite such a high rate of house price inflation, the increase was considered normal by government in the 1970s and 1980s. Average annual appreciation of house prices during 1973 to 1986 was six per cent, which is close to the average GDP growth of 5.4 per cent over the same period. This trend began to shift from 1986, when house prices rose more rapidly and sporadically, until the market crashed in 1993. The degree of competitiveness of the Hong Kong real estate sector was called into question by a Consumer Council study in 1996 which showed widespread existence of market failures in the property sector (Consumer Council 1996). In another study, it was also suggested that seven major developers had a market share of 75 per cent (Renaud, Pretorius and Pasadilla 1997). This was the first time a public organisation had openly admitted that the Hong Kong housing market was highly monopolised. In Figure 11.2, it can be seen that, since 1986, house prices had been on a steady rise. They fell slightly in 1995 when government used regulatory practices to limit bank mortgages to 70 per cent of property value. Even so, house prices began to rise again after a year. During the house price peak of March, 1977

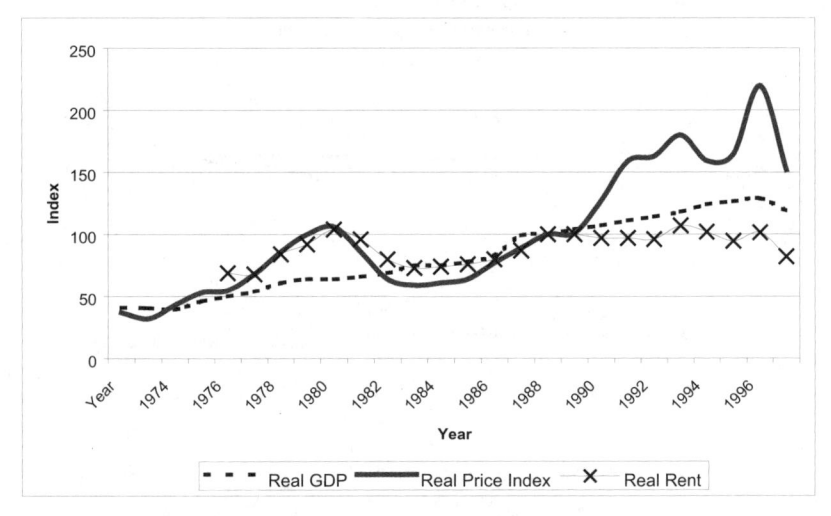

Figure 11.2 House Price Inflation and Economic Growth
Source: Lee, J., & Yip, N.M. 'Home Ownership under Economic Uncertainty: the role of subsidized sale flats in Hong Kong,' Third World Planning Review, Vol. 23 (1): 61–78.

(Rating and Valuation Department 2003), an average flat could easily fetch US$400,000. A 70 per cent mortgage ceiling meant that a family had to put down US$120,000 by way of deposit to obtain a 25-year mortgage for a bank loan of US$270,000.

At a nine per cent interest rate, the same family would have to pay a monthly mortgage bill of approximately US$3,200. Given a median household monthly income of US$2,200 in 1997, few could afford to buy.

Social exclusion and negative equity for the middle class

According to the 2001 census, about 860,000 households in Hong Kong (42 per cent of the total population) fell within the annual household income range of US$22,800–US$61,536.[2] Economically, they were the most active group, with earning power most likely to increase. However studies in the early 1990s (Lee 1992) indicated that people in Hong Kong were only barely satisfied with their current living environment, and many genuinely desired some improvement. Certainly this was the group putting the greatest pressure on the housing system.

Many middle-class people were excluded from government-subsidised rental housing because they were above the income limit; and most of them were not eligible for the government Home Ownership Scheme. Put simply they were excluded from the public housing sector. Yet they could not afford private home ownership either, at the going price. Even if they could, they would have to put up with a heavy mortgage burden and a stringent quality of life in order to make ends meet. Most of those entering the market before the 1990s, managed to gain financially. But many entering the market after 1995, suffer from negative equity since the property slump in late 1997.

The risks of home ownership are thus different for different cohorts of homeowners. Until 1998, there was no tax allowance for mortgage financed home ownership. So either you enjoyed a low rent in public rental housing, where you were entitled to what Castells et al. (1990) refer to as a *social wage,* or you had to be rich enough to buy a house and have the means to pay for a mortgage. The minimal tax allowance on mortgage interest introduced by the government since 1998 has lessened some of the burden for homeowners, but overall, home ownership is still extremely costly for many. Nevertheless, while western literature points to an increasingly marginalised and dilapidated social housing sector (Forrest, Murie and Williams 1990), the public rental housing sector in Hong Kong is thriving. It is the middle-class homeowners and private renters who are the more vulnerable in Hong Kong. Table 11.2 confirms that creeping privatisation has shifted the boundaries of social exclusion. At different levels of the housing ladder, middle-class people are now facing greater chances of being excluded; whereas for low-income people, the waiting time for public rental housing has improved from an average seven years to 4.7 years. Working class people in public housing are thus being the better provided for.

The Asian Financial Crisis and Home Ownership

The economic crisis that swept Asia in the second half of 1997 has fundamentally changed the landscape of home ownership in Hong Kong. House prices have fallen more than 65 per cent since 1997. Many of those who bought their homes shortly before 1997, are now in negative equity. Many households are shifting to private rental as an alternative, since it provides more flexibility, choice and less risk. For the first time, the demand for the state *Home Ownership Scheme* (HOS) has been dampened.

In September 2001, the government decided to put a moratorium on the sale of HOS flats. It was extended indefinitely in November 2002. This has been the combined result of a highly successful political campaign by key developers to stall government production of HOS flats and the negative publicity in the media with regard to the increasing number of negative equity cases. At the same time, the Housing Society (a small non-government housing agency concentrating on slightly up-market subsidised flats for sale) has been under pressure to trim its middle-class housing productions.

Once the most cherished tenure in Hong Kong, middle-class people now view home ownership with great scepticism.[3] In a manner quite unanticipated, the Asian financial crisis has exposed the various hidden risks of home ownership. It is now gradually being recognised by every stakeholder within the housing system – the real estate sector, the banking sector, the construction sector, as well as individual households – that home ownership can be a risky proposition. The Asian crisis has exposed a fundamental flaw in the whole housing policy setup: that the housing market works well only when the economy is in positive growth. Once the economy contracts, wealth trapped in property can quickly evaporate, giving rise to enormous negative consumption and investment consequences for individual households.

Table 11.2 Inclusion and Exclusion in Hong Kong's Housing Ladder

Housing Ladder	Inclusion	Exclusion
Private Housing (self-financed)	37 per cent households currently live in owner-occupied flats in the private sector. However, the economic recession and the unstable job market have already threatened households' ability to repay their loans.	Home owners in Negative Equity.[4] About 73,000 in Sept 2002, accounting for 16 per cent of the total mortgage borrowers. Presently, no measures are being provided to assist them. Many of them are on the verge of repossession.
Private Housing (with the assistance of the Home Starter Loan Scheme)	Since the launch of the Scheme in April 1998, and up to February 2001, 17,500 loans have been granted to eligible families and 1,000 loans to non-elderly singletons for home purchase.	Since April 1998 the property market has dropped a further 40 per cent and many households who bought their first home with the loan are now on the verge of negative equity.
Home Ownership Sale flats	297,600 flats have been sold so far to eligible households. Allocation is based on income criteria. The scheme has proved to be extremely popular since 1978 with an average over-subscription rate of 13 times.	In September 2001, the government decided to halt the sale of HOS flats for 10 months, so those households originally eligible would be excluded. In November 2002, the government has decided to suspend HOS indefinitely. This will exclude many middle-income groups who would otherwise be eligible for subsidised home ownership.

This in turn can adversely affect corporate profits, labour positions and ultimately the entire economy.

A structural defect within the colonial housing system: monopoly and market failure

The importance of the public housing sector to economic growth has been well recorded in various studies (Castells et al. 1990; Lee 1999). Castells et al. (1990) had put forth a strong argument suggesting that Hong Kong's economic growth in the 1970s and 1980s had been the indirect result of public housing investment. However, the adoption of the home ownership policy in the 1987 first Long Term Housing Strategy had fundamentally changed the ecology of public housing policy. In 1990, Chris Patten, the last colonial governor took another step for a new policy – to begin selling rental housing units at greatly discounted prices to sitting tenants, along the lines of the 'Right to Buy' policy introduced in UK in 1980 under the Thatcher government. The purpose of the policy was to promote 'quick home ownership' – an instant increase in the rate of owner-occupation, so as to meet the new 70 per cent home ownership target. This scheme was later known as the Tenant Purchase Scheme (TPS) under the new regime.

Together with a new annual housing production target of 85,000 (including both public and private housing), the new Special Administration Region Government aimed at righting the wrongs of colonial housing policy. The simple idea was that an overall increase in public housing supply would eventually lower house prices in the private market and hence curb speculation. Nonetheless these housing policy targets are now shunned, being widely regarded as a grave mistake which led to the collapse of the housing market later in 1997. Ho (2000) went as far as to suggest that it was the TPS, rather than the Asian Financial Crisis, which was responsible for Hong Kong's property slump in 1997 and after.

As it happens, however, Chris Patten's gubernatorial memoir offers exceptional insights into how Hong Kong's concluding colonial government came to interpret housing policy during the last days of British reign:

> Our greatest failings in the social field were in housing. Perhaps the problems we encountered were in the short term simply insuperable. We allocated more money to the Housing Authority, led with enormous political skill by Dame Rosanna Wong, and it continued to build more than 100 flats a day. More families become homeowners for the first time with government help. Yet Hong Kong continued to suffer from three interrelated problems. The price of home ownership remained extremely high in relation to real incomes, which were nevertheless rising. Public housing rents were so low in proportion to household income as to deter tenants from trying to move into their own property. Too many of the really poor waited for too long in sub standard accommodations for rehousing in better and cheaper flats. Housing was the area of Hong Kong's life where market forces had the least chance to operate. We suffered

from the worst eccentrically combined effects of monopoly capitalism and municipal socialism ... Any convincing attack on monopoly effectively enjoyed by a few extremely rich property developers in Hong Kong, making grotesquely large profits, could have a serious effect on market confidence at sensitive time. The stock market could have plummeted and the property market collapsed. While property prices rising too quickly causes political problems, my recent experience during the British recession suggested that falling prices, which leave many mortgaged homeowners with negative equities, cause a great deal more trouble.' (Patten 1998: 51)

Patten wrote his memoir in the second half of 1997 and had it published in 1998. Unfortunately most of what he predicted in 1998, has all happened in the ensuing five years. His memoir made clear two things.

First, there was a structural gap in the housing system which the then government knew of but refrained from doing anything about: the real estate sector being so powerful as to ensure that any attempt by the government to correct the gap would be seen as de-stabilising the economy. Henceforth this concluding colonial government chose the lesser evil – of allowing the housing market to further inflate.

Second, the colonial government continued with a programme of public housing to ameliorate the acute housing shortage, whilst knowing that this was going to do little to solve basic structural problems.

East Asian welfare debates

A cursory view of East Asian welfare values and institutions will surely produce enough varieties of experience to sustain research interest in East Asian social welfare. However, I think there are three things missing in the debate so far.

- First, the East Asian welfare model has not been subjected to rigorous testing under conditions of economic recession. Most studies clustered around the mid to late 90s, during which time the East Asian economies were largely booming.
- Second, these studies were based invariably on aggregate social expenditure data, without showing sufficient details and rationale behind their social policy components.
- Third, housing as a dimension of social policy has clearly been neglected.

Even if some studies managed to highlight selected welfare components, they contained largely data on social security, health, and education expenditures. For example, Gough (2001) based his entire work on health and social security data, while Goodman et al. (1998) based their study entirely on social security data. More recent studies, such as Aspalter (2002) and Ramesh and Asher (2000), have suffered from similar problems. Housing's omission from these analyses jeopardises the general applicability of the current discussions on the East Asian welfare model. This chapter seeks to highlight the importance of the housing dimension, particularly state-promulgated housing policies with an emphasis on owner-occupation, in the specific context of Hong Kong.

Conclusion

The Hong Kong experience has demonstrated that a system failure in the housing market can have serious repercussions on other parts of the system. I have suggested that one possible solution might be to develop a corporatist housing policy, whereby competing sectional interests in housing could be coordinated or negotiated in advance. Of course this would not be possible, without the most powerful groups within the housing system being persuaded to make concessions. If Hong Kong's post-colonial government is not prepared to give up the high-land-price policy – and if the developers are not prepared to give up their monopoly – such a corporatist-market model of shared power and responsibility will never materialise.

Meanwhile there remains the issue of social exclusion. Urban capitalism makes the housing system and home ownership the most powerful sector within East Asian cities. In colonial Hong Kong we witnessed a period of relatively stable housing policy in the 1970s, when the state accepted major responsibility for social rental housing provision (Castells et al. 1990). However, the rigorous housing privatisation processes of the 1980s and 90s have shifted Hong Kong towards full housing commodification in terms of home ownership.

Unfortunately, in Hong Kong, housing commodification seems to come hand in hand with house price volatility, income inequality and social exclusion. While the waiting list for public rental housing has been shortening in recent years as many households turn to home ownership, the same list looks set to lengthen again, as the number of households suffering from negative equity are set to be excluded from the housing system.

Jacobs (1988) once queried the notion of the 'light welfare states' of East Asia and suggested that there might be two explanations for their low expenditures:

- the high level of private finance/private saving oriented social security systems of Hong Kong and Singapore;
- the mass provision of family care work by women at home.

To that list I add a third set – capital gains from property investment. In collective terms, when everyone thinks that they can make easy money from home buying, they would be much less interested in the level of welfare, such as public housing, hence effectively minimising the political demand for more collective good. The trouble is that when the 'housing casino' collapses, all the other social problems that currently plague western societies emerge at East Asian societies' doorsteps. The absence of state welfare and hence the very 'lightness' of the East Asian welfare systems is thus unfounded. At best, it is just a transitional phenomenon during economic booms. The East Asian welfare model in fact offers no magic formula for social welfare and social well-being, as an alternative to the west, particularly during economic downturns. The tyranny of home ownership and its associated negative impact on the social well being of many middle-class households as seen in Hong Kong after 1997 provides an immense challenge for those who sought to mystify the way social policy problems are dealt with in East Asian societies.

Notes

1. Lord Maclehouse was the most progressive colonial governor Hong Kong ever had. He launched the 10-Year Public Housing Building Program in 1972 to house 1.8 million.
2. Income range from an annual household income range of HK$180,000–HK$479,988 in 2001 Census.
3. A series of public protests and demonstrations were organised in June and July 2000 amongst households with negative equities and substantial wealth loss in the housing market.
4. Results of an updated survey on residential mortgage loans in negative equity, Hong Kong Monetary Authority, March 18, 2002.

References

Aspalter, C. (ed.) (2002) *Discovering the welfare state in East Asia*, Westport, Conn: Praeger.
Castells et al. (1990) *The Shek Kip Mei Syndrome*, London: Pion Press.
Chan, K.W. (2000) 'Prosperity or Inequality: Deconstructing the Myth of Home ownership in Hong Kong' *Housing Studies*, Vol. 15 (1) January 2000, pp. 29–44.

Chen, F.L. (2000) *Working Women and State Policies in Taiwan: A Study in Political Economy*, London: Palgrave.
Cheung, S.Y.L. & Sze, M.H. (eds) *The Other Hong Kong Report 1995*. Hong Kong: Chinese University of Hong Kong Press, pp. 261–286.
Consumer Council (1996) *How Competitive is the Private Residential Property Market?*, Hong Kong: Consumer Council.
Doling, J. (1999) 'Housing Policies and the Little Tigers: How Do They Compare with Other Industrialised Countries?' *Housing Studies*, Vol. 14, No. 2 (1999), pp. 229–250.
Forrest, R., Murie, A. and Williams, P. (1990) *Home Ownership: Differentiation and Fragmentation*, London: Unwin and Hyman.
Goodman, R., White, G. and Kwon, H. (1998) *The East Asian Welfare Model: Welfare Orientalism and the State*, London: Routledge.
Gough, I. (2001) 'Globalization and Regional Welfare Regimes: The East Asian Case' *Global Social Policy*, Vol. 1(2) 163–189.
Gough, I. (2000) 'Welfare Regimes in East Asia and Europe' Paper presented to the Annual World Bank Conference on Development Economics Europe 2000, Paris, 27 June, 2000.
Ho, L.S. (2000) 'A Case Study of Economic Ecology' Centre for Public Policy Studies, Hong Kong: Lingnan University.
Holliday, I. (2000) 'Productivist welfare capitalism: Social policy in East Asia' *Political Studies*, Vol. 48(4), pp. 706–23.
Hort, S.E.O. and Kuhnle, S. (2000) 'The coming of East and South-east Asian welfare states' *Journal of European Social Policy*, Vol. 10 (2), pp. 162–184.
Jacobs, D. (1998) 'Social Welfare in East Asia: Low Public Spending but Low income Inequality?' CASE brief 7, July 1998, Centre for Analysis of Social Exclusion, LSE, London.
Jones, C. (1990) *Promoting Prosperity the Hong Kong Way of Social Policy*, Hong Kong: The Chinese University Press.
La Grange, A. and Yung, B. (2001) 'Aging in a tiger welfare regime: the single elderly in Hong Kong', *Journal of Cross-Cultural Gerontology*, 16: 257–281.
Lee, J. (1992) 'Housing and Social Welfare Revisited', in Lau, et al. (eds) *Indicators of Social Development 1990*, Hong Kong: CHUK Press.
Lee, J. (1999) *Housing, Home Ownership and Social Change in Hong Kong*, Aldershot: Ashgate.
Lee, J. (2002) 'Housing rescue package reduces government influence', *South China Morning Post*, 12 December, 2003.
Patten, C. (1998) *East and West*, London: Macmillan.
Ramesh, M. and Asher, M.G. (2000) *Welfare Capitalism in Southeast Asia*, Britain: Macmillan Press.
Rating and Valuation Department (2003) *Hong Kong Property Review 2002*, Hong Kong: Government Printer.
Renuad et al. (1997) *Market at Work*, Hong Kong: Hong Kong University Press.
Tang, K.L. (1999) 'Planning for the Unknown: Social Policy Making in Hong Kong 1990–1997' *International Journal of Sociology and Social Policy*, Vol. 19 (1/2) pp. 27–56.
Tang, K.L. (2000) *Social Welfare Development in East Asia*, Basingstoke: Palgrave.
Yu, V. and Cheung, J. (2003) 'One thousand hit the streets against cuts to welfare', *South China Morning Post*, 3 March, 2003.

12
The British Social Policy Legacy and the 'Australian Way'
Paul Smyth

Introduction

Australian social policy at the beginning of the 20th century was widely regarded (outside Europe) as 'leading the world'. A hundred years later, it is in crisis. Poverty and inequality grow while past instruments of social protection have either been dismantled or are highly constrained. Australia's characteristic 'notion of a "Fair Go"', according to Saunders (2002), 'has been abandoned, along with the basis of Australia's egalitarian tradition'. This sense of crisis has emerged during the conservative governments of Prime Minister John Howard (1996–) and arises from a programme of 'welfare reform' carried out in the name of ending 'welfare dependency'. Initially, this programme was presented in a terminology borrowed by the Government and its advisers from the United States. Blunting the edge of the American approach has been a revival of British social policy. Thus the initial, negative policy rhetoric of ending Australians' dependency on welfare was joined and possibly surpassed by the British – more positive sounding – language of promoting social inclusion or 'social participation'. The first significant British influence on Australian social policy since the 1970s, it raises important questions about the past and future of British social policy influence in Australia and the Commonwealth.

The British legacy

Thanks to a rather vigorous social policy historiography since the 1970s, we have now a good sense of the historical Australian model of 'wage earner welfare' which began to take shape in the early 20th century. Comparativists recognise it as one of the first of the now many exceptions to Esping-Andersen's three type categorisation of welfare states. But little has been written of the continuities and discontinuities of the Australian model with British social policy. What was the British social policy legacy? The question is not a familiar one in the Australian social policy literature. However, Anglo-Australian relations more generally are the subject of an ongoing historiography within which an 'old search for the "x" point on the Australian/British axis' has given way to narratives recognising multiple sources of national identity (*Australian Historical Studies* 2001, p. 78). Within the literature, the decline of British influence after World War II has become a particular focus of scholarly attention (Goldsworthy 2002). Ward (2001), for example, writes of the end of the 'British embrace' of Australian political culture and the decline of the 'imperial ideal'; and others detail the way non-British immigration and growing trade with the United States and Asia after the Second World War, taken together with British entry into the EEC, effected a watershed in the Anglo-Australian relationship (Galligan, Roberts and Trifiletti 2001). This chapter looks at Australia's distinctive social policy institutions, developed at the time of the Federation (2001), in relation to the 'British embrace'.

Anglo-Australian social policy (1) the social investment state

Accounts of the origins of federal social policy in Australia differ. The popular view is of an 'Australian Settlement' which is said to have left Australia ill-prepared for the challenges of globalisation in the 1980s. It rested on five policy planks: white Australia, industry protection, wage arbitration, state paternalism and imperial benevolence (Kelly 1992). It is claimed to have generated a self-serving, inward looking, 'protectionist' regime which lasted until the 1980s when globalisation made it unaffordable. This view has been criticised for being incomplete: for example, there is no mention of the doctrine of 'terra nullius' which enshrined white sovereignty over and denied the indigenous people's rights to the land (Stokes 2004). This chapter goes further, preferring to characterise Australian social policy history in terms of an 'Australian way'. This avoids the static, legalistic metaphor of a 'settlement' which has served to obscure the dynamic, creative and contested elements of the history (Smyth and Cass 1998). In this perspective there were three, not one, key 'historic compromises' in the evolution of social policy during the Anglo-Australian period: the 'social investment' state at

Federation, the Keynesian 'economic state' in the 1940s, and the 'welfare state' in the 1970s.

Productivist values

Between 'the years 1860 and 1914 the state played a bigger role in the Australian economy than in any other country ...' (Tsokhas 2001, p. 7). Arbitration and protection were key elements of the regime but so also was a social policy approach which can be well expressed in the term 'social investment' as already discussed by Patel and Midgley in this book (above, Ch. 6). As in New Zealand (see Ch. 13), this investment was associated with extensive government provision of capital infrastructure and utilities as well as extensive government-owned enterprises (Galligan et al. 2001, p. 121). It was designed to create a wealthy, diversified economy which could provide productive employment and have only minimal need for state-provided welfare. Macintyre (1986) expresses the aims in terms of 'meliorism, nation building and efficiency'. The productivist values of the regime were found for example in the orientation to employment creation rather than 'handouts' and the justification for the introduction of the Old Age Pension (1908) in terms of a social reward for a lifetime's work effort (Kewley 1973). The wider policy programme included free school education, slum clearance, provision of playgrounds and kindergartens, and public health measures (Beilharz, Considine and Watts 1992). An Invalid Pension (1910) and Maternity Allowance (1912) completed the development of this social investment regime.

The regime was oriented to a welfare society rather than a welfare state, with a preference for people to insure for their own health and welfare services through friendly societies and private saving. Australians were a 'remarkably thrifty people', Roe (1976, p. 17) writes, with an 'astonishing proportion' – by any international comparison – able to 'provide for themselves in the face of known social dangers'. Self insurance can be linked in turn to the system of 'wage earner welfare' in which a 'fair and reasonable' minimum wage was meant to afford male breadwinners the chance to satisfy 'the normal needs of the average employee regarded as a human being living in a civilised community'. Here, the 'welfare society' was not grounded in that atomised individualism characteristic of mid-19th century social thought but in those turn of the century social philosophies which emphasised that individuals were also family members and members of communities.

Various streams of British social thought coalesced in this development including Fabianism, ethical socialism and 'new liberalism'. For example, Sawer (2000) writes, of the 'new liberal' view that:

> 'freedom of choice' is meaningless if we don't have the material and cultural means for self-development ... social liberals knew that it was the duty of the state to intervene, whether in the labour market, the housing market or in other ways, such as through the provision of free schooling, libraries, museums and galleries, to ensure equality of opportunity.   (Sawer 2000, p. 23)

Important non-British influences were Marxism and Catholicism. The minimum wage, for example, owed much to Catholic social thinking where the emphasis was on a just, family wage to provide 'self trusting' individuals, families and community organisations with the opportunity to manage their own affairs with minimal state intrusion (Smyth 2003).

Unlike more recent social policy approaches where social politics are thought to be *against* markets, in this 'social investment state', state intervention was more a case of politics working *with* markets. This becomes clearer when we consider the Australian experience in relation to the broader themes informing the political economy of the Empire in the late 19th and early 20th centuries.

An Empire perspective

Australians, in this period, were as much citizens of the Empire as they were citizens of the newly formed Australia (Galligan et al. 2001). From Hancock's *Survey*, we can see how the ascendancy of the market had been at its height in mid-19th century Great Britain, by which time Adam Smith's vision of the 'Great Commercial Republic' arising from global free trade had overtaken the mercantilist economics informing the earlier rise of the Empire. Under mercantilism, the state had been central in establishing the conditions of national economic activity and then opening up the channels of international trade and colonial economic expansion. In the 18th century, however, increasing economic activity in the colonies meant that what Hancock called the 'economic frontiers' no longer matched the 'political frontiers' of the Empire; hence, North America's push for greater economic and ultimately political independence. The lesson that Adam Smith drew from these events, Hancock continues, was that free markets and free trade were the real source of the wealth of nations and not state power as the mercantilists had had it. By the mid-19th century the free trade view had become official British policy for the Empire; and as Hancock writes (p. 47), this made considerable sense:

> The industrial revolution gave her a flying start on all her neighbours. British industry and commerce and finance could now have for the asking an 'informal empire' far wider than the formal empire which Great Britain has lost, or any which she could hope to gain. If Great Britain chose to identify her interests with those of the Great Commercial Republic – and what other choice had she? – she could make herself its metropolis.

However, North Americans, continental Europeans and self-governing members of the Empire such as Australia did not share the Smith vision of a beneficent self-regulating global market place. According to Hancock, they believed that Smith's understanding of self-regulating markets had been exaggerated into 'a perfectionist pretence that the State could be altogether ignored'. They stressed the real world presence of 'economic disharmonies and clashes of interest'. They identified British promotion of global free trade with promotion of British manufacturing interests: in the 'Great Commercial Republic', England would prosper as the 'workshop' while dependencies (such as Australia) would be little more than suppliers of raw materials. It was the ideas of List in particular that Hancock (1940, p. 85) associates with the Australian political economy of the period:

> The ideas of List had penetrated the British Empire; they had crossed the Atlantic, they had entered the Pacific. This happened not because colonial statesmen pursued wide studies in economic theory, and decided that List was a more profound thinker than Adam Smith. Statesmen and people saw things as List saw them, and felt about them as he felt about them ...

The ideas of List do indeed reflect the Australian approach to social policy at that time. A global market was affirmed as a 'noble aspiration' but not accepted as a 'fact'. England's predominance of market power would mean trade that was free but not fair. Australia took the Listian path of using tariffs to protect and grow a more diversified economy. Australians did not want an economy that would function in the free market as merely a source of food and raw materials for the manufacturing centres of Great Britain. In Listian terms, the national system of political economy was seen to provide an important buffer between the citizen and global economic markets: it ought not disappear entirely into the *'cosmopolitical* economy' envisaged by Smith. And so, with Federation, Australia did adopt a uniform tariff policy, but like the minimum wage this needs to be seen within the framework of a Listian 'social investment state' seeking to build and broaden the productive capacities of the nation rather than a defensive manoeuvre designed to avoid market realities. In the period from Federation until World War II, Britain moved in a similar direction, establishing a system of imperial preferences, culminating in the Ottawa agreement of 1932.

Anglo-Australian social policy (2) the economic state

The second major development in the Australian way came with the transition from the Listian 'social investment state' to the Keynesian 'economic state' (Smyth 1994). Keynesianism changed the basic premise of orthodox economic thinking from the free market to the 'mixed economy' in which the enterprise of private enterprise was understood to be not enough and continuous and positive intervention by government was required for an optimal economic outcome. As Mullard and Spicker (1998, p. 29) write, the Keynesians sought:

> to break with the classical paradigm that a laissez-faire economy was the only solution for the well being of a society. Keynes showed that the market economy left to itself could not be trusted to generate sufficient investment and employment.

In the Keynesian model, consumers were no longer considered entirely sovereign in their self-interest but were understood to abridge their self-interest to the wider social interest. To generate the investment required for full employment without setting off inflation required the maintenance of a 'continuous contract' between the state, relevant social agencies and citizens. It is hard to over emphasise that this was as much a 'revolution' in social as it was in economic policy. Previously, social considerations came after the economic event. Thus in the Great Depression, nothing could be done but wait as market forces played themselves out in the individual decisions of market actors. Now that governments had assumed overall responsibility for the economy, market freedom was significantly modified to the extent that economic actors were now to work with government agencies to achieve democratically pre-determined social ends.

There was a relative paucity of welfare reform at the time: the 'safety net' was extended to include widows' pensions, unemployment and sickness benefits, child endowment and maternity leave as well as significant interventions in the area of housing (Kewley 1973). This was modest, but, it was modest by choice. Australians did not want a British or European-style welfare state. Social policy was to remain pre-eminently productivist with paid work to underpin the traditional goal of the welfare society. Traditional objectives of 'meliorism, nation building and national efficiency' found new impetus in a post-wartime ALP regime planning major public works together with a massive post-war immigration policy. The goal of social policy, according to the then Labor Prime Minister Ben Chifley, was to secure 'an increasing abundance and its equitable distribution'. Welfare, he continued, while vital to its recipient and a 'moral obligation' from the viewpoint of the nation, was not be seen as an end in itself (see Battin 1997).

This model of an 'economic state' elaborated under Labor in the 1940s was adopted in a more limited way by the successor conservative governments (1949–1972). Reluctant converts to full employment, they presided over an unanticipated strength in private investment across the 1950s and 60s which allowed for the maintenance of full employment with a maximum reliance on markets and a minimum of Keynesian style public investment and institution building. In one of the ironies of Australian social policy, this led to a narrowing and not a broadening of Australia's economic base. Australian reliance on agriculture and minerals increased while earlier hopes for diversified industrial capacities failed to materialise. As Capling (2001, p. 58) writes, the conservatives did not believe that the 'fostering of a viable dynamic and export-oriented manufacturing sector was a responsibility of the public sector'. Capling adjudges this a period of 'lost opportunities'. In the result, tariffs which had been justified originally in terms of building economic capacity and facilitating market opportunity became, by the 1960s, a way of avoiding market discipline.

The Commonwealth and a new global context

The Bretton Woods agreements for the post-war international economy provided the key global context of the new 'economic state' and they aimed for a more liberalised world trade order. This was accepted cautiously in Australia where the belief was that the US-led proposals would 'fossilise' the existing division of labour in favour of the already wealthy and industrialised (Capling 2001). According to Capling, Australia played a 'major part in determining the rules and norms of the emerging multilateral trade system' and in particular those 'positive rules' which sought to make full employment a precondition of trade liberalisation (Capling 2001, p. 13). As a 'middle power' this role also involved Australia in a lead advocacy role for developing countries whose economic future appeared to require a much more active promotion of national development than free trade was likely to deliver.

These developments occurred amid major changes in the Anglo-Australian relationship. Key factors were Britain's inability to protect Australia in the Pacific war as well as Britain's post-war economic weakness; the beginnings of a long term shift in trade to Asia and the United States in which the share of Australian exports to Britain fell from 40 per cent in the late 1940s to 5.4 per cent in the mid 1970s; and finally the break with immigration policies which had meant that until the 1940s, 98 per cent of Australians were of British origin (Greenwood and Harper 1958, Ward 2001). Nevertheless, while there was a loosening of what Greenwood (1958) called the 'soft clasp of British strength', Australia's links with Britain and the Commonwealth remained strong. Australia saw an important role for the Commonwealth in the context of the Cold War. Britain was seen as an important counter to possible 'limitations' and extravagances' in US policy and a basis for advancing the interests of the new small member states. The Commonwealth, Greenwood wrote, expressed:

> A belief bordering at times on faith ... that this meeting of East and West in fraternal association holds the promise of some advance towards a solution of one of the great problems of the day ... the experiment of assisting dependent peoples to self-government and full statehood, without a dispiriting attendant isolation. (Greenwood, pp. 90–91)

This belief, he thought had 'the allegiance of the Australian community'.

Anglo-Australian social policy (3) the welfare state

In the 1970s, Australia changed its traditional social policy orientation: away from the welfare society towards the British welfare state model. Economic policy was, of course, no longer salient in what Mishra (1984) called the 'differentiated welfare state'. With the productivist dimension of social policy apparently settled, attention turned more towards issues of consumption and distribution, or what the British

Fabian Tony Crosland had called the 'backcloth and fittings of society' (Smyth 1994).

The new social policy agenda gave attention to the consequences of the movement of married women out of the home into the paid workforce; and, associated with that, a major concern with aged care. Mass immigration created a momentum away from assimilation to multiculturalism and there was a re-emergence of an indigenous rights movement. Concern about the environmental and town-planning aspects of rapid economic growth was an early driver of the new welfare agenda. In this context the discovery that there were groups, aged pensioners in particular, who had not shared the benefits of economic growth raised awareness that more than economic growth was needed for good social policy. In addition the development of social sciences encouraged a view, on the Keynesian model, that better social outcomes might be achieved with a planned approach to meeting social needs. In a more industrialised society, it seemed that organising education, health and other social services had become too expensive and complex a task to be left to individuals, families and community associations. They would work with government in a new mixed economy of welfare (Smyth and Wearing 2002).

The Whitlam Labor government (1972–1975) shifted welfare from a residual towards a universal model. Among the initiatives were the creation of a national health service; setting up of local area development programmes; abolition of university fees; and extension of the aged pension to all people over 70 years of age. As it happened, Whitlam's welfare state reforms coincided with those changes in global economic conditions which meant that full employment could no longer be achieved as easily as it had been. Australia added its national chapter to the global 'crisis of the welfare state'. Perhaps, at no previous time in Australia's history had British welfare policy been seen in so positive a light. Curiously, it was also a time when the Anglo-Australian period drew to a close.

The end of the 'Imperial Ideal'

The demise of what Ward (2001) calls the 'Imperial Ideal' in Australia occurred with the ongoing decline of Britain's importance as a trading partner, a flowering of Australian culture, an endorsement of multiculturalism in place of the old British monoculture, an end of White Australia, and a belated granting of citizenship to the indigenous population in 1967. Macmillan's announcement (1962) of the intention to apply to join the Common Market proved a watershed when, 'even the most passionately pro-British Australian Ministers such as Robert Menzies and Alexander Downer, heard the old links snapping' (Davie 2001, p. 177). Indeed, by the time Britain finally confirmed its entry into the European Economic Community by referendum in 1975 there was little public reaction.

Nevertheless, British intellectual influences on Australian social policy remained strong, with the work of Titmuss and Marshall providing the intellectual underpinnings for the new macro social policy role of government. Institutions for positive welfare intervention were to match those of the 'economic state'. As the latter were founded in the obligation of the state to uphold the right to work, the new institutions of the welfare state were to be grounded in the newly acknowledged social rights.

Social Inclusion, globalisation and crisis in Australian social policy

Across the 1980s and 1990s, ALP (1983–1996) governments are said to have refurbished the 'Australian way' of doing welfare in response to the social policy challenge created by globalisation (Bryson 2001). Informed by an Accord of Scandinavian influence, this refurbishment was accomplished by winding back what was portrayed as the economically extravagant, universalist trend of the 1970s (Australia had in fact remained below average OECD social expenditures in the 1970s) and moving back towards a more traditional, productivist social policy regime based on full employment and 'wage earner welfare' (Smyth 2002). Under the Howard government (1996–), however, a diminishing government commitment to full employment under Labor was terminated altogether and the remaining instruments of social protection reduced in capacity. Under strong American influence, the goals of social policy shifted significantly towards 'ending welfare dependency'. To borrow the terms used by Harris in Chapter Three of this volume, welfare became less about solidarity and social justice and more about social order and participation. In this, the characteristic American concern with welfare dependency has been modified somewhat by the discourse of social inclusion or participation taken from Britain (Reference Group on Welfare Reform 2000). All of this occurred in the context of rising poverty and inequality amid strong economic growth.

People have made sense of these developments in different ways. Thus Shaver (2002) writes of the trend in current welfare reform as a transition 'from citizenship to supervision'. From this perspective, the post-World War II period is seen as a 'golden age' when we 'achieved something like T.H. Marshall's vision of social welfare ... albeit a flawed example of that vision'; with the flaw being the fact that on the whole, Australia's social rights were not granted on a universal basis but remained categorical, means-tested and paid from general revenue. Nevertheless, though means-tested, they were not miserly and have been seen by Australians as 'rightful'. Their recent diminishment follows a pattern found in other liberal welfare states of the Commonwealth such as New Zealand and Canada.

A second perspective emphasises the past centrality of 'wage-earners' welfare'. This system in tandem with highly redistributive, if targeted, welfare proved as sure a pathway to egalitarian social and economic outcomes as did more comprehensive – and more expensive – European welfare regimes (Smyth and Cass 1998). Across the 1980s and 1990s, however, progressive labour market deregulation gutted a relatively comprehensive award coverage of the work force leaving only a system of 'safety net' minimum wage arrangements. The resulting emergence of an 'un-Australian' working poor, has created an occupational illfare seriously compromising the traditional Australian social policy approach (Saunders and Taylor 2002; Saunders 2002).

Though accurate, these explanations do little to meet the central challenge facing Australian social policy today, that is, the economic critique of social spending as inefficient and unproductive. Without full employment and the 'economic state', 'wage earner welfare' and the social rights of citizenship have become problematic and not only for the ideologues of *laissez-faire* (Shaver 2002). Thus Pearson (2000) has been supported across the political spectrum for his campaign against passive welfare spending on indigenous peoples. He calls for a:

> new consensus around our commitment to welfare ... based on the principle that dependency and passivity are a scourge and must be avoided at all costs. Dependency and passivity kills people and is the surest road to social decline. Australians do not have an inalienable right to dependency, they have an inalienable right to a fair place in the real economy.

The social policy crisis in Australia, then, has arisen from the lack of fit between accounts of social policy in terms of social justice and redistribution, together with market-oriented economic policy goals focused on productivity and efficiency. Emerging social policy frameworks based on social inclusion must address this lack of fit. They cannot simply reiterate older claims based on social justice and redistribution. They must also be about production and the kind of productivist values expressed by Pearson. They must demonstrate how social policy can be rearticulated in economic policy in a more agreeable way. To this end this chapter has emphasised the neglected productivist dimension of social policy in the Anglo-Australian period.

Concluding reflection

This exploration of the British legacy in Australian social policy underscores the pre-eminently productivist basis of past Australian social policy. The Listian 'social investment state' was certainly about egalitarianism but it was an egalitarianism of opportunity arising from intensive investment in the productive powers of the national economy. From the Listian perspective, the so-called 'crisis of the welfare state' in the 1980s was arguably as much about the 'lost opportunities' to generate a broad, competitive industrial base in the 1950s and 60s than it was about any burden of welfare spending. Likewise the Keynesian state was premised first and foremost on the conviction that a people's 'inalienable right to a fair place in the real economy' would be better upheld in a mixed rather than a free market economy. Both the Listian and Keynesian frameworks offer radical ways of challenging the current neo liberal view of unaided markets as the pathway to productivity and efficiency.

The legacy also invites us to think again about the role of the nation state in promoting social inclusion. It suggests that there is unlikely to be a stark choice between the 'great commercial republic' and nation states living in complete economic autarchy. This is an urgent issue for Australia. Up to the 1970s her relationship with the global market was very much shaped by its membership of the Empire and Commonwealth, but now Australia is outside any regional trading bloc. In this regard it may well be a useful strategy for Australia to promote a stronger role for the Commonwealth in securing more favourable global economic arrangements for its multitude of small to medium member states.

Related to this lack of a regional place in the global economic order are issues of national identity. An accommodation of cultural diversity has come to replace the monoculture of the Anglo-Australian period. Australian social politics is now a more fluid, open and diverse identity. Recent attempts to Americanise Australian social policy are generally agreed to have foundered on a residual national aspiration to a

'Fair Go' (Dawkins and Kelly 2003). Attempts to renew this aspiration in the context of globalisation are likely to see Australian social policy paying more, not less attention to its British roots. Here the Commonwealth could prove a valuable forum.

References

Australian Historical Studies (2001) *Symposium Britishness and Australian Identity*, Vol. 116.
Battin, T. (1997) *Abandoning Keynes Australia's Capital Mistake*, London: Routledge.
Beilharz, P., Considine M. and Watts, R. (1992) *Arguing About the Welfare State*, Sydney: Allen and Unwin.
Bryson, L. (2001) 'Australia', in P. Alcock and G. Craig (eds), *International Social Policy*, Basingstoke: Palgrave, pp. 64–84.
Capling, Ann (2001) *Australia and the Global Trading System*, Melbourne: Cambridge University Press.
Davie, M. (2001) *Anglo-Australian Attitudes*, London: Pimlico.
Dawkins, P. and Kelly, P. (2003) *Hard Heads and Soft Hearts; a new reform agenda for Australia*, Sydney: Allen & Unwin.
Galligan, B., Roberts, W. and Trifiletti, G. (2001), *Australians and Globalisation: The Experience of Two Centuries*, Melbourne: Cambridge University Press.
Greenwood, G. (1958) 'The Commonwealth', in G. Greenwood and N. Harper (eds), *Australia in World Affairs 1950–55*, Melbourne: F.W. Cheshire, pp. 29–91.
Greenwood, G. and Harper, N. (eds) (1958) *Australia in World Affairs 1950–55*, Melbourne: F.W. Cheshire.
Goldsworthy, D. (2002) *Losing the Blanket Australia and the End of Britain's Empire*, Carlton: Melbourne University Press.
Hancock, W.K. (1940) *Survey of British Commonwealth Affairs Vol. 2, Problems of Economic Policy 1918–1939 Part 1*, London: Oxford University Press.
Kelly, P. (1992) *The End of Certainty*, Sydney: Allen and Unwin.
Kewley, T.H. (1973) *Social Security in Australia*, Sydney: Sydney University Press.
Macintyre, S. (1986) *The Succeeding Age 1901–1942, Vol. 4, The Oxford History of Australia*, Melbourne: Oxford University Press.
Mishra, R. (1984) *The Welfare State in Crisis*, New York: St Martin's Press.
Mullard, M. and Spicker, P. (1998) *Social Policy in a Changing Society*, London: Routledge.
Pearson, N. (2000) 'The Light on the Hill', Ben Chifley Memorial Lecture, http://www.capeyorkpartnerships.com/
Reference Group on Welfare Reform (2000) *Participation Support for a More Equitable Society. Final Report of the Reference Group on Welfare Reform*.
Roe, J. (1976) *Social Policy in Australia Some Perspectives 1901–1975*, Stanmore: Cassell.
Saunders, P. (2002) *The Ends and Means of Welfare*, Melbourne: Cambridge University Press.
Saunders, P. and Taylor, R. (2002) *The Price of Prosperity*, Kensington: University of NSW Press.
Sawer, M. (2000) 'The Ethical State: Social Liberalism and the Critique of Contract', *Australian Historical Studies*, Vol. 31, No. 114, pp. 67–90.

Shaver, S. (2002) Australian Welfare Reform: from citizenship to supervision', *Social Policy and Administration*, Vol. 36, No. 4, pp. 331–345.

Smyth. P. (1994) 'Australian Social Policy: The Keynesian Chapter', Kensington: University of NSW Press.

Smyth, P. and Cass, B. (eds) (1998) *Contesting the Australian Way State Market and Civil Society*, Melbourne: Cambridge University Press.

Smyth, P. and Wearing, M. (2002) 'After the welfare state ...', in S. Bell (ed.), *Economic Governance in Australia*, Melbourne: Oxford University Press.

Smyth, P. (2003) 'Reclaiming Community? From Welfare Society to Welfare State in Australian Catholic Social Thought', *Australian Journal of Politics and History*, Vol. 49, No. 1, pp. 17–30.

Stokes, G. (2004) 'The 'Australian Settlement' and Australian Political Thought', *Australian Journal of Political Science*, Vol. 39. No. 1.

Tsokhas, K. (2001) *Making a Nation State*, Carlton South: Melbourne University Press.

Ward, S. (2001) *Australia and the British Embrace: The Demise of the Imperial Ideal*, Melbourne: Melbourne University Press.

13
Redesigning the Welfare State in New Zealand

Susan St John

Introduction

New Zealand is a small exposed trading nation that has proceeded more quickly than many other nations with deregulation of the economy, removal of tariff protections, privatisation of state assets, labour market reform and promoting the ideals of free market competition. Rising social exclusion has been associated with both the neo-liberal economic reforms commenced in the early 1980s and the radical redesign of the welfare state in the 1990s. Rising social exclusion in New Zealand is linked with the growth in inequality that has been one of the fastest in the OECD (Statistics New Zealand 1999). Different ethnic groups have been affected differently. For example, Maori and Pacific Island peoples have fallen further behind the European population on income and other average social indicators of well being (Ministry of Social Policy 2001b; Mowbray 2001).[1] Moreover, the neo-liberal economic reform package also contained the seeds of disappointment. Economic outcomes have been lacklustre, inspiring a new willingness in the 2000s to discuss the meaning of social inclusion and a new view of the interrelationship between economic and social policies.

The official discourse now includes words like 'poverty' 'social inclusion' and 'social capability' but how these concepts are likely to be given practical manifestation is unclear.[2] The election of a centre left coalition in 1999 has seen some of the more dramatic changes of the 1990s reversed,[3] but the cold winds of economic reality for a small open commodity-based country in a globalised world have encouraged a cautious and conservative approach.[4] It is now critical for New Zealand to reexamine the traditional reasons for the welfare state and explore the shape of a new welfare state that can better shield citizens from the harsher aspects of globalisation. While developments in welfare in New Zealand, a small isolated nation, need to remain consistent with regional trends, her experience of the radical market approach to globalisation will be of significance to her global policy networks including the Commonwealth.

The past informs the present

New Zealand's colonial legacy is only partially reflected in the unique welfare state that developed from the late 1890s. Thomson (1998) describes the New Zealand of the 19th century as 'a world without welfare'. When the largely young and hardy immigrants from the old country came to New Zealand they sought to reinforce with even greater vigor the strong anti-welfare mood of 19th century Britain. The dominant ideology was that individuals should be self-reliant and that families should care for their own

Early laws in New Zealand formalised family responsibility. Destitute Persons' legislation imposed obligations on the relatives of the needy with deductions from wages by employers often enforced for this purpose. While the workhouses and Poor Law were hated parts of the old country and not explicitly recreated in the 'new country', other strictures such as charitable aid had much the same impact. In spite of romantic notions of New Zealand being the cradle of civilisation in terms of the development of the welfare state, the moves to wide collective responsibility were both reluctant and late.[5] Even following the introduction of the old age pension in 1898 the remnants of an anti-welfare attitude were strong. So strong indeed that throughout much of the first 30 years of the 20th century, only around 30 per cent of those eligible by age for the pension collected it (Thomson 1998).

Origins of the modern welfare state

The British influence in the development of social and economic policy continued strongly in the 20th century. The welfare state bearing the 'cradle to grave' image that originated in the Social Security Act of 1938 can be viewed as not only a response to the relief of hardship but also as a practical answer to obvious failures of private insurance markets.[6] The risks of old age, ill health and unemployment exposed by the Great Depression required a social insurance approach broadly inclusive of all citizens.

The 1942 UK Beveridge report was influential in the post-war period, although New Zealand did not adopt a similar national health service. Nevertheless the post-war period saw the full flowering of an inclusive, non-contributory, welfare state based on principles of egalitarianism and full employment. Later, the Royal Commission on Social Security (1972) emphasised the inclusive 'participation and belonging' objective of welfare provisions rather than the mere relief of poverty. Innovative polices in the 1970s included the introduction of a no-fault accident compensation scheme, a new benefit for sole parents, and expansion of universal pensions for all over the age of 60. In the 1980s, however, unprecedented increases in unemployment placed new pressures on social welfare benefits. Traditional welfare benefits such as sickness, domestic purposes (sole parent), and unemployment remained subject to income testing, while additional welfare assistance was subject to wider tests of means, including asset testing.

The 1991 reforms

The reforms in the UK in the Thatcher years found reflection in a more extreme form in New Zealand's market liberalisation of the 1980s and the welfare reforms of the 1990s.[7] The post-war presumption of the benefits system was that the realistic alternative to a benefit was a full-time, adequately paid job. However, for increasing numbers of people displaced by economic reform, part-time insecure and casual work was all that was available. This underlying conflict was recognised in Treasury papers throughout the 1980s which expressed concern about fragmentation and inefficiency in the delivery and administration of welfare payments. They also stressed the problems of overlapping income tests and the work disincentives of the high effective marginal tax rates (EMTRs) that are implicit in such tests. In some ranges of income, EMTRs could approach 100 per cent.

In 1990 the Treasury said:

> As a general rule, the more people facing higher effective marginal tax rates over longer ranges of potential income, the greater the costs to society and the greater the probable loss of output.
>
> An indication of the effect of such scales is the fact that very few people are in jobs with an income at the level where the maximum rate of benefit abatement applies; instead they tend to have no job at all, rather than work for little gain. This is worrying since it

discourages part-time work, which may be the most appropriate employment for some beneficiaries.

High levels of benefits were identified as a major factor preventing a more gradual abatement system. In December 1990, it was announced that benefits would be cut significantly (see Box 13.1) and a taskforce (the Change Team on Targeting Social Assistance) was established to design a new system of targeted social assistance. The policy document that emerged was the background paper for the wide-ranging reforms announced in the 1991 Budget.[8]

The 1991 Budget document *Welfare that Works* (Shipley 1991) claimed to present an 'integrated approach to social security and social assistance'. The problem of high effective marginal tax rates that compound as social assistance becomes increasingly targeted was to be solved:

> Although any targeting system involves a reduction of total support as family income rises, the system will be designed in such a way that people are better off earning additional income and moving from dependence to independence.
>
> The reduction in assistance will not be in sudden steps because that would mean some people might be discouraged from earning more if the final result is a drop in the total of earnings and income assistance. (This is sometimes known as a 'poverty trap'.) Instead, assistance will be phased out over a range of income so the effects of the drop in assistance on total earnings will be less severe. Support for different services will be phased out service by service.

Welfare that Works put forward a vision of a seamless, global system of abatement of all social assistance. A single family income test and a single phase-out rate were to apply across all forms of social assistance using family accounts. Unfortunately, the more that is included for abatement, the longer the income range over which abatement applies, and the more people are affected.[9] Family accounts proved to be unworkable not least because of the nature of the modern fragmented and fluid family whose circumstances are not readily summarised for abatement purposes using a smart card.[10]

Although many other aspects of *Welfare that Works* also proved unworkable, the move towards an ever more tightly targeted welfare state proceeded.[11] Far from the 1970s ideals of 'participation and

Box 13.1   Welfare Changes (NZ) 1990–1993

- Most benefits, such as the Sickness, Domestic Purposes Benefit and Unemployment Benefit were cut by between five per cent and 27 per cent from April 1991. These cuts have not been restored.
  The age for youth rates for the unemployment benefit was extended to the age of 25. Stand down periods were lengthened and generally the eligibility rules, especially for the unemployment benefit, were tightened. The rates of abatement of benefits for other income were not changed, and the level of exempt income was held at levels last adjusted in 1986.
- The universal family benefit, a non-taxable per child universal benefit of $6 a week, was amalgamated from 1991 with Family Support and from that time all family assistance became targeted using the test of combined parental income.
- Allowances for tertiary students under 25 became fully conditional on parental income even in cases when parents are divorced and whether or not both parents actually contribute to their son or daughter's support. Students who borrow from the state for fees and living costs must repay this assistance plus interest, at the rate of 10 cents in each extra dollar earned above a low minimum. In 1999 interest on the loans of students still studying was removed.
  Certain health subsidies, formerly universal, were restricted to those in low income families through the introduction of the Community Services Card. Later, in 1996, as a concession to the real difficulties faced by families visits to the GP were made free for all children under six by the provision of a $32.50 subsidy. A visit to the GP can be approximately $40–50. With the card, a subsidy of $15 applies for an adult and $20 for a child. These subsidies remain unadjusted for inflation.
- Housing reforms that took effect from 1 July 1993 brought about a rationalisation of all former assistance into an income and assets-tested accommodation supplement.
- The state pension was to become a tightly targeted social welfare benefit to be applied for only by the poor. However the legislation, which was passed on Budget night 1991, was subsequently overturned in response to public pressure. The age of eligibility was raised from 60 to 65 between 1992 and 2001.

belonging', the social policy of the early 1990s was driven by concepts of self-reliance, targeting and a movement away from universal provisions of all kinds (Boston et al. 1999). Families, for example saw all their family assistance become dependent on joint parental income with the abolition of the universal child benefit, while student allowances also become tested against parental income up to the age of 25.[12]

The rise of the New Right and the demolition of the traditional welfare state in the 1990s might be seen to hold portents of a return to the values of the 'world without welfare' of the past. But, as Thomson (1998) suggested, the early 'world without welfare' depended crucially for its success on the state playing an active role in other ways. Land and home ownership was actively encouraged by state assistance, while for much of the early period, massive government public works made employment readily available. As neither of these underpinnings were apparent in the 1990s, the exhortations to self-reliance for many people became somewhat empty rhetoric.

Once the technocratic solution to overlapping income tests in the form of family accounts was discredited, it could be argued that the rationale for a total targeting approach also disappeared. However many of these reforms proceeded in isolation one from another, intensifying rather than solving the welfare mess and poverty traps identified by the Treasury in the 1980s (St John and Rankin 1998, 2002).

Although the government was determined to balance the budget, cutting government spending was not the main reason given for these changes. It was claimed that the welfare state actually created poverty by encouraging state dependency. So lower social welfare benefits and tighter targeting were required to push people into finding paid work. However, the numbers on benefits actually rose in the 1990s, especially the numbers on sickness, invalid and domestic purposes benefits (Work and Income NZ 2001).

The economic framework

The goals of economic and social policy since the mid 1980s have stressed achieving and maintaining low inflation, removing economic distortions, level playing fields and the growth of Gross Domestic Product (GDP). In the pursuit of free trade NZ has proceeded more quickly than many other nations in removing tariff protections. The negative impact of the reforms has been charted by various commentators e.g. (Dalziel 1999a, 1999b; Easton 1997a, 1997b; Jesson 1999; Kelsey 1997, 1993). Rapid deregulation and privatisation and the progressive withdrawal of the state from the economy have been accompanied by lacklustre growth, high interest rates, a widening of the income distribution, a ballooning current account deficit and overseas debt.

At the end of December 2002, New Zealand's net international investment position stood at minus 100.7 billion.[13] The accumulated impact of high and persistent current account deficits have serious implications for further indebtedness and the increasing foreign ownership of New Zealand's productive assets. While low inflation has been achieved, and growth in the early 2000s has been relatively strong, there are indications that this has been due to a number of fortuitous factors. High immigration, a booming real estate market and high world prices for primary commodities has seen unemployment levels fall to historically low levels, while domestic prices have been held in check by a high exchange rate. In 2003 some of these influences are waning, suggesting a slowing economy and emerging pressures on the welfare system.

Three major Acts tightly define the economic framework in New Zealand. The Reserve Bank Act 1989, has a singular focus on keeping inflation low (one to three per cent) by using interest rate adjustments. There is no obligation placed on the operation of monetary policy to consider the distributional implications of tight monetary policy.

The Fiscal Responsibility Act 1994 requires fiscal prudence and places emphasis on achieving operating surpluses and repaying public debt. There is no requirement to monitor social impact. The choices between tax cuts, spending on infrastructure such as schools, roads, water systems and hospitals, repaying debt, or buying shares, are not required to be evaluated in social impact terms.

The economic framework also includes the Employment Relations Act 2000 which replaced the early Employment Contracts Act of the 1990 reforms.[14] While it has been suggested that a 'Social Responsibility Act' might balance the otherwise narrow economic focus of these three defining Acts, the concept has received only limited attention (Boston, St John and Stephens 1996).

Tax reform

New Zealand's tax system was radically reformed from the mid 1980s with the intent to level playing fields and remove distortions (Scollay and St John 2000). In 1986, the Labour Government brought in a comprehensive Goods and Services Tax (GST) on almost everything except accommodation. Benefits were adjusted for the impact of GST when it began but a rise in the GST from 10 per cent to 12.5 per cent in 1989 was made without any further compensation. Moreover, the benefit cuts in 1991 effectively undid the original compensation.

The tax and benefit package of 1996

A new, lower tax structure, justified by emerging fiscal surpluses was announced in the 1996 budget. Taxes were cut substantially and family assistance increased (see Table 13.1 and 13.2).

The government claimed that these measures would benefit low and middle-income families, but in fact, high-income earners gained the most. For every dollar of extra expenditure or forgone revenue in the programme, 40 cents went to non-family groups, 31 cents went to families in the top two income quintiles, and only 29 cents went to the 'target' group of low and middle-income families (Dalziel 1999a). Single-earner families gained far more than low-income two-earner families, with some low-income families gaining very little.

Social welfare benefits after income tax were unchanged by these tax reductions, and families on benefits were not entitled to the new child

Table 13.1 New Zealand Tax Schedule for Personal Income Tax

Bracket	Effective marginal tax rate* 1988–1996 (%)	Effective marginal tax rate* 1 July, 1998 to 1 April, 2000 (%)	Effective marginal tax rate* from 1 April, 2000 (%)
$0–9,500	15	15	15
$9,501–30,895	28	21	21
$30,895–38,000	33	21	21
$38,001–60,000	33	33	33
$60,000+	33	33	39

* Includes the low income earner's rebate

Table 13.2 Weekly Maximum Rates of Family Support and Child Tax Credit

	Prior to July 1996	From 1 July 1998 Family support	From 1 July 1998 Family support and child tax credit
For the eldest child:			
Aged 0 to 15 years	$42.00	$47.00	$62
Aged 16 years or over	$42.00	$60.00	$75
For each additional child:			
Aged 0 to 12 years	$27.00	$32.00	$47
Aged 13 to 15 years	$35.00	$40.00	$55
Aged 16 years and over	$35.00	$60.00	$75

tax credit of $15 a week per child.[15] The increase to Family Support, especially for the first child (Table 13.2) was miniscule compared to the tax cuts delivered to high-income earners. Dalziel (1999a) calculated the combined impact of the tax and family support package as only 7.4 per cent to those in the lowest quintile of household income, and one third to top quintile.

Overall the tax system imposes a high burden on low-paid workers. The first $9,500 of income is still taxed at the relatively high rate of 15 per cent. Despite inflation since 1986 of over 60 per cent, the threshold for this bottom rate has not been adjusted. Meanwhile the top threshold of $30,875 has been raised to $38,000. On income of between $9,501 and $38,000, the tax rate is now 21 per cent. On income over $38,000, the top rate was 33 per cent until July 2000, when the Labour/Alliance government raised it to 39 per cent for those earning over $60,000 per annum, thus restoring some progressivity.

OECD figures (2002) show that government spending at 36.4 per cent of GDP is modest compared to other successful countries (e.g. UK 37.8 per cent, Norway 39.4 per cent, Denmark 51.1 per cent, Germany 44.5 per cent, Canada 41.9 per cent). However, New Zealand is perceived by the business community to be a large government, high tax country, especially in comparison with Australia whose ratio is 32.9 per cent.[16] International comparisons can, however, be misleading in debates over the size of the state. For example, in contrast to many other countries the state pension in New Zealand is fully taxed, with tax flows straight back to government, inflating both the tax and the spending figures. In Australia most old age pensioners pay no tax. Adjusting for tax on pensions alone would reduce New Zealand's government spending ratio about two percentage points. Thus there needs to be a better understanding of these measurement issues if the debate over regional convergence in social policy matters is to be meaningful.

The rise of social exclusion

The consequence of policy changes documented above has been that during a time of limited economic growth, income has been redistributed toward the highest deciles (see Figure 13.1) and away from the middle and lowest deciles. In spite of a much stronger economic performance in New Zealand since the late 1990s, relative poverty, especially among families with children, remains a major social problem in New Zealand (Child Poverty Action Group 2003).

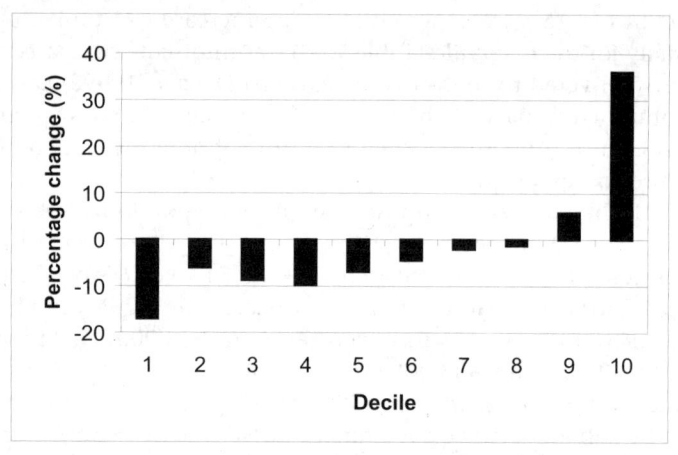

Figure 13.1 Mean Household Equivalent Disposable Income Changes (NZ) 1982–1998
Source: Mowbray (2001).

While New Zealand has no official poverty line, the government itself uses a 60 per cent of equivalent net-of-housing costs disposable income measure (Ministry of Social Development 2002). According to this measure, there was a dramatic increase in the percentage of children in poverty between 1988 and 1993. While there had been some improvement by 1998, by 2002 that gain had slipped away with 29 per cent of children living in poverty. The proportion of children in sole parent families below the threshold rose from 18 per cent in 1988, to a huge 66 per cent in 2002 (Ministry of Social Development 2002). Unlike the UK where there has been a determined focus on eliminating child poverty, New Zealand has not yet grasped the mettle of this social blight.

Rediscovery of social and economic policy links

More recently, there has been an official recognition of the links between economic and social policy and a new willingness to debate the issues of social exclusion. One of the policy platforms of the 1999 Labour/Alliance government was 'Closing the Gaps' a strategy designed to reduce the disparities between Pakeha (non-indigenous peoples) and Maori. In a major break with tradition, the Treasury commissioned work on social inclusion accompanied by work in other departments on social development and sustainable development. The social indicators including low absolute incomes are acknowledged as being far from healthy (The Treasury 2001).

> While acknowledging New Zealand's strengths, it is not difficult to point to areas in which New Zealand currently falls short. Average material living standards have fallen relative to most other OECD countries; income inequality increased particularly in the late 1980s; the incidence of household poverty is too high; there are wide gaps in ethnic averages across a range of social indicators, there are poor outcomes in health and education among lower socio-economic groups; there are quite sharp divisions in values and attitudes on key socio-economic issues; and there are institutional weaknesses that trouble Crown-Maori aspirations and our levels of social capability more generally. Added to this is a regional picture of increasing deprivation in Northland and parts of Auckland, and stagnation in East Cape. Finally, there is the threat of more skilled young New Zealanders leaving for what they see as more prosperous foreign countries that are putting out the welcome mat for them.

Talk about an inclusionary policy regime, however, shows little evidence that sounder and more secure social insurance schemes are being considered:

> While necessary as a short-term safety net, the tax-benefit transfer system is not a realistic or desirable option to tackle in a sustainable way the problem of low absolute levels of income. Limits on the effectiveness of 'passive' tax-benefit redistribution arise from the costs to growth of high marginal rates of tax, the international mobility of high-skill, high-income people, and the risks to social cohesion from having a large and expensive group of taxpayer-funded beneficiaries. An 'active' approach to raising low incomes through policies that improve education and labour-market opportunities in the lower part of the distribution offers the best prospect to make a difference to distributional outcomes over the medium term. This is supported by a considerable weight of empirical evidence.

The old: a success story of social inclusion?

The intention of the new government is clearly to address issues of social exclusion, but, some piecemeal changes to housing apart, there has been little dramatic action.[17] The official strategy is to downplay the need for direct redistribution while emphasising the desirability of work.

In the ambivalence over the need for redistributive tax and welfare reform, inconsistency has emerged, especially between the treatment of the old and the young. Thus the state pension, New Zealand Superannuation, for those over 65 is fully universal and is the one part of the welfare state to have emerged relatively unscathed by the reforms of the 1990s. It may now, ironically, provide a new model for social inclusion in the 21st century (St John 2001b; St John and Gran 2001; St John and Willmore 2001). New Zealand Superannuation is neither income, asset or retirement-tested with entitlement established by residency criterion alone. Being individually based and linked to average wages, it enables older people to largely achieve 'participation and belonging' even in the face of social change such as divorce, separation and remarriage, and changes in the labour market.[18] New Zealand Superannuation is treated as taxable income with rising marginal tax rates providing a degree of clawback as incomes from other sources rise.

New Zealand may thus be viewed as one of the first countries to have a basic minimum income guarantee for its citizens, albeit only those over 65 years of age. In terms of the objective of social inclusion, it must be judged a success, with the older population enjoying a relatively high standard of living compared to many of working age (Ministry of Social Policy 2001a). Nevertheless, in the context of a welfare state that is tightly targeted, a tax system that offers limited progressivity, a system in which children have lost the right to universal healthcare and a universal family benefit, and students no longer have universal tertiary education, universal pensions are likely to become increasingly questioned.

Conclusion

It is useful to view the issues in comparative international terms. Currently the welfare state choices can be usefully framed in terms of either building a unique national approach that draws on the early British legacy of an inclusive welfare state, or following an American one which is targeted, limited and stigmatising. Treasury continues to portray the choice in economic terms with statements that policies to promote increased opportunities for meaningful employment should be a priority to promote the inclusive economy. However there is little debate around the need for enhanced safety nets in the absence of such meaningful employment, nor is it clear what policies will produce the widespread well-paid jobs on the scale that is required.

New Zealand enjoys a pension system that appears to be inclusive for the elderly, and may even be a good model for other countries, especially as an alternative to the World Bank prescription for privatised pensions.[19] In contrast to NZ superannuation, assistance to families with children and those on benefits has been highly targeted, and ungenerous. Family assistance in particular has been the poor relation in the welfare system (St John 2001a). Serious attention to the tax system including a review of the 1996 tax reductions may be needed to find the extra revenue to extend more universalistic ideas to the working age population. In particular, redesign of welfare benefits is necessary to take more account of the fact that casual and part-time work rather than secure full-time work is the reality for many people. Ideally benefits should gradually move towards establishing a guarantee basic minimum income for all citizens such as New Zealand already has in place for everyone over 65.

The commonwealth legacy of countries such as Australia and New Zealand may predispose them to resist the powerful thrust to the Americanisation of social policy. In the era of globalisation of economic activity and the new risks that this poses, it is important to emphasise the need for a strong welfare state, including a return to the past objective of belonging and participation.

As Barr (2001) – an influential British economist – asserts:

> ... contrary to widely-held views, the welfare state exists for reasons additional to and separate from poverty relief, reasons that arise out of pervasive problems of imperfect information, risk and uncertainty. [The] welfare state is here to stay since twenty first century developments do nothing to undermine those reasons – if anything the reverse.

New Zealand's own unique style of social insurance in the post-war period has the potential to halt the rise of social exclusion. This remains to be realised. For the old, at least, New Zealand offers a unique contribution in developing a unique commonwealth alternative to the American model.

Notes

1. An example of relative disadvantage is that a Maori baby boy living in the most deprived area of New Zealand can expect to live 15 years less on

average than a European baby girl in the least deprived area (Howden-Chapman, Blakely, Blaiklock and Kiro 2000).
2. Following a briefing to the incoming government in 1999 on living standards (The Treasury 1999), there has been a rash of reports on the social inclusion theme, for example, 'Towards an inclusive economy' (The Treasury 2001). This work is supported by other research projects both within Treasury and in other government departments such as the Ministry of Social Development.
3. For example, the Labour/Alliance government acted decisively to return the collective Accident Compensation scheme (ACC) to its former status as a social insurance programme after significant parts of it were privatised by the former government. Likewise, indexation changes to the state pension that reduced its generosity were reversed. In employment law the Employment Contracts Act 1991 was replaced by a softer version, the Employment Relations Act 2000.
4. This is particularly true on the fiscal front where the emphasis has been on generating fiscal surpluses and using part of these to partially prefund the state pension.
5. In Thompson's words we have had 'a rather arrogant view of history and our own hallowed place in it'.
6. Barr (1998, 2001) provides a critical insight that the welfare state as been as much about insurance for the middle classes as about the relief of poverty.
7. This section draws on St John and Rankin (1998) and (2002).
8. These reforms included redesigning ACC, housing assistance, employment law, superannuation, health, students loans and allowances. Entitlement to social assistance was to be restricted to the 'genuinely needy', not as of right as a citizen. See Boston, Dalziel and St John (1999) for full analysis of reforms.
9. It seems likely that the rate of abatement would have needed to be as high as 50 per cent. Lower rates were considered but these would prolong the abatement range unrealistically. Unfortunately, a rate of abatement of 50 per cent coupled with marginal tax rates of 21 per cent or 33 per cent gives rise to effective marginal tax rates of 71 per cent or 83 per cent. And, even with a 50 per cent abatement rate, the range of income over which a couple or an individual might be affected is wide.
10. Reports of the Prime Ministerial Review Committee on the Reform of Social Assistance (1991) obtained under the Official Information Act show how impractical the idea of family accounts really was. Eventually, in a brief, barely-reported announcement the family accounts project was abandoned in 1993.
11. Along with the abandonment of Family Accounts, part-user charges for hospitals were abolished, and superannuation changes were abandoned.
12. Box 1 sets out the major reforms.
13. This is a measure of the extent to which New Zealand's international liabilities exceed its international assets. It represents over 80 per cent of GDP.
14. The intent of the original Act was to 'free up' the labour market and expose it to market forces by allowing individual bargaining. The power of the unions was weakened considerably. The Labour/Alliance government moderated this legislation in the new Act when it came to power in 1999, but unions remain weak.

15. The child tax credit is highly discriminatory as it only goes to those children whose parents meet the criteria of being independent from the state (Child Poverty Action Group 2000).
16. The New Zealand Business Roundtable is an influential grouping of wealthy and powerful business leaders who have fought assiduously for lower taxes and a smaller size of the state. See, for example, 'Government Spending could be slashed' The Independent 29th August 2001.
17. The government has sought to reverse some of the damaging impact of market-related rents introduced in 1991. The principal policy so far is the reintroduction of income-related rents for those in the state houses This has improved the income position of the very poorest of those renting, but the majority of low-income families, markets rents still remain a significant factor in ensuring their ongoing poverty. There were some limited moves to encourage home ownership announced in mid-2003.
18. The rate of NZS is a minimum 32.5 per cent of the net average wage for a married person, with higher rates for single and living alone.
19. New Zealand has eschewed the approach of three pillars recommended by the World Bank and followed by countries such as Chile and Australia. Thus there are no compulsory private savings and no tax subsidies to voluntary provision.

References

Barr, N. (1998) *The economics of the welfare state* (3rd edition), Oxford: Oxford University Press.

Barr, N. (2001) *The welfare state as piggy bank. Information, risk uncertainty and the role of the state*, Oxford: Oxford University Press.

Boston, J., Dalziel, P. and St John, S. (eds) (1999) *Redesigning the welfare state in New Zealand: Problems, policies, prospects*, Auckland: Oxford University Press.

Boston, J., St John, S. and Stephens, B. (1996) 'The quest for social responsibility', *Social Policy Journal of New Zealand*(7), 2–16.

Child Poverty Action Group (2000) *CPA Submission to the government on extending the child tax credit to all children*, Auckland: Child Poverty Action Group.

Child Poverty Action Group (2003) *Our Childen. The priority for policy* (2nd edition), Auckland: Child Poverty Action Group.

Dalziel, P. (1999a) 'Macroeconomic constraints', J. Boston, P. Dalziel and S. St John (eds), *Redesigning the welfare state in New Zealand: Problems, policies, prospects*, Auckland: Oxford University Press.

Dalziel, P. (1999b) *New Zealand's economic reform programme was a failure*, Unpublished manuscript, Christchurch.

Easton, B. (1997a) *The commercialisation of New Zealand*, Auckland: Auckland University Press.

Easton, B. (1997b) *In stormy seas. The post-war New Zealand Economy*, Dunedin: University of Otago Press.

Howden-Chapman, P., Blakely, T., Blaiklock, A. and Kiro, C. (2000) 'Closing the health gap', *NZ Medical Journal*, 113 (1114), 1–2.

Jesson, B. (1999) *Only Their Purpose is Mad*, Wellington: The Dunmore Press.

Kelsey, J. (1993) *Rolling Back the State*, Wellington: Bridget Williams Books.

Kelsey, J. (1997) *The New Zealand Experiment* (2nd edition), Auckland: Auckland University Press/Bridget Williams Books.
Ministry of Social Development (2002) *The Social Report 2002*. Wellington: Ministry of Social Development.
Ministry of Social Policy (2001a) *Older New Zealanders*, Wellington: MOSP.
Ministry of Social Policy (2001b) *The social report 2001. Indicators of social well-being in New Zealand*, Wellington: Ministry of Social Policy.
Mowbray, M. (2001) *Distributions and disparity. New Zealand household incomes*, Wellington: Ministry of Social Policy.
OECD (2002) *OECD in figures*, Paris: OECD.
Royal Commission of Inquiry on Social Security in New Zealand (1972) *Social Security in New Zealand*, Wellington: Government Printer.
Scollay, R. and St John, S. (2000) Taxation, *Macroeconomics and the contemporary New Zealand economy*, Malaysia: Pearson Education NZ Limited.
Shipley, H.J. (1991) *Social Assistance: Welfare that Works*, Wellington: Government Printer.
St John, S. (2001a) 'Financial Assistance for the Young: New Zealand's incoherent Welfare State' (Policy discussion paper 23), Auckland: Department of Economics, The University of Auckland.
St John, S. (2001b) 'New Zealand goes it alone in superannuation policy'. Paper presented at the Reform of Superannuation and Pensions. The 9th Annual Colloquium of Superannuation Researchers, UNSW Sydney.
St John, S. and Gran, B. (2001) 'The world's social laboratory: Women friendly features of New Zealand pensions'. In J. Ginn, D. Street and S. Arber (eds), *Women, Work and Pensions*, Maidenhead, Berkshire, UK: Open University Press.
St John, S. and Rankin, K. (1998) 'Quantifying the Welfare Mess' (Policy Discussion Papers 22), Auckland: Department of Economics, University of Auckland.
St John, S. and Rankin, K. (2002) 'Entrenching the welfare mess' (Policy discussion paper 24), Auckland: Economics Department Auckland University.
St John, S. and Willmore, L. (2001) 'Two legs are better than three: New Zealand as a model for old age pensions', *World Development*, Vol. 29, No. 8, 1291–1305.
Statistics New Zealand (1999) *New Zealand now: Incomes*, Wellington: Statistics New Zealand.
The Treasury (1990) *Briefing to the incoming government*, Wellington: The Treasury.
The Treasury (1999) *Towards higher living standards for New Zealanders*, Wellington: The Treasury.
The Treasury (2001) *Towards an inclusive economy*, Wellington: The Treasury.
Thomson, D. (1998) *A world without welfare: New Zealand's colonial experiment*, Auckland: Auckland University Press.
Work and Income NZ (2001) *Statistical report 2000*, Wellington: WINZ.

14
Canada, Social Inclusion and the Commonwealth

Malcolm J. Stewart

Introduction

From a Canadian perspective, a potential role for the Commonwealth in advocating greater social inclusion is attractive; but there are two major reasons for skepticism. The first is the conceptual ambiguity arising from social inclusion discourse. While social inclusion is readily associated with notions of equality, social justice and redistribution, critics note that adherents of competing ideologies have used the term to support active labour market policies such as compulsory work-for-welfare; and have suggested in moralistic diatribes that some groups of people *choose* to exclude themselves from economic and social benefits through self-destructive behaviour or lack of motivation (Levitas 1998; Silver 1994, p. 101). The second centres on the Commonwealth itself, an organisation of former British colonies known primarily for its role in promoting goodwill through international sport. It has no obvious role in promoting unity within its disparate membership on such matters as economic globalisation or social development. An immense credibility gap will have to be filled to convince the uninitiated that it can be transformed into a viable political force for social justice on the world stage. (cf. Ch. 1 of this volume)

In the following pages, I begin by considering the meaning of social inclusion and clarify its use in the present discussion. I then explore the important historical influence of Britain on the development of Canadian social policy, within the unique dynamics of the country's political culture. Next, I comment on the potential of social democracy in Canadian politics to marshall broad support for the contemporary, British-led Third Way movement, within the context of the changing 'geometry' of the Atlantic triangle. I conclude with some thoughts on the likelihood of Canada's supporting a new role for the Commonwealth as champion of social inclusion on the global stage.

Social inclusion as a continuum

Popular discourse often frames social inclusion and social exclusion as mutually exclusive categories, but it may be more useful to think of social inclusion and social exclusion as opposite poles of a continuum. At one pole are absolute forms of exclusion such as genocide and apartheid. Historically, indigenous peoples were regularly subjected to mass enslavement and extermination by invading colonisers. In more recent times the massive losses of life in Stalin's ethnic purges; the horror of the Jewish Holocaust; state-sanctioned 'disappearances' of tens of thousands in Latin America; genocidal tribal conflict in Rwanda; and 'ethnic cleansing' in Bosnia remind us of the depths of inhumanity to which systematic exclusion can sink. At the opposite pole is absolute inclusion, which entails complete acceptance of all persons as equals, with full access to and equal sharing of all of a society's resources and benefits. Examples of truly inclusive societies in modern times are rare, but certain tribal societies and religious communities may approach such unconditional inclusiveness. In between are the various 'shades of gray' that characterise most societies. No society is completely inclusive or exclusive: its position on the continuum fluctuates over time (Drache and Stewart 2001). Just as social inclusion can be conceived along dimensions of human rights, equality and social participation of the people within a nation, so it can be conceived as applying to relations among nations or regions. From this perspective it is clear that, even though measures of social inclusion may be high overall, examples of social exclusion may be found within any given society (cf. Ch. 1 again). Similarly, wide variations in social inclusion may be found in comparing nations or regions. Thus, while social inclusion may be relatively high in more economically advanced nations or regions, the vast majority of the world's people – those living in nations and regions that together control only a small fraction of the world's resources – are excluded.

Canada may serve as a case example of a country that is relatively advanced overall, in terms of civil, political and human rights guarantees, and in which human rights and redistribution policies help to reduce extremes of disadvantage and social exclusion. Indeed, Canada is counted today as one of the most humane and inclusive societies in the world. The Canadian model of moderation, tolerance and compromise has achieved a remarkable level of political harmony, social stability and economic prosperity. However, there are many examples of social exclusion that place the country's stellar reputation at risk. After seven consecutive years at the top of the United Nations' Human Development Index ranking, Canada fell from first to third position in 2001 and to eighth in 2003, behind Norway, Iceland, Sweden, Australia, the Netherlands, Belgium and the United States (United Nations Development Program 2003: *Human Development Report 2002*). Its status as *the* best country in which to live has been diminished by chronic failure to resolve a number of long-standing issues of social inequity. In contrast with its overall high quality of life rating, Canada currently ranks 11th on the UN's Poverty Index. Neo-liberal economics and the politics of compromise have too often produced income security measures characterised by inadequate benefits and stringent means testing, leaving disadvantaged persons such as the chronically unemployed, persons with mental illness, physically-disabled persons, sole-support mothers and the elderly poor, especially unattached women, on the margins of society. Resistance to full gender equality and the recognition of the economic value of unpaid caring work continues to disadvantage women across the life course (Baines, Evans et al. 1991). Policies and practices directed towards Aboriginal peoples and non-European immigrants of colour are too often tainted by institutionalised racism. Progress towards greater inclusion in some areas is offset by setbacks in others. Some examples:

- With a substantial infusion of new funding for the income-tested Canada Child Tax Benefit and National Child Benefit for the country's poorest families, child poverty declined to 16.5 per cent in 2000, the lowest level since 1989 (Campaign 2000 [2002]). But several provinces, released from national standards by reduced federal cost-sharing, have introduced work-for-welfare programmes and have cut the benefits of families receiving social assistance by the amount of federal child benefits. Moreover, there is still no sign of a national programme of affordable child care to support working families, which many family policy advocates note is the strongest single policy tool for assisting young families toward financial security.
- Some recent court decisions have advanced Aboriginal land claims, but the issue of compensation for hundreds of abused former residents of the government mandated and church-operated residential

school system for Indian children remains in political and legal limbo.
- There is no commitment to equal pay for work of equal value among women and men across all employment sectors; nor to measures to reduce the high rates of poverty found among women living alone in old age.
- Perhaps most distressing, senior governments continue to evade responsibility for a national strategy to provide permanent, affordable housing for tens of thousands of low income individuals and families. Temporary shelters and half-measures to stimulate the private construction industry attest to a colossal failure of political will.

The recent 'slippage' in Canada's social inclusiveness will now be examined more closely with reference to historical, political and economic developments.

The British legacy of Canada's political culture

Canada's early political culture congealed around unwavering loyalty to the British crown (Lipset 1990). Wrested from the French on the Plains of Abraham in 1759, Canada symbolised Britain's determination to maintain a presence in North America following the American Revolution of 1776. During and after the Revolution Canada was the chief refuge of British United Empire Loyalists, many of whom later rose to prominence in the English-speaking stronghold of Upper Canada. In a series of skirmishes along the Canadian border which culminated in the War of 1812, the British army successfully fended off American invasion.

Since they were a Tory 'fragment' rather than a cross-section of 18th century British society, the first British settlers in Canada tended to be less egalitarian and more accepting of hierarchy than their predominantly liberal American contemporaries. They were predisposed to trust state authorities and civil society elites and were little inclined to focus on class divisions or demand the empowerment of labour. Subsequent waves of 19th century immigrants diluted the original Tory fragment, introducing elements of Whig liberalism and Fabian socialism (Horowitz 1972). Thus the British legacy, in particular tolerance for ideological differences, facilitated conditions that contributed to the achievement of an inclusive society. The influence of the British Tory tradition tended to modify the otherwise right-of-centre Conservative party, enabling it to embrace state intervention in economic and social affairs; while the centrist Liberal party learned to retain power by adopting popular socialist policy ideas. Indeed, socialism may have come to enjoy greater respectability in Canada than in America because it was advocated by *British* socialists and was therefore seen as part of the political fabric. By contrast, American socialist thinking, with its roots in continental Europe, was 'foreign' to the entrenched liberal values of individual freedom and liberty (ibid.). In any event, tolerance for difference and willingness to seek compromise has come to characterise Canadian politics.

As in other colonies throughout the Empire, early Canada was infused with British authority and tradition. The Governors appointed to lead the new colony towards responsible government personified British imperial responsibility. Capable and often visionary leaders, well-schooled in colonial management, they readily adapted British social, political, legal and economic institutions to the needs of the developing colony. Following Confederation in 1867, a succession of prime ministers and cabinet members maintained the young nation's economic and political ties to Britain; and well into the first half of the 20th century, while the country was still developing a university establishment of its own, members of Canada's professional, intellectual and business elites studied in Britain, most notably at Oxford (Owram 1986; and cf. comments in Ch. 2 and elsewhere in this volume).

During its early development the country's position on the 'internal' social inclusion/exclusion continuum was conditioned by three broad objectives of the British colonial government. The first was to achieve the peaceful accommodation, despite linguistic differences and inevitable tensions between conquerors and conquered, of the founding French and English cultures to one another. The second was to enlist the cooperation of the Aboriginal peoples in defending British North America. The third objective, once the British had secured control of the territory, was to absorb large numbers of immigrants to settle the land and facilitate territorial expansion and economic growth. The legal and institutional frameworks imported from Britain aided the achievement of these objectives in a relatively orderly and peaceful manner.

Towards the end of the 19th century the moral suasion of the reformist Social Gospel movement and the political pressure of a growing labour movement sowed the seeds of Canada's social democratic movement and spurred the Canadian state's interest in social security. As the increasingly visible needs of injured workers,[1] war-widowed mothers[2] and the destitute elderly[3] began to attract official attention, the list of publicly funded and administered social programmes began to grow. By the middle of the 20th century, the accumulated experiences of generations who settled the land, provided labour power for nascent industries, and endured economic deprivation and wartime adversity together led to a sense of solidarity and collective responsibility for the security and inclusion of all citizens.

Geographic, constitutional and cultural constraints

Until the mid-1970s Canada proceeded in conformity with the three stages of social policy development outlined by Heclo: experimentation, consolidation and expansion (Heclo 1981). Yet for a number of reasons Canada lagged considerably behind the United States and the more advanced industrialised nations of Europe in the experimentation and consolidation stages (Guest 1984). This 'lag effect' is attributable to a slower pace of industrial development and urbanisation, magnified by the thin dispersion of a relatively small population across a huge land mass; but in addition, divergent regional economic interests and cultural differences mediated against the early emergence of a strong sense of national unity and common purpose. Constitutional arrangements, which were designed to accommodate regional differences, often presented obstacles to strong central government leadership in such areas as social policy. Under the *British North America Act*, the provinces had primary responsibility for health, education and welfare, and in turn the provinces left the relief of need to local authorities. Even as the need for social protection increased with population growth and industrialisation there was no clear role for the federal government. The emergence of social policy therefore entailed, with few exceptions, an incremental process of negotiation over which level of government had jurisdiction for what and how the costs of new policy initiatives would be divided amongst them. To this day the Canadian version of federalism permits the more populous provinces to exercise veto powers over significant change and requires a high level of consensus among 10 semi-autonomous provinces and three territories, each with its competing priorities (Pal 1985).

Formation of the welfare state

The creation of the post-war welfare state was the highest expression of the collectivist sentiments fostered by the Great Depression and two

World Wars. Britain's influence on the development of Canada's welfare state was crucial. Leonard Marsh and others, who provided the intellectual guidance for Canada's post-war reconstruction planning, were deeply influenced by Lord Beveridge, the acknowledged architect of Britain's welfare state. Many senior civil servants also contributed a strong British element to government management in the post-war period. The growing voices of the political and intellectual left, amplified by the experience of the Great Depression and reinforced by the writings of British social scientist, T.H. Marshall and economist J.M. Keynes, challenged a succession of Canadian governments to move beyond the 'modified individualism' of economic liberalism toward universal, collectivist policies of social protection. Despite their nominal ideological differences, the national Liberal and Conservative parties, anxious to attract the broad centre of the political spectrum, ultimately heeded much of this advice. When in power during the mid-1940s to late 1960s both parties expanded the range of means-tested benefit programmes for the poor, introduced a number of new social insurance schemes for the working classes and implemented some modest but nonetheless universal social welfare programmes for families with children and the elderly (Owram 1986; Armitage 1990; McClelland and Stewart, Inc. and Guest 1985). During the 1970s the enhancement of individual rights and freedoms received primacy within Prime Minister Pierre Trudeau's vision of 'the Just Society'. Then, just as institutionalised welfare – the pinnacle of social inclusion – appeared to be within grasp, the 'Keynesian consensus' of capital and labour began to collapse in the aftermath of the 1973 oil crisis. In subsequent decades the idealism of the Trudeau era was displaced by neo-liberal obsession with fiscal responsibility and public debt reduction. Thus Canada's tryst with post-war Britain's 'model welfare state' was never fully consummated. The hard swing to the political right led to 25 years of neo-liberal retrenchment and welfare state decline.

Retrenchment and reform

From the national election of 1983 onward, concern over growing public debt preoccupied Canadian political leaders. However, the excesses and hostilities that characterised the attacks on the working classes by Thatcher in Britain and Reagan in the United States were less evident in Canada. Canada's neo-liberal, Progressive Conservative (PC) government led by Brian Mulroney and his fiscally conservative Finance Minister, Michael Wilson, while strong on rhetoric, were only moderately successful in carrying out their avowed agenda of welfare state retrenchment (Myles 1988). The Mulroney government was wary that any wholesale assault on popular social programmes could trigger electoral penalties from the broad middle class; so instead of direct confrontation, they adopted a strategy that became known as 'social policy by stealth' to avoid close public scrutiny. This involved the incremental erosion of social programmes by means of subtle changes in tax laws and removal of full inflation protection from benefits.[4] Though less effective in reducing government deficits in the short term, such 'systemic' measures have considerable potential for reducing spending in the long run (Rice and Prince 2000).

In the 1993 election the PCs were handed a humiliating defeat, reduced to only two seats in Parliament. Ironically, where the Progressive Conservatives had failed to significantly reduce the welfare state, the Liberal government, elected on the promise of a more caring and consultative approach, succeeded. While in opposition they learned well from the mistakes of the PCs, who by the middle of their second majority term were widely regarded as arrogant and elitist. In short order the new majority Liberal government commenced the Social Security Review under the leadership of a popular Cabinet Minister, the Hon. Lloyd Axworthy. However, the true cost-cutting purpose of the Review soon became apparent when the Department of Finance released a series of discussion documents appealing for public support to overhaul a wide range of social programmes to bring them into line with the '... changing needs of Canadians in a rapidly changing world' (Department of Finance, Ottawa 1994a). Any hope that the Review would 'reform' the nation's social policies to address their inadequacies and inequities were soon dashed, and a new approach dubbed 'social policy by budget' was instituted (Collins 1998).

Accommodation to Western conservatism and Quebec nationalism

The near-demise of the Progressive Conservative government in 1993 left a vacuum that changed the political landscape dramatically. Significant numbers of Members of Parliament were elected from two new parties: the right-wing Reform Party, based in the Western provinces of Saskatchewan, Alberta and British Columbia, and the separatist *Bloc Québecois*.

Disaffection towards the federal government, based on the widely held perception in Western Canada that federal politics is controlled by Central Canadian interests, has a long and convoluted history. The populist Reform Party (re-named Canadian Alliance in 2000) grew out of a grassroots movement aimed at reducing the powers of the federal government and seeking more control by the provinces over their own affairs. It won 52 of 295 seats in the 1993 election, 60 in 1997 (enough to become the Official Opposition) and 66 in 2000.

Formation of the *Bloc Québecois*, a federal political party dedicated to the separation of Quebec from the rest of Canada, was precipitated by Parliament's failure to reach agreement on the Meech Lake Constitutional Accord in 1990. The *Bloc* won 54 seats in the 1993 election and, with a solid base of support in Quebec, has retained official party status, winning 44 seats in the 1997 federal election and 38 in the 2000 election.

The continuing presence of the *Bloc Québecois* in the federal parliament and the potential for expanded support for the Canadian Alliance Party in Central and Eastern Canada have dramatically reshaped national politics. The very future of the country and the viability of federalism now hinges on the ability of any national government to balance the demands of Western conservatives with those of Quebec, without alienating the rest of Canada.

Social inclusion in Canada today

Social inclusion in Canada was advanced greatly by enactment of the 1982 *Charter of Rights and Freedoms*. The Charter gave the Supreme Court primacy over Parliament as the arbiter of individual rights. However, broad social rights as conceived by T.H. Marshall have rarely been on the Court's agenda. An attempt by the province of Ontario's only social democratic premier in the mid-1990s to enshrine social rights as part of the 1992 Charlottetown Constitutional Accord came to naught when the Accord failed to achieve sufficient support in a national referendum (Laycock and Clarke 2002).

After nearly a decade of Liberal deficit cutting and fiscal austerity, spending on the Canadian welfare state has been steeply reduced; and concomitantly, social inclusion has lost ground. In the 1995 federal budget the Minister of Finance announced plans to reduce overall government expenditures by $25.3 billion, or 19 per cent over three years, $7.5 billion of which would be realised from reductions in social spending (Martin 1995). Part of the latter reductions would be achieved through the *Canada Health and Social Transfer* (CHST), a block funding method of transferring federal funds to the provinces for health, education, and social services, which would take effect in the 1996–97 fiscal year. Other reductions would be realised by removing 45,000 positions from the federal civil service through attrition and early retirement plans. It was estimated that, when combined with reductions in funding for the health care system, about one quarter of social programme spending would be lost by the turn of the century (Wiseman 1996).

In 1999 the federal and provincial governments signed the *Social Union Framework Agreement* which prohibits the federal government from introducing new social programmes without the approval of at least six provinces, including the three largest. This effectively ensured that there would be no new, national social programmes and no nationally uniform social policy standards (Lightman 2003).

The province of Quebec is an exception to the overall decline of social inclusion in Canada. Within the context of the cultural and political tensions outlined above, Quebec politicians have achieved special status for the province within the Confederation. They have negotiated with considerable success for control in such strategic areas as pension policy and immigration, while retaining federal funding commitments. Beginning in the 1970s and 1980s, Quebec instituted a network of integrated, community-based health and social service centres and adopted a series of supportive family policy initiatives – including cash transfers and low-cost, universally available regulated child care – that set it apart as the most progressive and socially inclusive province in the nation. Recently, a broad-based coalition of community organisations succeeded in having *Bill 112, An Act to Combat Poverty and Social Exclusion* passed unanimously by the National Assembly of Quebec (Noel 2002).

The New Left

Until recently, prospects for rescuing social democracy from oblivion in this country seemed remote indeed. The New Democratic Party, Canada's counterpart of Britain's Labour Party, has never ranked higher than third in national politics. It currently ranks fourth with only 14 seats in Parliament, just ahead of the last place, centre-right Progressive Conservatives who hold 12 seats. As noted above, the right-wing Canadian Alliance and the *Bloc Québécois* share the bulk of opposition votes in Parliament. However, under newly-elected leadership,[5] New Democrats may part with the orthodoxy of the past to offer voters a social rights alternative, modelled after British Labour's Third

Way (cf. multiple references elsewhere in this volume), in the imminent federal election. Gaining the support of Quebec voters, without which no political party has a realistic chance of forming a national government, would be essential to the success of such a strategy. The recent election of a majority Liberal government in Quebec,[6] which is widely interpreted as a rejection of the old-guard separatist dream, may herald a new openness to the rest of Canada. Moreover Quebec, where labour involvement is strong and where progressive social policy enjoys wide support, may prove to be fertile ground for the revival of a national social democratic party. However, the likelihood is that a majority Liberal government will again be elected early in 2004 under the leadership of the popular, one-time Finance Minister Paul Martin who is positioned within his party as 'Prime Minister-in-waiting'. At best, the NDP stands a chance of increasing its influence in a minority Liberal government; but the chances of its forming the Official Opposition are remote indeed.

The Atlantic Triangle

It was once common among comparative welfare scholars to explain Canada as '... an effect of ongoing and changing relationships with the two great imperial powers of modern capitalism', Britain and the United States (Myles 1989). While this explanatory framework has fallen out of currency, it contains an enduring truth.

Patriation of the Constitution in 1982 formalised the end of Canada's political dependence on Britain, and the decades since World War II have seen a precipitous reduction of trade between the two countries. As political and economic links to Britain have lessened, geographic proximity to the United States, combined with the larger nation's vast economic power have increased Canada's economic and political dependency on its closest neighbour. The 1989 *Free Trade Agreement* and the 1993 *North American Free Trade Agreement* signified Canada's increasing economic orientation towards the U.S. and tied Canada even more closely to the American economy and business model. Although NAFTA currently contains no explicit references to social programmes, critics have warned that programmes such as universal, publicly-funded health care may be targeted in future as giving unfair competitive advantage to Canadian businesses. The U.S. now receives over 87 per cent of Canada's exports. An increasing proportion of businesses operating in Canada are under American ownership and control. Discussions are well advanced on a *Free Trade of the Americas*

Agreement, which would further crystallise the trend towards economic integration within the Western Hemisphere.

Since the September 11, 2001 terrorist attacks on the World Trade Center and Pentagon, Canada's loyalties and capabilities are being put to the test. Under the sharp scrutiny of American politicians, immigration rules have been tightened and significant expenditures have been made to upgrade security and step up surveillance on both sides of what was to have been an open, free trade border. Canada bravely resisted the Bush Administration's efforts to draw it into active participation in America's war against Iraq, insisting that the United Nations should determine the conditions, nature and timing of reprisals against Iraq. True, after years of retrenchment, Canada's military establishment is manifestly strained and its capacity for sustained foreign commitment very limited. Nevertheless Canada's heavy economic dependence on the United States makes it unlikely that longer term American military initiatives – such as the 'Star Wars' scheme to build a defensive shield over North America – will be successfully resisted.

The Commonwealth

Today's Commonwealth is a loose association of 54 small and middle power countries. As former colonies of Britain, they share a common working language and similar systems of law, public administration and education, although they differ greatly in size, economic development, religious beliefs and culture. The functions of the Commonwealth are in the realms of co-operation, exchange, consensus building and sustainable development among its developed and less developed member nations: '... a force for: Peace, Democracy, Equality and Good Governance'; '... a catalyst for Global Consensus Building'; and '... a source of assistance for Sustainable Development and Poverty Eradication' (Commonwealth Secretariat website 2002).

Canada was a founding member of the Commonwealth in 1931. It has supported the organisation through bad times and good. Canadian leaders regularly champion human rights and social justice in international fora advocating, for example, the forgiveness of Third World debt and promoting a G8 consensus on an economic development plan for Africa. It is fair to assume that these positions are reinforced by Canada's membership in the Commonwealth.

In his recent review of the contemporary Commonwealth, McIntyre asserts that even though the combined populations of the organisation's member nations add up to a quarter or more of the world's people, it is not presently a large player on the international scene (McIntyre 2001, p. 112). Moreover, there is little evidence that its members are swayed by Commonwealth censure to refrain from discriminatory, inhumane or undemocratic behaviour.[7] These observations cast doubt on the organisation's potential to achieve a sufficient convergence of interests to become a champion for global social inclusion. However, the Commonwealth is a complex organisation – or rather, organisation of organisations. Its ambitious programme has political dimensions, through its Inter-governmental Organisations. It is connected to civil society through its many affiliated non-government organisations. It has a corporate constituency through its business and trade affiliates. It provides an important forum for small countries and an inclusive, 'one country, one vote' governance structure that is not found in many other international organisations. In addition, it fosters the sharing of much valued technical assistance with its less developed members. The organisation does, however, suffer from the low visibility of much of its work. With the exception of the quadrennial Commonwealth Games, there appears to be little public awareness of what the organisation is or what it does. It is not widely known that the organisation underwent somewhat of a renaissance during the 1990s. After decades of ignoring the contradictions of oppression and racism practiced by several of its members, the Heads of Government recommitted themselves in the 1991 Harare Declaration to the principles of racial equality and human rights first adopted in the 1971 Singapore Declaration. In the context of de-colonisation, the end of apartheid in South Africa and the end of the Cold War, they also expressed intent to address the vulnerability of the Commonwealth's smaller and poorer nations, and to promote sustained development to tackle global problems including environmental degradation, migration and refugees, communicable diseases and drug trafficking. An action plan to implement the Harare Declaration was elaborated in 1995 at the Heads of Government meeting in Milbrook, New Zealand (Harare Commonwealth declaration 1991; Commonwealth Action Programme on the Harare Declaration 1995). McIntyre suggests that this lack of public awareness reflects an inadequate resource base in relation to an ambitious agenda; and a tendency to rely too much on voluntary and non-governmental organisations to fulfill a large part of the mandate. He argues that little financial commitment or official attention has been requested from member nations (Ibid. and cf. all of the above to Chs. 15 and 16 in this volume).

Conclusion

Canada owes much to its British legacy of sound institutions and political tolerance, which have enabled it to become one of the most inclusive societies in the world today as it also becomes one of the most racially, linguistically and culturally diverse. These institutions have benefited many other nations as well.

As the nations of the world are drawn inexorably into the global, capitalist economy, it is imperative that economic growth and business objectives be balanced with policies of human rights and redistribution that enhance social inclusion and social development. Continuation of the increasing gaps – intra-national, international and inter-regional – between developed and developing nations perpetuates hatred and deadly, no-win conflict. To the extent that the Third Way, inspired by British intellectual and political leaders, may offer a humane alternative to neo-liberal retrenchment and dismantlement of social protection, it deserves serious attention and support.

Clearly, if Commonwealth leadership seriously aspires to become a global catalyst for the advancement of social inclusion, it will need to raise its profile considerably, make greater demands on the governments of its member nations and compete for their attention with other international organisations in which they participate. This is a tall order, but in view of the stakes, well worth the effort.

Notes

1. Workmen's Compensation, the first social insurance scheme in Canada, was enacted in Ontario in 1914, and in other provinces thereafter.
2. Mothers Allowance was introduced first by British Columbia in 1916. By 1922 all nine provinces had enacted similar legislation.
3. The Old Age Pension Act, passed in 1927 and cost-shared by the federal and provincial governments, was the first truly national social programme.
4. In 1989, universal Old Age Security benefits were incrementally 'clawed back' through the tax system from recipients with incomes over $50,000. Beyond incomes of $76,333 benefits disappeared. Partial indexation – omission of the first three percentage points of inflation from the calculation of annual benefit increases – was adopted for all federal government benefits.
5. At its national leadership convention in January, 2003 the NDP elected a new, charismatic and telegenic leader in preference to a more traditional, labour-backed candidate.
6. On April 14, 2003 the provincial Liberals defeated the Parti Québecois government which had held power for 14 years.
7. Examples include recent election abuses in Zimbabwe, the suspension of Pakistan's dictatorship and lack of consensus on the Kyoto Accord.

References

Armitage, A. (1990) *Social Welfare in Canada*, Toronto: McClelland and Stewart, Inc.
Baines, C.P., Evans, et al. (eds) (1991) *Women's Caring: Feminist Perspectives on Social Welfare*, Toronto: McClelland and Stewart.
Banting, K.G. (1987) *The Welfare State and Canadian Federalism*, Kingston and Montreal: Mcgill-Queen's University Press.
Campaign 2000 (2002) *2002 Report Card on Child and Family Poverty*. Online document. Available http://www.campaign2000.ca/rc/rc02/intro.html.
Collins, S.B. (1998) The challenge of equity in Canadian social welfare policy, *Canadian Social Policy Review*, Vol. 4: 2 (Winter): 1–14.
Commonwealth Action Programme on the Harare Declaration (1995) Online document. Available http://www.thecommonwealth.org/whoweare/declarations/millbrook.html
Commonwealth Secretariat website. Available http://www.thecommonwealth.org/whoweare/comsec.html.
Department of Finance (1994a), *Agenda: jobs and growth*, Ottawa: Government of Canada.
Drache, D., Stewart, M. (2001) *The Human Services Deficit and What Can Be Done About It*, Toronto: Robarts Centre for Canadian Studies, York University. Available online: http://www.robarts.yorku.ca.
Guest, D. (1984) Social Policy in Canada, *Social Policy and Administration*, Vol. 18, No. 2: 130–47.
Guest, D. (1985) *The Emergence of Social Security in Canada*, Vancouver: University of British Columbia Press.
Harare Commonwealth Declaration (1991) Online document. Available http://www.thecommonwealth.org/whoweare/declarations/Harare.html
Heclo, H. (1981) Towards a New Welfare State?, P. Flora and A.J. Heidenheimer (eds), *Comparative Public Policy: the politics of social change in Europe and America*, New Brunswick, N.J.: Transaction Books.
Horowitz, G. (1972) *Canadian Labour in Politics*, Toronto: University of Toronto Press.
Laycock, D., Clarke, G. (2002) Framing the Canadian Social Contract: Integrating Social, Economic and Political Values Since 1940, Canadian Policy Research Networks (2002). Online document. Available http://www.cprn.com/cprn.html.
Levitas, R. (1998) *The Inclusive Society? Social Exlusion and New Labour*, London: Macmillan.
Lightman, E. (2003) *Social Policy in Canada*, Don Mills: Oxford University Press.
Lipset, S.M. (1990) *Continental Divide: the values and institutions of the United States and Canada*, New York: Routledge.
Martin, Paul Jr. (1995) *1995 Budget Speech*, Ottawa: Canada Department of Finance.
McIntyre, W.D. (2001) *A Guide to the Contemporary Commmonwealth*, Hampshire: Basingstoke; New York: Palgrave.
Myles, J. (1988) 'Decline or Impasse?: 'The current state of the welfare state', *Studies in Political Economy*, Vol. 26 (Summer): 73–107.
Myles, J. (1989) 'Understanding Canada: comparative political economy perspectives', *Canadian Review of Sociology and Anthropology*, Vol. 26, No. 1: 1–9.

Noel, A. (2002) 'A Law Against Poverty: Quebec's New Approach to Combating Poverty and Social Exclusion'. Online document. Available http://www.cprn.org/docs/family/lap_e.pdf

Owram, D. (1986) *The Government Generation: Canadian Intellectuals and the State 1900–1945*, Toronto: University of Toronto Press.

Pal, L. (1985) Federalism, Social Policy and the Constitution, in J. Ismael (ed.), *Canadian Social Welfare Policy*, Kingston and Montreal: McGill-Queen's University Press.

Rice, J.J., Prince, M.J. (2000) *Changing Politics of Canadian Social Policy*, Toronto: University of Toronto Press.

Silver, H. (1994) 'Social exclusion and social solidarity: three paradigms', *International Labour Review*, 1333 (5–6): 531–78. Cited in Graham, J.R., Swift, K.J. and Delaney, R. (2003) *Canadian Social Policy: An Introduction* (2nd edition), Toronto: Prentice-Hall Canada.

United Nations Development Program (2003) *Human Development Report 2002*, New York: United Nations.

Wiseman, J. (1996) National social policy in an age of global power: lessons from Canada and Australia, in J. Pulkingham and G. Ternowetski (eds), *Remaking Canadian Social Policy*, Halifax: Fernwood.

Part Three
The Commonwealth as a Transnational Institution

15
The Commonwealth and Social Inclusion

W. David McIntyre

The Commonwealth would not, at first glance, seem a promising instrument for the advancement of social inclusion. Its chief preoccupations are seeking credibility for its structures, conducting multilateral consultations on world affairs, seeking harmonisation (or simply understanding) of policies on trade, investment, and infrastructure development. As its budgets and activities have to stem from consensus, and its membership is largely made up of governments unable to afford large sums, its programmes are of necessity usually limited in scope.

However, the very nature and membership of the Commonwealth and the historical evolution of its structure, have forced it more and more into the direction of inclusion. An association that began as an élite group of self-governing Dominions within the world's most powerful empire, emerged, by the start of the 21st century, as the world's premier forum of small states. While the main preoccupation of the old Dominions had been gaining a voice in the operations of the premier world power, the main needs of the contemporary small state-majority are alleviating poverty, disease, homelessness, malnutrition, educational under-achievement, disability, and gender inequality. If the 'old Commonwealth' was obsessed with the balance of power, the 'new Commonwealth' focuses increasingly of the problems of globalisation.

When the Heads of Government addressed this issue at Fancourt, South Africa, in 1999, they balanced assertions about new opportunities for wealth creation with demands that the process should be 'participatory' and with recognition of a 'growing sense of social exclusion' (Durban Communiqué 1999: 5). Social inclusion, as the obverse to this is, however, a contestable concept. As Patricia Harris argues persuasively in chapter three, there is a need for more comprehensive conceptual analysis and for a wide range of ameliorative measures. It also depends on whether the approach is from a 'top down' concept of social order or a 'bottom up' demand for more justice for the excluded. Both approaches have been evident in the Commonwealth. Inclusion, as discussed in this chapter, evolved historically at several distinct levels – individual, national and global – with social inclusion coming comparatively late in the sequence.

Inclusion can first be found in the evolution of the name. As a synonym for empire, in the sense of family-of-countries, 'Commonwealth' first appeared before the American Revolution and occasionally in Victorian times. It became the preferred label for a democratic, federal state, as popularised in James Bryce's *The American Commonwealth* published in 1888. The United States was depicted displaying 'the type of institutions towards which as by the law of fate, the rest of civilised mankind are forced to move' (Bryce 1959: 1). In this sense 'Commonwealth' went into the federal title of Australia (La Nauze 1971: 59–71).

At a second level came political inclusion. The 'principle of the Commonwealth', as enunciated by the 'Round Table' movement before the 1914–18 War, was a rather exalted concept of citizenship derived from the ancient Greek model. It meant 'entrusting sovereignty to all those, whose sense of duty to their fellow-citizens is strong enough to justify the trust' (Curtis 1916: 181). In practical terms it became the question of how British subjects in the Dominions could become responsible for foreign affairs equally with those in the British Isles. The probable influence behind the principle was the classical scholar Alfred Zimmern, whose *Greek Commonwealth* was published in 1911 and who went on to apply the label to a third level – that of international affairs. In an essay of December 1914, he quoted Lord Acton's dictum that the existence of several nations in the same state was one of the tests of freedom. Zimmern suggested that such a mix was the basis of what he called the 'British Commonwealth of Nations' (Zimmern 1914: 21). This has been identified as the invention (Hall 1971: 189) of the label that was first used in an official document in the Irish Treaty of 1921; then 'sanctified' by use in the Balfour definition of 1926, and put into law in the preamble to the Statute of Westminster in 1931. It remained current only until 1948 when 'British' was dropped in front of 'Commonwealth of Nations'.

Equality of status became the founding principle. Unequal as they were in population, size, wealth, and power, Britain and the

Dominions, determined in 1926 to treat each other as equal in their mutual relations. After initial reluctance, Dominion status (i.e. independence and equality) was given to India, Pakistan and Ceylon in 1947–48. In the 1950s, there was reluctance to widen the association further, and the idea was floated of a 'mezzanine status', for countries that would become independent but not Commonwealth members (Jeffries 31 March 1953). This idea proved indefensible and large countries like Ghana, Malaya and Nigeria joined the Commonwealth on independence.

Another pause occurred when Cyprus became independent in 1960 with a population of only half-a-million. The British Cabinet Secretary said that hitherto Commonwealth members had all been 'significant countries that could expect to exercise some influence in world counsels, to be viable economically, and to be worthwhile partners in some regional defence system' (Brook 26 April 1960). Cyprus would create a precedent for nearly 30 really small countries. During uninhibited talk at Downing Street in 1960 between Prime Minister Harold Macmillan and two of his ministers, one of them said: 'If Cyprus was admitted as a fully independent member then all the other tiddlers would demand this treatment' (Bligh 20 July 1960). But a study group of Commonwealth senior officials pointed out that to exclude newly independent small countries 'would be a frustration of much that the Commonwealth stands for' (CAB 133/200 1960). The admission of Cyprus in 1961 led to the eventual entry (by the 1990s) of 28 member states that had populations of less than 1.5 million. Of these, five were mini-states of between 100,000 and 200,000 and eight were micro states of less than 100,000. All gained an equal voice in Commonwealth conclaves. Political inclusion was well-established (McIntyre 1996: 244–277).

Concern for social inclusion only emerged as the preoccupations of the political Commonwealth changed. For about 30 years, from the 1950s to the 1980s, two issues – the Cold War and decolonisation – dominated Commonwealth affairs. The association was used as an instrument for trying to persuade newly independent countries to keep out of the communist bloc. Both issues had their most bitter focus in Southern Africa where the linked problems presented by the rebel white regime in Rhodesia, the apartheid system in South Africa, and the latter's occupation of Namibia, put the British on the defensive in the Commonwealth. This probably contributed to Britain's willingness to relinquish co-ordination to a Commonwealth Secretariat responsible to the Heads of Government collectively. This idea came from new members, but the Secretariat began with minimal opportunities for initiative. Interest in social inclusion awoke only gradually.

The creation of the Secretariat was the most significant landmark in the organisation of the contemporary Commonwealth. It arose unexpectedly. By 1964 the British Prime Minister was finding the new leaders 'not the easiest of associates' (Douglas Home 3 June 1964). He suggested to the old members (Australia, Canada, and New Zealand) that new practical measures might present the Commonwealth in more attractive light for the newcomers. A package of five proposals under the title of *The Way Ahead* was promulgated. They were designed for strengthening administrative infrastructure rather than focusing on social policy. They covered technical assistance in development; a foundation to foster professional links; capital assistance for tertiary education; training and research in public administration; and regional centres of advice in planning. These proposals were overtaken by an intervention from President Nkrumah of Ghana during the global trends debate at the start of the 1964 Prime Minister's Meeting. He deplored the focus on the Cold War. He said the real problem was the gap between the 'haves' and the 'have-nots'. He called for a Commonwealth 'clearing house' to prepare plans for trade, aid and development, and to circulate information about this (Nkrumah 8 July 1964). Senior officials realised that it would bad to put down the initiative, but they strove fiercely to ensure that the Secretariat was designed for pooling and disseminating information rather than for policy-making or executive action.

A Secretariat along these lines was approved in 1965 (*Communiqués 1* 1987: 105–111). The first Secretary-General, Canadian diplomat Arnold Smith, was a 'cold warrior', quite inexperienced with the new Commonwealth. It was Arnold Smith, however, who began to steer the association in the direction of social inclusion. His chief institutional legacy is the Commonwealth Fund for Technical Co-operation (CFTC) based on the concept of 'third party technical assistance'. A country's contribution goes to a fund to facilitate work by an expert from another country going to assist in a third country. Approved in 1971, the CFTC is the Secretariat's operational arm for providing experts, consultancy services and training (Smith 1981: 108–20). In the same year the Commonwealth Declaration of Principles was adopted, by which members *pledged support* for peace, liberty, and international co-operation and *condemned* racial discrimination, colonial domination, and wide disparities of wealth (*Communiqués 1*: 156–7). These were, again, generalised tenets with no social policy specifics.

But Arnold Smith ended his term as Secretary-General in 1975 by declaring that the growing gap between living standards in the developed and developing worlds was 'neither decent nor sane'. He called on members to 'reject the habits that have kept the rich relatively rich and the poor absolutely poor' (*S-G Report* 1975: 9). Sonny Ramphal, who took over between 1975 and 1990, added urgency to this quest. He also added that achieving racial equality was the 'unfinished revolution of our time' (*S-G Report* 1977: 7).

The association grew in size through the 1970s to 1990s – to 32 members in 1970, 45 in 1980, 50 in 1990, to 54 in 1995. The biggest threat to this growing structure was the development of the three great regional trading blocs – the EU, NAFTA, and APEC. Britain's entry into the European Communities (later Union) in 1973, after a decade of agonising, sparked the growth of rival groupings for keeping access to trade and aid. The Commonwealth's majority of developing countries banded together with other ex-colonies in the Africa-Caribbean-Pacific (ACP) group under the Lomé and Cotonou Conventions. The old Dominions sought neighbourly or regional trade relations. Canada entered NAFTA, the North American Free Trade Area. Australia and New Zealand made their CER, Closer Economic Relations, arrangements. Later, under Australian initiative, they both looked to the Pacific Rim through APEC, Asia-Pacific Economic Co-operation (McIntyre 2001: 123–5). The Commonwealth declined in economic significance.

Meanwhile, Cold War and Southern African issues continued to dominate Commonwealth discussions. Then, with the sudden end of the Cold War and of apartheid, the Commonwealth had to seek new legitimacy in an age of declining state activity, new-found faith in free market forces, emphasis on private enterprise and voluntary action. Surprisingly, the Commonwealth was not unprepared for these changes because of its growing attention to social inclusion issues.

The new agendas did not derive from any systematic study or strategic plan. They arose incrementally and evolved independently. Little cohesion was attempted until the Harare Declaration of 1991. Yet a trawl through the communiqués of the Commonwealth Heads of Government Meetings (CHOGMS) reveals the cumulative interest in social policy. Issues came up as follows: youth (1973), women's rights (1975), non-governmental organisations, NGOs, (1977), small states (1979), the homeless and disabled (1981), students (1985), HIV/AIDS (1987), Sport (1989). A High Level Appraisal Group of Heads of Government was appointed in 1989 to plan for the Commonwealth in the 1990s. The Harare Commonwealth Declaration, adopted at the 1991 CHOGM, attempted to give some cohesion to the somewhat untidy incremental growth of the previous decades (*Communiqués 2*: 82–5). After re-affirming the 1971 principles, the Heads of Government now pledged themselves to focus on five main areas. These were:

- the fundamental political values of democracy, the rule of law, independence of the judiciary, good governance, human rights, and equal opportunities;
- equality for women;
- universal access to education;
- sustainable development and the alleviation of poverty based on sound management, free trade, the market economy, and human development;
- help for small states.

Trying to balance the relative importance of these fields became the main focus for debate in the 1990s. These developments will be discussed under the headings: (i) small states, (ii) civil society, (iii) the free market, (iv) gender equality, and (v) youth.

Small states

The small state dimension represents the most significant structural feature of the contemporary Commonwealth. Over half the members are small states. In 1979 the CHOGM discussed for the first time the 'special disadvantages that beset the growing number of smaller member countries, particularly the island developing countries' (*Communiqués 1*: 213). The 1983 CHOGM appointed an expert group to advise on small state security. Its report, *Vulnerability: Small States in the Global Society,* recommended a more equitable international economic order, regional arrangements for collaboration, and measures to strengthen domestic security. Member countries were encouraged to assist the small states. Ministerial Meetings on Small States began during the 1993 Chogm and in 1997 a second *Vulnerability* study was produced entitled *A Future for Small States*. This included the first balanced definition of 'globalisation':

> Globalisation is most easily comprehended as a process of accelerating interdependence which has at its core the liberalisation of trade, the deregulation of financial markets, the spread of trans-national production of goods and services, and the development of new tech-

nologies, particularly information technology. There are also cultural elements to the phenomena associated with the diffusion of consumerist values, environmental concerns focused on the protection of seas and habitat, and political issues to do to the effectiveness of the state. (*Vulnerability 2*: 3–4)

As champion of the small states, the Commonwealth Secretariat joined with the World Bank in reiterating the call for special consideration of small states for investment and debt adjustment. A small states dimension is also incorporated into the activities of the Commonwealth Parliamentary Association, which, since 1981, has mounted Parliamentary Conferences of Small States. The small states vote contributed to the election of Don McKinnon from (comparatively small) New Zealand as the fourth Secretary-General in 1999.

Civil society

Civil society emerged as the dynamic dimension of the Commonwealth in the second half of the 1990s. Although it had always been present from the days of Victorian charitable organisations, it was now subjected to systematic study and accorded more formal recognition. When the founding document for the Secretariat was approved in 1965, an equivalent document provided for the creation of the Commonwealth Foundation 'to administer a fund for increasing interchanges between Commonwealth organisations in professional fields' (*Communiqués 1*: 111–13). This became an autonomous body, housed alongside the Secretariat, in Marlborough House, London. Over the years, the Foundation assisted in the formation of some 40 pan-Commonwealth professional associations. But at a conference at Dalhousie University, Nova Scotia, in 1976, it was realised that, as well as the professional organisations, there were many other voluntary bodies at work in the Commonwealth. Thus NGOs had a brief appearance on the CHOGM agenda in 1977. This led to the appointment of an advisory committee, which produced *From Governments to Grassroots*, calling for national NGO liaison units and NGO desks in the Secretariat and foreign ministries. It also suggested that the Foundation's mandate should be expanded. This was heeded by the Foundation's Board of Trustees which adopted a vastly enlarged portfolio in 1980 that included food production, health, education, social welfare, science and technology, culture, the media, and public administration.

There was, in the 1980s, an explosion of activity in the voluntary sector. The Foundation sponsored, for a time, a network of national

NGO liaison units in 40 countries (Special Report 1993). New voluntary bodies in the broad field of development began to adopt a 'bottom up' approach. In 1988 the first of a series of 'Working for Common Wealth' conferences was held at Goa, India. It arose from discussions by a small group of Australian, British and Canadian specialists in job creation and local development. The Goa conference was organised in new ways – a transition from 'structure to flexibility'. The participants were asked how best their time might be spent. 'Organisers have to let go', said rapporteur Colin Ball. 'If people don't have ownership, they do not develop responsibility and realise their potential'. He regretted the old-fashioned charitable implication of the appellation NGO and coined the phase Local Development Organisation (LDO).

He called for an integrated approach to social and economic development, empowering people, rather than setting up services or activities by 'imperialist professionals or outsiders however well-meaning'. He extolled the role of the facilitator and catalyst. 'The LDO creates opportunities, space, choices; it makes it possible for things to happen, rather than creating the 'happenings' itself' (WCW 1 1988: 6–8). The Goa Conference insisted that development should not alienate the disadvantaged; gain for some should not lead to other people's loss, and that social, ecological and environmental conditions must not be harmed. The outcome was the formation of the Commonwealth Association for Local Action and Development (COMMACT) which took the Gandhian motto 'Think Global, Act Local'. This association was represented at the first quadrennial NGO Forum organised by the Foundation before the 1991 CHOGM.

The Forum issued a call for an NGO charter. Instead, a survey was conducted of the growth of the voluntary movement and its characteristics, with recommendations for the future. Colin Ball was joint author with Leith Dunn, of *Non-Governmental Organisations: Guidelines for Good Policy and Practice* for the Second NGO Forum in 1995. This was published at the 1995 CHOGM where it was described as 'a Geneva Convention for NGOs'. These were defined as voluntary, independent, not-for-profit, and not self-serving (*NGO Guidelines* 1995: 19). The professional associations, which had been the initial core of the Foundation's brief, were excluded. The emphasis was now to be on organisations working with people to improve their social and economic position. Such organisations worked with people to encourage emancipation from dependency, alleviation of poverty, and advancing human development. Since they increasingly worked with governments, the *Guidelines* called for the refinement of legislation and official procedures for the regulation and public accountability of NGOs and for frameworks of appropriate consultation and cooperation. To this end the Foundation began to facilitate NGO representation at Commonwealth ministerial meetings. The Secretariat also had its own NGO Liaison Officer from 1993.

After the *Guidelines* had been discussed at regional forums, the Foundation embarked on its most ambitious research project in 1997 – a broad study of citizen's views on the role of civil society. Ten thousand people in 47 countries were asked three rather sophisticated questions:

- What in your view is a 'good society'? To what extent does such a society exist today?
- What roles are best played by citizens and what roles are best played by the state and other sectors in such a good society?
- What would enable citizens to play their roles in the development of society more effectively in the future?

The results were ready for the 1999 CHOGM in the booklet *Citizens and Governance: Civil Society in the New Millennium*. The bulk of the report comprises often-moving quotations from ordinary citizens. The conclusions were surprisingly clear and ran counter to the free market orthodoxies of the victors of the Cold War. People were concerned with *basic needs* (economic and physical security), they wanted *association in their communities* (including respect for culture, sharing and caring), and they *expected to participate* (in responsive and inclusive governance, equal rights, and justice). It was clear that women and young people felt excluded; men felt included but threatened. The good society seemed far off. It was also evident that many people saw a significant role for the State as *provider* of services and law, as *facilitator* of citizen's participation, and *promoter* of equal rights and justice (*Civil Society* 1999: 72, 92).

The 1999 NGO Forum sent the Civil Society report to the Heads of Government with the warning that 'Poverty is still the reality for most people in the Commonwealth ... . Globalisation not only disempowers; it also further impoverishes the many whose daily life is a daily struggle to survive'. The Forum recommended that there should be partnerships among civil society organisations, and between civil society, government and private corporations to temper the harmful effects of globalisation. (Third NGO Forum 1999: 1)

The Heads of Government seemed unprepared for this message. They 'noted the significance of civil society in empowering people to benefit from globalisation, in contributing towards the goal of poverty elimination, equal opportunity and fair distribution of resources ... '. They referred the report and the NGO Forum Communiqué to senior officials for study and recommendations before the next CHOGM. The 1999 CHOGM also appointed a High Level Review Group (HLRG) to draw up a blueprint for the Commonwealth in the 21st century. The draft of the HLRG's report in 2001 was generally regarded as a disappointing document, but it did call for collaboration between governments, inter-governmental agencies, the private sector, and civil society. It recommended that NGOs and professional associations should band together in 'focus groups' based on functional interests and that there should be 'better-structured relations' between the official and unofficial Commonwealth (*TRT* 2002: 249–263).

The ambitious CHOGM planned for Brisbane in October 2001 was postponed after the 9/11 atrocities in the United States, but a parallel 'Commonwealth People's Festival' went ahead with a disappointingly low level of support. The postponed CHOGM finally took place in retreat-like seclusion near Coolum, Queensland, in March 2002. The conference communiqué failed to mention civil society, and the Coolum Declaration on 'The Commonwealth in the 21st Century' adopting the HLRG report, gave civil society only one mention. It called on the inter-governmental, professional, and civil society bodies to 'join with us in building closer Commonwealth 'family links' and strengthening consultation and collaboration' (*TRT* 2002: 280).

In spite of this less-than-inspirational vision from the political/official Commonwealth, the new century witnessed considerable vigour in the civil society sector. The Commonwealth Education Ministers Meetings in Halifax, Nova Scotia, in 2000, and the Commonwealth Health Ministers Meetings in Christchurch, New Zealand, in 2001, were both preceded by NGO consultations and involved parallel professional forums and trade fairs. Civil society input was also sought, for the first time, for the Commonwealth Finance Ministers Meetings in London in 2002 – a move that received more visibility. A series of regional civil society consultations was held in Sri Lanka, Ghana, Fiji, Jamaica, and Britain, the findings of which were considered in a major conference of civil society organisations in London in July 2002 organised by the Commonwealth Foundation and the Treasury. They were hailed by Graça Machel, chairperson of the Commonwealth Foundation, as a 'gigantic initiative'. Key demands from these consultations were increased finance for a global fund to combat HIV/AIDS, TB, and malaria; 'fair trade not free trade'; cheap pharmaceuticals, and debt cancellation.

Similarly, the call for focus groups was well taken. The longest-established group was the Commonwealth Human Rights Initiative (CHRI) formed in 1987 by five Commonwealth associations – journalists, trade unionists, lawyers, legal educators, and medics – later joined by parliamentarians and the press. CHRI has published authoritative reports about human rights abuses in countries under military rule and on violations of the rights of prisoners. It has emphasised that the Commonwealth is not only an association of nations, but also a 'Commonwealth of Peoples'. In 1999 it held a 'Dialogue on Indigenous Rights' which led to the creation of the Commonwealth Association of Indigenous Peoples (CAIP).

Another group of professional associations came together to combat HIV/AIDS. At the CHOGM in 1999, one of the most influential initiatives from the voluntary sector was a submission from the Association of Commonwealth Universities, the Commonwealth Medical Association, the University of Natal, and five other associations of medical professionals about the impact of HIV/AIDS in the Commonwealth. Member countries that make up 30 per cent of the world's population account for 60 per cent of the HIV/AIDS infections. In Southern Africa life expectancy rates have fallen alarmingly, and many of the teachers and nurses vital for ameliorative programmes are expected to die. Heads of Government were urged to declare a global emergency, which they did in paragraph 55 of the Durban Communiqué. To keep up the momentum, the Commonwealth Medical Association separated its professional and welfare arms, entrusting the latter to a new Commonwealth Medical Association Trust (COMMAT) which co-ordinates the work of the 'Para 55 Group'. Sixteen Commonwealth associations make up this group to publicise the extent of the HIV/AIDS pandemic, promulgate best practice in prevention and care, and put pressure on governments and drug companies to take action (Para 55 2002).

During the discussion over the HLRG's draft report for the 21st century in 2001, a further group of 12 Commonwealth associations formed the Commonwealth Consortium for Education in order to stress the role of education in policies for good governance and poverty eradication. Another group of 19 NGOs produced *A New Vision for the Commonwealth* to make up for the feebleness of the HLRG draft. It was not considered by the Heads of Government to whom it was submitted at Coolum in March 2002, but it was stronger on social inclusion than the official report. Above all, it exuded a sense of optimism. It sees the Commonwealth as 'an experiment in international relations that is only just beginning'. It went on: 'Through skilful use of its network from the top of government to the smallest non-governmental organisation the Commonwealth can contribute much towards setting an agenda for the wider world'. At the head of this agenda it places the attack on poverty. To achieve a more just and inclusive global economy it suggests that the 'greatest need in the fight against poverty is investment'. Commonwealth agencies should work to ensure good governance to attract investment. To encourage stability, the Commonwealth 'must embrace the cultural diversity agenda as a core element in its policy programme alongside development, good governance, human rights and civil society' (New Vision 2002: 5, 12, 17).

The free market

This NGO document, which was so much more positive than the Coolum Declaration, brings out the most striking development in the Commonwealth in the 1990s, namely the new emphasis given to the market, to private enterprise and the role of corporate investment. With the ending of the Cold War; the apparent vindication of capitalism; the extolling of the advantages of globalisation, a whole new dimension of Commonwealth aspiration was revealed. Private investment, technology transfer, and information technology were now seen as vital for achieving the goals of sustainable development and poverty alleviation. From the Commonwealth Finance Ministers Meeting of 1989 had come the idea of a Commonwealth Equity Fund. The plan was approved by the 1989 CHOGM where the Secretary-General announced the 'Hibiscus Issue'. This was followed by a series of regional investment funds approved at the 1995 CHOGM as the Commonwealth Private Investment Initiative (CPII). A second fund for Africa was launched in 2002.

For the 1997 CHOGM the British hosts made 'Trade, Investment and Development' the theme. In the run-up, a joint Commonwealth/European Union seminar embraced the rising 'globalist' philosophy. It asserted three propositions: that foreign capital investment was not 're-colonisation in disguise'; that aid did not contribute to economic growth; and that tariffs and subsidies were damaging to economies that used them (*Commonwealth and Europe* 1997: 5). This stark ideological stance set the tone for the first Commonwealth Business Forum that preceded that 1997 CHOGM. The meeting identified poor infrastructure as a hindrance in many countries and called for codes of good practice in government, business, and finance to counter corruption. The conclusions of the Forum were to be fostered by a Commonwealth Business Council as an ongoing private sector voice. These ideas were endorsed by Heads of Government in the *Edinburgh Commonwealth Economic Declaration*. Trade, investment, new technologies, and market forces were seen as the 'engines of growth'. Market principles, open trade and investment, development of human and physical resources, gender equality, good governance and political stability were the 'major components of economic and social progress' (*Edinburgh Communiqué* 1997: 3). Such ideological simplicity was tempered for the Commonwealth by the special consideration accorded to the small states, the policy of debt alleviation for poor economies, a call for codes of good practice to eliminate corruption, and by the acceptance of the goal of halving the proportion of people living in extreme poverty by 2015.

Two years later, the 1999 CHOGM addressed the problems arising from globalisation more specifically in the *Fancourt Commonwealth Declaration on Globalisation and People-centred Development*. On the positive side, globalisation had created 'unprecedented opportunities for wealth creation and the betterment of the human condition'. But the benefits were 'not shared equitably'. The declaration argued for social inclusion. 'If the poor and the vulnerable are to be at the centre of development, the process must be participatory, in which they have a voice'. The gap between the rich and poor was highlighted and a 'growing sense of social exclusion' admitted. Gender inequality, youth unemployment, poor support for the aged, children and disabled, and threats to cultural diversity were all acknowledged. Solutions would require security, political stability, and peace, for which government and civil society should collaborate (*Durban Communiqué* 1999: 3–5). The unresolved question, at the start of the new century, was the relative balance between the political, civil society and private enterprise Commonwealths (McIntyre 2002).

Gender equality

Amid the generalities that characterise most Commonwealth debates, two subjects with more specific relevance to the advancing of social inclusion, concern women and young people. A call for facilitating women's 'full participation in national and international affairs' first appeared on the CHOGM agenda in 1975 (*Communiqués 1*: 180). An Adviser on Women and Development was added to the Secretariat staff in 1979 and the 1987 CHOGM agreed to an Expert Study Group on the subject and to triennial meetings of Ministers for Women's Affairs.

The report *Women and Structural Adjustment* in 1989 indicated that the 1980s were times of setback and growing gender inequalities because of economic restructuring. A Commonwealth Plan of Action on Gender and Development in 1995 emphasised the importance of education and training for women and the mainstreaming of gender issues. Providing mechanisms, such as 'gender responsive budgeting' as pioneered in Australia, were advocated (Cox 2001: 22). In 1996 the Women's Affairs Ministers Meeting set a target of 30 per cent for women members of parliaments. By the end of the century, the average had reached 13 per cent overall; only New Zealand exceeded 30 per cent. The Commonwealth Parliamentary Association that had earlier begun to hold conferences of parliamentarians from small states, moved on to hold parallel conferences for women parliamentarians. At the 2000 conference the Canadian representatives reported that all bills before the federal parliament in Ottawa were now subject to 'gender analysis' to ensure absence of discrimination.

Youth

If women make up roughly half the Commonwealth's adult population, young people under 16 comprise three-quarters of the total population. Thus the Commonwealth has tried to address young peoples' needs in several dimensions. The Commonwealth Youth Programme was launched in 1974, and built up regional youth centres in the Caribbean, Africa, South Asia and the South Pacific where diploma courses on 'Youth and Development' became available for training youth leaders. In his 1995 review of the Secretariat's economic and social programmes, Professor John Toye singled out the CYP as the 'clearest case' of a Commonwealth programme which 'enjoys an absolute advantage' (Toye 1995: 17). Triennial Youth Ministers Meetings provide overview of the CYP. In the 1990s the Secretariat began to stress youth employment and the need for new technical skills. Programmes of investment and youth enterprise, mentoring and leadership were re-packaged in 2002, under the *Youth for the Future Initiative*, as part of the goal of poverty reduction.

The specific needs of students had long been catered for by scholarship schemes, but student mobility came under threat in the 1980s because of the full cost-recovery fee regimes for overseas students charged by tertiary institutions in the developed member countries, notably Britain. A Commonwealth Committee on Student Mobility monitored the problem and urged Heads of Government to make better arrangements for Commonwealth students. In 1985 the

CHOGM tried a new approach. It authorised the Secretary-General to investigate the potential in distance education for bridging the widening education gap. A group of experts under Lord Briggs, Provost of Worcester College, Oxford, and Chancellor of Britain's Open University, surveyed the considerable wealth of experience with distance education in Commonwealth countries. It drew a distinction between 'distance education', in which a significant part of the teaching was done by someone removed in space and time from the learner, and 'open learning', a process widely available to learners no matter who or where they were and when they wished to study. The Open University enrolled more students than any other British university outside the federal University of London. Average costs per graduate were relatively lower than elsewhere. Briggs's group reported to the 1987 CHOGM in favour of an agency that would work through existing institutions and not enrol its own students. They proposed a 'University of the Commonwealth for Co-operating in Distance Education' with the visionary goal that 'any learner, anywhere in the Commonwealth, shall be able to study any distance teaching programme available for any bona fide college or university in the Commonwealth' (Briggs 1987: 2).

The Commonwealth of Learning (COL) started work on 1 January 1989 in Vancouver, Canada, after the British Columbia government made a generous grant to secure the venue. The COL did not enrol students, but maintained an online advisory service on the availability of distance education courses. It conducted training in the technology for distance education. It specialised in continuing professional education, teacher training, environmental issues, and the role of women in development. In the 1990s, it began to tackle issues of academic credit transfer, quality assessment, and institutional accreditation. It assembled training modules from around the Commonwealth and made them available elsewhere. After various funding crises, it was agreed that national contributions for the COL should be determined at the triennial Commonwealth Education Ministers Meetings. But there was never enough money to satisfy the requirements of member countries. The COL had to temper the original 'any learner anywhere' vision and concentrate on more basic needs. The COL's president, Gajaraj Dhanarajan, said that the Commonwealth was home to 'the world's largest source of illiteracy, under-education and under-provision for learning'. Thus emphasis switched to open schooling especially for females; technical and vocational training and non-formal education; and continuing professional training, especially for teachers

(Dhanarajan 2001). The traditional tertiary education role, though not abandoned, was supplemented by more basic contributions to social inclusion.

Sport

The most popular aspect of the Commonwealth is the Commonwealth Games (cf. Ch. 1, p. 2 above). For some people it is their *only* point of identification with the Commonwealth. When team sports like soccer, rugby, hockey, cricket and basketball are also brought into the picture, a vast area of popular enthusiasm and young peoples' endeavour are involved. Yet sport became divisive in the Commonwealth, partly because of apartheid in South Africa and the use of sporting boycotts to combat it, and partly because of the uneven spread of resources for training and in hosting big sports events. The Commonwealth Games were held only in Australia, Britain, Canada or New Zealand until 1966 when they went to Kingston, Jamaica, and in 1998 to Kuala Lumpur, Malaysia. In the debate in 1988 over the venue of the 15th Games for 1994, the Indian Minister for Sport argued the claims of New Delhi:

> Are you permanently going to keep us in Asia and Africa away from the pride and pleasure of hosting the Games for the Commonwealth family ... are we permanently going to be the guests at the table of the affluent ... Do we not have the right to participate as equal members of the Commonwealth family? (Alva 1988)

When the choice went to Victoria, BC, the Canadian government was sufficiently concerned about the implications of the debate (and the escalating costs of hosting) that it put the future of the Games on the 1989 CHOGM agenda. Here the Secretary-General was authorised to set up a working party of sports administrators, governments, and the Commonwealth Games Federation. This group reported to the 1991 CHOGM and was reconstituted as the CHOGM Committee on Co-operation Through Sport (CCCS) chaired by Roy McMurtry, then associate Chief Justice of Ontario. Every two years in the 1990s, the CCCS presented eloquent reports on the importance of sport especially for young people. In 1993 it declared that:

> The future of the Commonwealth will not rest on economic factors alone. It is vitally important for the continual relevance and strength of the association that the meaning and spirit of the

Commonwealth reaches the grassroots, particularly young people. Sport can serve the Commonwealth well in this regard, becoming the first point of information about the Commonwealth for young people (CCCS 1993: 24).

At the national level sport helped create unity and pride. At the grassroots level it gave young people goals, discipline, self-respect, good health, and engaged them in community concerns. Hosting sport events became incentives for infrastructure improvements and community developments.

In the 1999 CCCS report particular attention was given to the impact of the Mathare Youth Sports Association in slum settlements on the outskirts of Nairobi, Kenya. It began with a group of boys seen by an aid worker kicking around a home-made football. After he provided them with a proper ball and some coaching, their game improved. Word spread, and soccer became a local focus of enthusiasm, leading to a 10,000-member association with 80 leagues. After they won success in a national tournament, one of the Mathare teams competed in an international contest in Norway. Here the tidiness and cleanliness of the towns astonished the players. They determined to clean up at home. Thus, from football a community organisation arose, which encouraged youngsters to stay at school, get qualifications, and help clean up the district they lived in, and help combat HIV/AIDS. Self-discipline, skills, educational improvement were by-products and some of the 'Norway graduates' went on to tertiary education and became community leaders (CCCS 1999: 19).

In this way sport is seen as a useful instrument in development. As Sport Canada's administrator Greg Rokosh writes:

> For those young people with limited economic and social prospects, sport can provide positive alternatives to juvenile delinquency and other problems associated with low self-esteem, boredom, alienation and poverty. With its enormous appeal, sport can assist marginalised young people in rejoining society and the education system (Rokosh 2002: 8).

To symbolise this new emphasis, the 17th Commonwealth Games in Manchester 2002 was accompanied by a 'Spirit of Friendship Festival' illustrating the multi-cultural nature of the city and the Games. Events for élite athletes with disabilities were fully integrated into the programme for the first time. For the last leg of the Queen's Baton Relay, in the opening ceremony, a six-year-old girl, with a terminal illness and attached to an oxygen cylinder, handed the baton to the Queen, who went down from the dais to receive it.

The paradox of the contemporary Commonwealth can be seen in the contrast between promise and performance, between rhetoric and results. In a somewhat devastating analysis of the economy of the Empire/Commonwealth since 1914, Brian Tomlinson suggests that 'British rule did not leave a substantial legacy of wealth, health, and happiness to the majority of the subjects of the Commonwealth.' As compared with the lot of this majority, he shows that a 'Physical Quality of Life Index' for 1985 placed the top half-dozen member countries in the following order: Australia, Canada, Britain, New Zealand, Barbados and Jamaica. These rankings correlate fairly consistently with the ranking for per capita gross national product and public spending on education (Tomlinson 1999: 375–7). Over half of the Commonwealth's budgets are met by the ABC members, (Australia, Britain, Canada). At the other end of the scale, over half the member states of the Commonwealth are in the small state category that features in the Secretariat's index of countries exposed to external economic forces and environmental hazards (Vulnerability Index 2000).

Yet because of its historical evolution from the former Commonwealth of Nations, based on the doctrine of equality of status, the Commonwealth that emerged out of the maelstrom of decolonisation gradually became an valuable structure for giving the small states a voice in international affairs. By its very nature, the 'New Commonwealth', with its inter-governmental agencies – Secretariat, Fund for Technical Co-operation, Foundation, Youth Programme, COL, CHOGMs, and ministerial conclaves – increasingly took on the commitment to social inclusion. Where governments faltered in their execution of social policies, civil society organisations stepped in with impressive expertise. More recently, the hopes invested in the free market rest on the supposed advantages of a 'Commonwealth business culture' based on the use of a common language and administrative heritage. As yet, the appropriate balance between state, civil society and market influences has not been resolved. The paradox of the contemporary Commonwealth was also clearly evident in two recent Commonwealth meetings.

Firstly, the Commonwealth Health Ministers Meetings at Christchurch, New Zealand, in November 2001, began with an NGO Consultation that contributed to the ministerial agenda. The Ministerial Meetings took place adjacent to a Parallel Health Symposium and Trade

Fair. There were daily joint sessions and there was NGO and Symposium input into the ministerial communiqué. There was also media access throughout. This tri-sector approach was innovative and valuable, but the respective responses to globalisation were significantly different. The health professionals welcomed the opportunities presented by globalisation for access to information, training, and even diagnosis and therapy. The ministers were preoccupied with the resulting problems of poverty. The professionals concentrated on winners; the ministers on the losers. The professionals showed academic detachment; the ministers had to face their electorates and meet budgets. Civil society organisations were in an intermediary position. They spoke up for the vulnerable, but they were not the decision-makers. However, the dialogue was impressive, appreciated, and indicated the Commonwealth's growing potential as an instrument for furthering social inclusion (McIntyre 2002: 16–20).

The second example of the paradox comes from the 2002 CHOGM at Coolum, Queensland. At a gathering where they should have concentrated on enunciating a vision for the 21st century, and resolving the relative roles of state, civil society, and market, Heads of Government managed to spend most of their time failing to reach agreement about the future of Zimbabwe's membership in the light of recent human rights violations. It was the sort of structural and ideological wrangle that has so often absorbed energies in the past. At the same time, in a brief ceremony, the Secretary-General presented an Award for Action on HIV/AIDS to President Museveni of Uganda. In a country that had a 30 per cent adult infection rate and only two blood-testing machines, Museveni led a multi-sectoral campaign to address the pandemic that reduced the infection rate to 6 per cent (Para 55 2002: Ch. 2: 3). Civil society organisations, in touch with grassroots problems, went away from Coolum feeling rebuffed by the political/official Commonwealth.

Yet the rich structure endures. Heads of Government and ministers are willing to meet in Commonwealth conclaves. They authorised the Secretariat and the Foundation in 2002 to facilitate further civil society and business consultation and collaboration. In this respect the Commonwealth has greater width and depth – more people-to-people contacts – than any other international agency. The voluntary, independent, professional, philanthropic and sporting organisations (Vippsos) provide multi-dimensional popular representation that makes the Commonwealth unique as a global instrument. The needs and aspirations of the majority, as expressed in the civil society and governance project, are clearly in favour of inclusion, participation, and security. The Commonwealth provides mechanisms for multi-sectoral approaches and solutions. Will the Commonwealth be remembered for rhetoric or results?

References

Alva, M. (1988) From the 1994 venue bids during the Commonwealth Games Federation Assembly.
Bligh, T. (20 July 1960) Note for the record of meeting held on 13 July 1960. [British] P[ublic] R[ecord] O[ffice], Kew: PREM[IER] 11/3649.
Briggs, A. (1987) *Towards a Commonwealth of Learning: A Proposal to Create the University of the Commonwealth for Co-operation in Distance Education*, London: Com[monwealth] Sec[retariat].
Brook, Sir Norman (26 April 1960) Minute for the PM. PRO: PREM 11/3220.
Bryce, J. (1959) *The American Commonwealth*, new edition by L.M. Hacker, New York: Putnam.
CAB 133/200 (1960) Report of a group of Commonwealth officials, 23 July 1960, in Cabinet Records, PRO.
CCCS (1993) CHOGM committee on co-operation through sport, 1993 Report, London: ComSec.
CCCS (1999) = CHOGM Committee on Cooperation Through Sport, *1999 Report*, London: ComSec.
Civil Society (1999) *Citizens and Governance: Civil Society and the New Millennium*, London: Commonwealth Foundation.
Communiqués 1 (1987) *The Commonwealth at the Summit*: Vol. 1, *Communiqués of Commonwealth Heads of Government Meetings 1944–86*, London: ComSec.
Communiqués 2 (1997) *The Commonwealth at the Summit*, Vol. 2, *Communiqués of the Commonwealth Heads of Government Meetings 1987–1995*, London: ComSec.
Commonwealth and Europe: Investment and Trade – Opportunities for Partnership, London: Economist Intelligence Unit (1997).
Cox, W. (2001) 'Gender responsive national budgets', *Commonwealth Currents*, 4: 22.
Curtis, L. (1916) *The Commonwealth of Nations*, London: Macmillan.
Dhanarajan, G. (2001) *Reflections on Ten Years of the Commonwealth of Learning*, Vancouver: COL.
Douglas Home, Sir Alec, to Pearson, Menzies and Holyoake (3 June 1964) National Archives of Canada, Ottawa. Record Group 25, box 10662, part 2.
Durban Communiqué (1999) London: ComSec.
Edinburgh Communiqué (1997) London: ComSec.
Hall, H.D. (1971) *Commonwealth: A History of the British Commonwealth of Nations*, London: Van Nostrand.
Jeffries, Sir Charles to Romney Sedgwick (31 March 1953) PRO: D[ominions] O[ffice] 35/5056.
La Nauze, J.A. (1971) 'The Name of the Commonwealth of Australia', *Historical Studies* [Melbourne] 15(57).
McIntyre, W. David (1996) 'The Admission of Small States to the Commonwealth', *Journal of Imperial and Commonwealth History* 24(2).

McIntyre, W. David (2001) *A Guide to the Contemporary Commonwealth*, Basingstoke: Palgrave.
McIntyre, W. David (2002) 'The Commonwealth's Tri-Sector Dialogue', *New Zealand International Review*, 27(2): 17–20.
New Vision (2002) *A New Vision for the Commonwealth: A Report for the Commonwealth Heads of Government 2002*, London: 19 contributing Commonwealth organisations.
NGO Guidelines (1995) C. Ball and L. Dunn, *Non-Governmental Organisations: Guidelines for Good Policy and Practice*. London: Commonwealth Foundation.
Nkrumah, Kwame (9 July 1964) PMM (64) 3rd mtg. PM 153/50/4, part 11 in Record Group ABHS 950. Archives New Zealand, Wellington.
Para 55 (2002) *Para 55.Org: HIV/AIDS – a global emergency*. London: Commonwealth Medical Trust.
Rokosh (2002) Greg Rokosk, 'Development Through Sport', *Commonwealth Currents*, 2002, 1–2.
S-G Report (1975) Fifth Report of the Commonwealth Secretary-General. London: ComSec.
S-G Report (1977) Sixth Report of the Commonwealth Secretary-General London: ComSec.
Smith, Arnold (1981) *Stitches in Time*, with Clyde Sanger. London: André Deutsch.
Special Report (1993) *The Commonwealth Foundation: A Special Report 1966 to 1993*, London: Commonwealth Foundation.
Third NGO Forum (1999) Report of the Third Commonwealth NGO Forum: The People's Future – Citizens and Governance in the New Millennium, Durban, South Africa, 6–8 November.
Tomlinson, B.R. (1999) 'Imperialism and After: The Economy of the Empire on the Periphery', in *The Oxford History of the British Empire*, Vol. iv, *The Twentieth Century*, (eds) J.M. Brown and W.R. Louis, Oxford: Oxford University Press.
Toye, J. (1995) Review of the Economic and Social Programmes, London: ComSec.
TRT (2002) Report of the Commonwealth High Level Review Group to Commonwealth Heads of Government, Coolum, Australia. *The Round Table*, 91(364).
Vulnerability 2 (1997) *A Future for Small States: Overcoming Vulnerability*, London: ComSec.
Vulnerability Index (2000) *A Commonwealth Vulnerability Index for Developing Countries*, London: ComSec.
WCW 1 (1988) 'Working for Common Wealth', Series No. WCW1: The International Conference on Local Economic Development, Goa, India, 21–28 Sept.
Zimmern, A.E. (1914) 'German Culture and the British Commonwealth' in his *Nationality and Government*, London: Chatto and Windus 1918.

16
Prospects for a Commonwealth Future
Catherine Jones Finer and Paul Smyth

British social policy tradition and development could be of continuing significance for the nations of the Commonwealth; this uniquely world-wide association of small states; in conjunction with a few larger richer states, of which the United States is not one. The extent to which, if at all, this hybrid association of the Commonwealth might be mobilised and energised in the cause of social inclusion – both within and between its member states – has been the underlying theme of this collection. With globalisation and the decline of communism, the world is frequently said to be facing a stark choice between American versus mainstream European[1] notions of the good society and how best such a society is to be secured. This book has raised the possibility of a third choice: that of a pragmatic, Commonwealth-backed and interpreted – i.e. not simply as propounded by Britain's Mr Blair – 'Third Way'.

The making of the British welfare state may have seemed of heady international significance during and immediately after World War II, but its glamour proved short-lived, at least outside of Britain (e.g. Jones 1993: 30–33). It took just one decade (to the early 1960s) for Britain to start being cast as the 'laggard' low social spender of welfare state Europe. Yet in this matter Britain was not so much alone, as more in tune with the Dominions of the Commonwealth than with either Continental Europe or – at the other developed country extreme – the residualist United States. (Jones Finer 1999; Castles and Mitchell 1993: 21–22).

This was a 'middle way' trait scheduled to persist.[2] Whatever Margaret Thatcher may have intended by her attempts to 'roll back' the British welfare state in the 1980s, there was no way her government(s) could have transformed Britain into a replica of Reagan's United States (e.g. Pierson 1994); any more than could her true successor, Mr Tony Blair, even had he so wished, have transformed turn-of-the-21st-century Britain into a replica of still-extant social-democratic Sweden (e.g. Greve 2004). The middle way – variously entitled Third Way; stakeholder society; social investment state and other epithets besides – was evidently here to stay for the time being thanks, not least, to its immense capacity for variable interpretation and pragmatic reinterpretation within and across the Commonwealth. The frequency of reference to versions of the Third Way throughout this collection, bear witness to both its appeal and its adaptability.

As should be obvious, this book has not been an exercise in retrospective spin with regard to the social policy significance of either Empire or Commonwealth. All of the contributors have presented unvarnished pictures of the challenges, as they see them, facing the countries of the Commonwealth, individually and collectively, as they struggle to reconcile the twin, prime policy objectives of economic competitiveness and sustainable social cohesion, in the context of globalisation. Each and every country seems to be recoiling in its own way from the idea of a United States-led, laissez-faire framework for global integration seemingly guaranteed to impose a form of welfare residualism upon all its participants. It is in this context, for the mainly small-sized member states of the Commonwealth, that the policy appeal of Britain's Third Way (itself allegedly part-inspired by south-east Asian Commonwealth example – Jones Finer 1998: 155, 170), is to be appreciated. Might this Third Way offer a socially inclusive approach alternative to both socialism and neo-liberalism for a globalised world; one less 'culturally foreign' to most of it than either 'the social quality of Europe' (Beck, van der Meisen, Walker 1997) or the vaunted individualism of the United States ?

These are large, important, yet in some ways remarkably un-asked as well as un-answered questions. In the field of comparative social policy, the global impact of the British tradition has been conspicuously underplayed. This being so, our collection has sought more to open up a rich scholarly terrain than to provide a complete and comprehensive set of answers to the questions raised. Naturally, it has not been possible to fill in even all the geographical gaps at a single throw. Some of the gaps – with regard to the ex-colonies of Central, East and West Africa in particular – are indicative of generations of educational deprivation. Others seem more a comment on the continuing uncertain status of *social policy*, in the Third World, as a useful subject for study. But complete comprehensiveness was never a practical, publishable proposition in any case, given the size of the one-time Empire and thence of its marginally reduced product, the Commonwealth of Nations. A 'representative spread' – geographic, cultural and political – of coverage and countries, is what we have aimed for.

The social politics of nation states still matter, but, as Patricia Harris argues persuasively in her chapter, a national focus alone can no longer suffice (see also Yeates 2000; Sykes, Palier and Prior 2001; Deacon, Hulse and Stubbs 1997). More effective institutions for international social policy collaboration are essential. The important point about the Commonwealth in this regard, is that this could be more a matter of revivifying older practices than creating fresh practices *ex nihilo*. The countries of the Commonwealth have – albeit in vastly different institutional forms and with varying degrees of attachment – a shared British social policy legacy which could act as a starting point for considering ways to combat contemporary forms of social exclusion. We understand the importance of historical 'pathways' in the development of national welfare regimes; we ought also to profit from a consideration of the Commonwealth as a 'pathway' for global policy action in the future. Given that the Commonwealth is the premier association of small states, such a development would not be insignificant.

Could social inclusion develop as a supranational social policy objective investing the organisations of the Commonwealth with new purpose? In the context of globalisation it is surely an idea worth visiting. It is the very pervasiveness and multi-faceted quality of notions of social inclusion/exclusion which would seem, ideally, to pitch them within a pragmatic Commonwealth frame of reference. Should issues of inclusion/exclusion be as much about behaviour as money (as much between nations, as between families and communities) then the scope for constructive, productive, three-way solidarity deals[3] within the Commonwealth could be as great as it is conspicuously not great within the much grander – and more segmented – UN.

Social inclusion has, of course, emerged in this book as a highly contested item in itself. Moncrieffe and Harriss-White, for example, question the usefulness of the term when the majority of a given country's population was to be regarded as excluded and/or 'adversely incorporated'. Nonetheless the term was seen to fit in well with new policy agendas for Commonwealth states in terms of 'social investment' (e.g. Australia, Canada and South Africa) as well as for the

Commonwealth as a whole (McIntyre). What our book does suggest is that social inclusion, if used in a critical way, may further the development of a kind of comprehensive policy framework which brings together the previously discrete interests of rich member states concerned with 'social policy', and poor member states concerned with 'social development'. This could be an exciting, major challenge for research and policy communities.

In this regard the distinction drawn by Harriss-White between promotive and protective social policy (where the former is about 'reducing the need for help' while the latter is about providing help for those in need) is useful. In countries like India and Botswana 'promotive' social policy has historically been very much associated with community development practices. As McIntyre indicates, such practices are at the forefront of the inclusionist agenda within the Commonwealth today. However community capacity-building has also come back to a central position within the Third Way policy approaches of the richer member states, where it is typically embedded in 'social investment' thinking. Clearly all members – not just the poorer states – now have an interest in the promotive dimension of social inclusion. At the same time systems of social protection can no longer be thought to be the luxury preserve of richer, industrialised countries. Here, as Tan Ern Ser indicates, the Commonwealth has a wealth of experience of diverse modes of social protection (from social insurance, to provident funds, to social assistance) upon which its members could draw. Above all, however, the message from all our authors in both rich and poor countries is that the social inclusion agenda must be developed in a way that looks to both its promotive and its protective dimensions. The inclination amongst Third Way apologists to argue for the former as a substitute for the latter, does not stand up as a sustainable position.

A resurgent Commonwealth social policy may strike some as remote, quixotic idea. Has the Commonwealth not become more or less irrelevant in global terms with the post-war decline of Britain as an economic superpower, the 'maelstrom of decolonisation' in the 1950s and 1960s, British entry into the European Union and the rise of the United States as *the* dominant world power? Many Commonwealth countries find themselves today enmeshed in important regional relationships within Europe, North America, Africa and Asia, relationships which have seemingly eclipsed the old Commonwealth ties. For others, independence might in any case have been considered an end to colonising influence *per se*.

All of this is true and yet, as our collection shows, the Commonwealth link and the Commonwealth legacy still matter, albeit in myriad ways in different settings. In Botswana, for instance, it may be a matter of re-defining traditional values in relation to the colonial legacy; whereas in Canada it may be sense of trying to preserve learnt social values in the face of Americanisation. But in all cases we see the Commonwealth element as a factor still present and still contributing to the determination of current social policy practice.

From this perspective, the putative decline of Britain itself as a source of influence may not be so important. British social policy traditions were ever only one of many sources for social policy development in individual Commonwealth countries. If these countries are to come together in a renewed Commonwealth social dialogue, then it will be chiefly because they recognise that they share a common interest in developing a Commonwealth pathway to social reform within the global economy; a pathway different from that of the American or the European: one with which they can feel more at home. Thus, while developments within British social policy remain important, prospects for renewal are to be located right across the network of policy learning and cooperation among member countries, which the Commonwealth affords.

Certainly the following points stand out:

- the very pragmatism and ideological impurity of the British social policy tradition continues to make it of infinite adaptability and potential relevance to countries not steeped in either European or North American tradition;
- the British Empire/Commonwealth must be the most experienced international institution in the world at *creating* institutions designed to demarcate social lines of social exclusion; and hence, by the same token, might be presumed the international institution best equipped (certainly best placed by desert) to cope with combating the same from the bottom up;
- nevertheless, since there are not enough rich enough states in the Commonwealth capable of subventing the rest (even supposing they might wish to be doing so, over and above every other international obligation), it comes down to questions of money in the end. Safe money, moreover, rather than money down the proverbial corruption drain.

In which case, why might not the famous, cautious, but infinitely flexible ex-imperial expedient of the *Provident Fund* – as already referred to in so many of the smaller-country chapters above – serve as trial model for a Commonwealth *inter-state* mechanism for communal financing – via the institution of compulsory state income-related contributions into a central Commonwealth trust fund, to be dedicated to Commonwealth social objectives, as periodically to be agreed on by the member states?

The political implications of the latter scenario might be short-term horrendous, yet of long-term self-educating and self-sustaining importance. Merely putting such a question to the test, cross-nationally, could serve to demonstrate the significance (or lack of it) member states attach to their membership of this institution. This in itself could enhance our understanding and appreciation of the worth of the contemporary Commonwealth.

At the time of writing (end 2003), with the issue of Zimbabwe having yet again 'split the Commonwealth' and diverted yet another CHOGM from what Commonwealth *aficionados* think should be its mainstream business; prospects for the rational review and deployment of Commonwealth resources on an ongoing consensual basis, look dim indeed. Yet the issue of Zimbabwe, as with comparable others before it, may yet diminish, if not go away, in time.

Notes

1. Principally either corporatist German or social-democratic Scandinavian.
2. Cf. The Keynesian-inspired *Third Way* movement of mid-1930s Britain, under the leadership of Harold Macmillan (e.g. Greenleaf 1983: II.250, 253, 258).
3. i.e. Bottom-up and lateral, as well as top-down.

References

Beck, W., van der Meisen, L., Walker, A. (eds) (1997) *The Social Quality of Europe*, The Hague: Kluwer Law International.

Castles, F.G., Mitchell, D. (1993) 'Worlds of Welfare and Families of Nations', in F.G. Castles (ed.) *Families of Nations: Patterns of Public Policy in Western Democracies*, Aldershot: Dartmouth, pp. 93–128.

Deacon, B., Hulse, M., Stubbs, P. (eds) (1997) *Global Social Policy: International Organizations and the Future of Welfare*, London: Sage.

Greenleaf, W.H. (1983) *The British Political Tradition: Vol. II: The Ideological Heritage*, Oxford: Blackwell.

Greve, B. (ed) (2004) Nordic Regional Issue, *Social Policy & Administration*, 38.2.

Jones, C. (1993) Beveridge Abroad: From Student to Statesman, in N. Deakin, M. Willis (eds) *Social Services Research 1993 No. 1: Beveridge – Special Edition*, Birmingham: Department of Social Policy and Social Work, University of Birmingham, pp. 22–34.

Jones Finer, C. (1998) The New Social Policy in Britain, in C. Jones Finer and M. Nellis (eds) *Crime and Social Exclusion*, Oxford: Blackwell; pp. 154–170.

Jones Finer, C. (1999) 'Trends in the Development of Welfare States' in J. Clasen (ed.), *Comparative Social Policy*, Basingstoke: Macmillan; pp. 15–33.

Pierson, P. (1994) *Dismantling the Welfare State? Reagan, Thatcher and the Politics of Retrenchment*, Cambridge: Cambridge University Press.

Sykes, R., Palier, B., Prior, P. (2001) *Globalization and European Welfare States: Challenges and Change*, Basingstoke: Palgrave.

Yeates, N. (2000) 'Social Politics and Policy in an Era of Globalization', in N. Manning and I. Shaw (eds), *New Risks, New Welfare: Signposts for Social Policy*, Oxford: Blackwell; pp. 36–56.

Name Index

Atlee, Clement 17

Bentham, Jeremy 25n, 109
Bevan, Aneurin 19
Beveridge, Lord William 18, 35, 114, 130, 203
Bismarck, Count Otto von 13
Blair, Tony 24, 29, 236, 237
Bush George W. 208
Bustamente, Alexander 55
Butler, Richard Austen (R.A.B.) 19

Churchill, Winston 26n

Dahrendorf, Ralf 20
Douglas Home, Sir Alec 218
Durkheim, Emile 32, 33, 34, 35, 36, 41

Esping Andersen, Gosta 168
Etzioni, Amitai 39

Howard, John 167

Jayawardene, J.R. 118

Keynes, John Maynard 35, 43, 172–3, 203

Lee, Kuan Yew 17, 20, 126–7, 134
List, Friedrich 171, 172, 178

MacDonald, Ramsey 112
Macmillan, Harold 175, 217
MacLehose, Sir Murray 165n
Mahathir, Mohamad 139, 141, 145, 146, 147, 148
Malthus, Thomas 25n, 32

Mandela, Nelson 81, 87
Manley Michael 55, 59
Marsh, Leonard 203
Marshall, T.H. (Thomas Humphrey) 17, 35–36, 41, 43, 45, 114, 176, 177, 203, 205
Marx, Karl 32, 34, 139
Mill, James 109
Mulroney, Brian 203–4
Murray, Charles 39, 40

Nkrumah, Kwame 218

Patten, Christopher 162–3

Queen Elizabeth II 2, 232

Ramphal, (Sir Shridath) Sonny 219
Reagan, Ronald 203, 237
Ricardo, David 32

Seaga, Edward 60
Smith, Adam 32, 33, 34, 170, 171
Smith, Arnold 218–19
Spencer, Herbert 32

Thatcher, Margaret 24, 183, 203, 236
Titmuss, Richard Morris 16, 17, 18, 19, 33, 34, 35, 41, 43, 176
Tonnies, Ferdinand 32, 34
Townsend, Peter 33, 37, 38, 42, 43, 44
Trudeau, Pierre 203

Webb, Sidney (Lord Passfield) 112
Whitlam, (Edward) Gough 175

Subject Index

Aboriginal and indigenous peoples, treatment of   15, 74, 77, 78, 82, 83, 111, 118, 139, 140, 168, 175, 177, 181, 190, 193n, 198, 199–200, 201, 225
Asian Financial Crisis   26n, 138, 151, 160ff.
(cf Western economic crisis)
Asian [welfare] model   126, 136, 151, 163, 165

Beveridge Report   18–19, 35, 115, 120n, 183
British Empire   1, 2, 11, 12, 13, 15, 17, 21, 25
  Characteristics of   1, 12–16, 25, 171, 240
  British legacy & influence *per se*   77, 138, 148, 167ff., 175, 178, 182, 197, 200ff., 210, 236, 239, 240

Churches   see *under* missionaries
Citizenship   36, 38, 41, 62, 120, 125, 149, 175, 176, 216, 223
  Charter of rights and freedoms (Canada)   205
  Citizens charter (Jamaica)   61
  Citizens' rights   36, 56, 61, 69, 89, 128, 177
  Participatory citizenship   69, 74, 120
Civic associations/civil society   40, 71, 76, 77, 88, 149, 209, 221ff., 227, 232, 233
Colonies   2, 15, 69, 71, 112, 130, 136, 179, 197, 201, 208, 219, 237
  colonial/ex-colonial elites   15, 20, 56, 83, 110, 111, 140, 148, 201
  colonial government/rule   51, 52, 71, 76, 111–112, 113, 156, 201
  colonial heritage/legacy   25, 54, 56, 57, 76, 81, 82, 86, 91, 94,
109, 112, 130–31, 136, 138, 139ff., 147, 148, 156ff., 193, 240
Commonwealth (of Nations)
  Beginnings/evolution   1, 23, 173–74, 208, 215ff.
  Characteristics   7, 11, 25, 43, 208–9, 215, 217, 219–21, 232–33, 236, 237, 238, 240
  Declaration of principles   218 [cf Commonwealth website declaration   208]
  Functions   25, 75, 77, 78, 139, 150, 208, 217, 219, 232
  New Commonwealth   2, 20, 23, 24, 215
  Old Commonwealth/ Commonwealth Dominions   2, 4, 5, 7, 13, 15, 20, 23–25, 26n, 215, 217, 219, 236
  Potential   3, 4, 7, 25, 36, 43, 44, 65, 91–2, 107, 139, 174, 178, 179, 195, 197, 198, 210, 215, 226, 232, 238, 239, 240, 241
  Secretariat   2, 208, 217–19, 221, 228, 232, 233
  and social exclusion   3, 29, 215, 227, 240
  (*See also* social exclusion)
  and social inclusion   1, 3–4, 25, 29, 43, 44, 77–78, 80, 197, 209, 210, 215, 217, 218, 219, 225, 227, 232, 236, 238, 239, 240
  (*See also* social inclusion)
Commonwealth Games   2, 199, 211, 230–231
Commonwealth of learning   229–230
Communitarianism   38, 39, 40, 42, 68, 70, 74, 120
Community development   68, 69, 70, 71, 72, 73ff., 89, 241

Subject Index 245

Corruption 95, 101ff., 145, 226–27, 240
CPF *see* Provident funds

Democracy 25, 55, 56, 68, 69, 85, 87, 113, 220
Liberal democracy 25, 69, 73, 74, 77
Social democracy 117, 119, 120, 197, 201, 206, 207, 237
Developmental social welfare 81, 82, 87–8, 91
Developmental state 69, 71–3, 75

Education 15, 51, 52, 68, 69, 82, 83, 87, 111, 113, 114, 115, 116–117, 118, 127, 129, 134, 169, 175, 185, 202, 206, 220, 225, 228–30, 232
Europe[an]
Common market 175
Economic Community (EEC) 7, 23, 24, 168, 176
Single Market 24
Union (EU) 3, 7, 29, 219, 239

Family
the role of 70, 71, 73, 82, 89, 128, 151, 182
Difficulties facing 153, 175, 185, 199
Benefits/services in support of 184–85, 188–89, 199, 206
Women's work in 35, 44, 165, 199
(*See also* women/women's rights)

Global[isation] 3, 4, 7, 29, 30, 37ff., 38, 41–43, 44, 56, 62, 64, 77, 81, 82, 91, 146, 148, 168, 173, 176, 179, 181, 184, 193, 197, 210, 216, 220–21, 223, 224, 226, 227, 233, 237, 238

Health care policy 14, 15, 51, 52, 57ff., 68, 82, 83, 87, 98, 112, 113–14, 115–16, 118, 127, 129, 133, 135, 169, 175, 185, 202, 205, 206, 207, 224, 232

Housing policy 6, 52, 127, 129, 132–33, 151ff., 185, 200
east Asian policy models 152–5
HIV/Aids 68, 73, 90, 224, 225, 231, 233

Immigrants/immigration
to Australia 168, 173, 175
to Canada 199, 200, 206
in Malaysia 140, 141, 147
to NZ 182, 187
to UK 16, 19, 20, 21, 23
Immigration policy (Australia) 173, 174; (Canada) 208, (Sri Lanka 112, (UK) 21–23; (UK re Canada) 201
(*See also* Migrant labour, Migration)
Indentured labour 21, 112
Industrialisation, impact of 32, 34
Britain 12, 13, 171
Canada 202
Germany 13
S. Africa 83, 84
Islam[ic] 141, 143, 144, 145, 146, 147

Keynesian (economic state) 169, 172–173, 178, 241n

Labour movements/trades unions 55–6, 86, 87, 96, 112, 130, 194n, 201, 225
Liberalism 34, 57, 120, 203
Neo liberalism 24, 57, 77, 89, 91, 117, 118, 120, 178, 181, 199, 203, 237

Market, characteristics of 30ff., 44, 53, 61
Market society problematic 30, 38, 41, 53, 61, 62, 64, 119, 125, 172, 177
Migrant labour 72, 85, 112
(*See also* indentured labour)
Migration
around the empire 21
from Jamaica 59
children from UK 14
(*See also* immigration)

246 Subject Index

Missionaries   15, 15, 21, 51, 68, 76, 111
Churches, role of   82–3, 113

Nation state   1, 3, 4, 30, 37, 41, 42, 44, 178, 197, 238
Government limitations of   64
Hollowing out of   37, 42
New Labour   24, 29
(*See also* Third Way)
Non-governmental organizations (NGOs)   77, 91, 128, 209, 221ff., 232, 233

Pensions   7, 86, 87, 90, 95, 96, 97ff., 169, 176, 182, 189, 191–2, 193, 210n
Poor law   see public/social assistance
Poverty: anti-poverty policies   3, 29, 84, 90, 94ff., 114, 118, 183, 186, 199, 203, 206, 215, 222, 224, 226, 228, 233
Distribution/extent of   53–54, 73, 81, 82, 84, 86, 100ff., 113, 177, 189, 190, 191, 199
Standards/definitions of   97, 101–105, 108n, 188
Productivist welfare [capitalism]   126, 169, 173, 176, 178
(*See also* wage-earner welfare)
Provident Funds
British colonial legacy of   130–31, 136
Commonwealth Provident Fund   240–41
CPF (Sing.)   6, 126, 129, 130ff.; limitations   135–6
EPF (Sri Lanka)   115
Public/social assistance   83, 86, 90, 95, 96, 98ff., 115, 128, 184–5, 239
Poor Law   12, 14, 113, 114, 182
(*See also* social security)

Race/ethnic discrimination   5, 6, 22, 53, 59, 70, 77, 81, 83, 85, 86, 92, 116–117, 138, 139, 140, 149, 181, 191, 199, 218
Colonial legacy of   54, 70, 77, 84, 85, 86, 87, 110, 138ff., 147, 209
Race relations   22, 23

Slaves/slavery, legacy of   21, 51, 53, 82, 84, 111
Social assistance   see public/social assistance
Social exclusion   3, 4, 5, 6, 37, 38, 39, 52, 53, 62, 63, 70, 95, 151, 152, 181, 189–191, 193
Middle class exclusion   6, 159ff., 189, 192
Poor people's exclusion   36, 40, 63
Self-exclusion   197
Social exclusion/inclusion discourse   3, 4, 37–38, 39, 53, 63–64, 65, 181, 198ff., 215–16, 238
Social inclusion   3–4, 5, 7, 25, 29ff., 52, 56, 64, 65–66, 68, 74, 167, 176ff., 181, 191–2, 197, 205ff., 216
Components of   30–31, 41
Discourse on   3, 29ff., 43, 63, 197, 238, 239
Social insurance   86, 96, 182, 193, 193, 203, 239
Social investment state   168, 169, 170, 172, 178, 238–39
Socialism/socialist   34, 55, 59, 125, 126, 170, 201, 237
Socialist market   152–55
Social justice   30ff., 64, 65, 118, 119, 176, 178, 197, 218
Social policy evolution of   11–12, 16, 17, 44, 63–4, 68–9, 74, 77, 109ff., 167–76, 202, 239
British legacy/tradition of   168, 178, 179, 236, 238, 238, 240
Commonwealth formulations   219, 238, 239, 241
Social rights   36, 89, 176, 177, 178, 203, 205
Social security   5, 6, 53, 86, 87, 90, 94ff., 115, 164, 183, 184, 199, 201, 204
'Protective' vs. 'promotive'   94ff., 239
(*See also* public/social assistance)
Social services   53, 57, 68, 74, 86, 89, 91, 114, 115, 175, 206
Social welfare (benefits)   51, 52, 53, 62, 69, 70, 71, 73, 81, 82, 83ff., 96, 113, 114, 151, 175, 183–5, 188, 192, 193, 202, 203

Subject Index 247

Social work   71, 84, 89
State welfarism   126ff.

Taxation strategies   37, 183–4, 187–9, 192, 204
Third Way   6, 7, 24–25, 91, 119, 127, 206–7, 210, 236, 237, 239, 241n
Third World   5, 6, 86, 208, 237
Tiger economies (east and southeast Asia)   23, 24, 72, 78n
Traditional principles and practices   51, 69, 70, 74, 76, 110, 240

Voluntary agencies   84, 86, 89, 91, 211, 221ff.
(*See also* NGOs)

Wage-earner social security/welfare   115, 167, 169, 176, 177
(*See also* productivist welfare)
War, import of   13, 16–19, 21, 23, 83
Welfare states   7, 21, 44
 Australian   7, 169, 173, 174–5, 176, 178
 British   4, 11, 17–19, 21, 24, 35, 114, 203, 236
 Canadian   202–3, 205
 International   44
 Jamaican   57
 'light welfare states' of East Asia   65
 New Zealand   181–2, 184, 185, 193
 Singapore (state welfarism)   126–8, 129
 Sri Lanka   6, 109, 114–17, 118, 119
 Tamil Nadu   97, 107
Western Economic Crisis   23–24, 60, 85, 86
(cf Asian Financial Crisis)
Women/women's rights/status   52, 70, 71, 74, 76–77, 78, 84, 85, 86, 90, 94, 97, 100, 103, 175, 200, 219, 220, 223, 227–8, 229
(*See also* Family)

Youth/young people   14, 70, 78, 94, 219, 223, 227, 228–229, 230, 231